T0169941

Other Books by Paul Pines

The Tin Angel
Redemption
Pines songs (A little rooti tooti chapbook)
Hotel Madden Poems
Onion; poems
Breath
Adrift on Blinding Light
Taxidancing

MY BROTHER'S MADNESS

a memoir by

Paul Pines

CURBSTONE PRESS

First Edition: 2007
Copyright © 2007 by Paul Pines
ALL RIGHTS RESERVED

Printed in the U.S. on acid-free paper
Cover design: Susan Shapiro
Cover photo used by permission of the author.

This book was published with the support of
the Connecticut Commission on Culture and
Tourism, the Connecticut State Legislature
through the Office of Policy & Management,
the National Endowment for the Arts, and
donations from many individuals. We are
grateful for this support.

Library of Congress Cataloging-in-Publication Data

Pines, Paul.
  My brother's madness : a memoir / by Paul Pines.
     p. cm.
  ISBN 978-1-931896-34-4 (pbk. : acid-free paper)
  1. Pines, Claude—Family. 2. Authors, American—20th century—
Biography.
3. Brothers—Biography. I. Title.

  PS3566.I522Z46 2007
  811'.54—dc22
  [B]   2007021694

published by
  CURBSTONE PRESS 321 Jackson St. Willimantic, CT 06226
      phone: 860-423-5110   e-mail: info@curbstone.org
                  www.curbstone.org

I have been blessed with friends, some of who have contributed directly to the writing of this book: Robert Audi, Dan Asia, Paul Benveniste, Esther Broner, Ed Gorn, Jeff Hoffman, Rochelle Ratner, Howard Rayfiel, Jean Rikoff, Betsy Sandlin, Susan Sherman, David Unger, Fred Waitzkin, Bernie Weitzman, Dalt Wonk, and Asa Zatz. My brother had the love and support of many, some of whom I know he would have wanted me to acknowledge: Paul Bachman, Linda Eckstein, Kenneth and Catherine Gericke, Nancy Harrigan, Mark Hoffman, Florence Infantino, Gary Jones, Micaela Kelly, Jack Nicholson, Karen Padowicz, Joanne Rachlin, Susan Scherer, Deb Sweet, Patti Weiss, David & Mary Young, and Bob Zagorn. For their support of this book, I would like to thank Chuck Wachtel, Matthew Proser—the latter also for his sensitive editorial work with me on the manuscript—and Jane Blanshard for her fine copy editing. I am doubly grateful for the meticulous attention and commitment this book has received at Curbstone Press from Alexander Taylor, Judy Doyle, and Jantje Tielken. Finally, the love and courage of my wife, Carol, and the soulful presence of our daughter, Charlotte, have been, and continue to be a constant source of renewal.

MAD, adj. (madder, maddest) 1 insane; having a disordered mind. 2 wildly foolish. 3 (often foll. by *about* or *Brit. On*) wildly excited or infatuated... 4 *colloq.* angry. 5 (of an animal) rabid. 6 wildly light-hearted. *V.intr.* (madded, madding) *archaic* bemad; act madly (*the madding crowd*) * like mad *colloq.* Extremely eager. [Old English *gemaeded* 'made insane'] * MADNESS n.

OXFORD MODERN ENGLISH DICTIONARY

BOOK ONE: THE INVISIBLE WORM

THE SICK ROSE

The invisible worm
That flies in the night,
In the howling storm,
Has found out thy bed...
   William Blake, *Songs of Experience*

PART 1

LUNCH WITH CITIZEN X

My brother Claude arrives late for my wedding on Columbus Day, 1985, looking drawn, his blond hair limp with sweat, blue eyes peering from dark wells over a pasted smile. He has driven his Datsun for over four hours from West 75th Street on a day when the last autumnal flares of red and gold burst like Roman candles in the Adirondack foot hills. On the steps of the Friends Lake Inn, his pale face stands out from the hundred-odd guests as Judge Austin hears our vows, and Bill Bronk, former New York State poet laureate, reads a poem. My attention drifts between my bride Carol, stunning in a halo of baby's breath, and my brother, who appears as glazed as the ice-filled tureen on the buffet.

After the ceremony, I buttonhole him in front of the salmon mousse. The problem, he tells me, is his new job at University Hospital. Co-workers at the lab are laughing at him and whispering behind his back. Going to work is becoming more difficult every day. He isn't sure how long he can continue to do it.

Claude's phone calls over the following months become increasingly urgent. He says his colleagues are not even attempting to disguise their contempt for him. Men in suits watch him from the doorway, follow him to lunch, report on his movements.

I press him to explain; why should he be subjected to such relentless ridicule and extraordinary surveillance?

My brother doesn't know.

I report to our Uncle Irving over the phone: "I can't tell if what he's saying is real, imaginary, or both."

My concern for Claude peaks in February, just as my agent at Curtis Brown finalizes a deal with a French film company to option my novel, THE TIN ANGEL, based on my experience as the owner of a Bowery jazz club I sold at the end of the 70s. The contract includes a round-trip ticket on Air France, an apartment on the Left Bank, and a substantial fee for the first draft of a screenplay. We are expected in Paris at the beginning of April.

Over the following month, Claude's calls are less frequent, but he is harder to reach. As Carol and I prepare for our trip, my brother's predicament weighs heavily on my mind. I am reluctant to leave him alone, but feel compelled to make the journey. In response to my cry for help, Uncle Irving flies up from his pool-side lanai in West Palm Beach.

On April 5, 1986, three days before we leave for Paris, I drive south from Glens Falls, New York, to meet Claude and our uncle for lunch in Manhattan at a Greek coffee shop on Second Avenue, near University Hospital. Sprays of forsythia along the Thruway, their manic intensity, remind me of Van Gogh's yellows, the luminous cry of his irises and stars.

By the time I feed the meter in front of Kips Bay Plaza, I'm twenty minutes late. I find Claude and Irving already seated, my brother hunched over a half-eaten cheeseburger. Irving picks at a chef's salad. In expensive tweeds, at seventy-six he reminds me of an old RAF pilot more than a retired physician. "Sorry to start without you." He embraces me. "Claude has to get back to work."

My brother stands. His rumpled hair and wrinkled shirt recall the way he looked after dropping out of medical school at Einstein. When I hug him, his body stiffens. Rather than return my embrace, he pats my back as if he were burping a baby.

I order a bowl of chili.

"See that black guy?" Claude gestures at a man in a short-sleeved shirt by the cashier. "He'll pretend not to see me."

The man my brother indicates is built like a Steeler linebacker. Instead of shoulder pads and a helmet, he wears a badge and gun as well as the insignia of nearby University Hospital.

"I can take him," boasts Irving.

"When I left the hospital, he was standing at the entrance. Sometimes he sits outside the lab. They think they're subtle, but I know what's going on."

"Introduce yourself, then give him a kiss." Irving talks out of the side of his mouth, his imitation of George Raft. He used to address his Garment District patients that way before retiring from a practice that was mostly workman's comp.

My brother and I exchange a knowing glance.

"Why should that man be watching you?" I ask.

Claude shrugs.

Weeks from the end of a temporary employment contract to replace a woman on maternity leave, his job at the hospital has become a nightmare. At first, his co-workers welcomed him, but they now make him the butt of their jokes. "Lately they give me a wide berth, like I might be wired with plastique. Men in suits wander in and out of the lab, watch me when I go to the bathroom. They're keeping an eye on me."

What's it all about?

"Do they think I might pull out an Uzi and shoot the place up? They're treating me like a criminal, but no one will tell me what I've done or name my accuser. It's right out of Kafka." He studies his cheeseburger. "You remember Citizen K? Well, meet Citizen X."

"Why not leave?" asks Irving.

"Let them drive me out? No. I can get through three more weeks."

The black security guard at the register pockets his change, grabs two brown paper bags in one huge hand, then leaves without a look in our direction.

Perspiration beads Claude's forehead. He waves nicotine-stained fingers in front of his face as if clearing away cobwebs. "Don't worry. It'll be over soon."

But I am worried. What does he mean by, It'll be over soon! *How can I go to Paris with Carol under these conditions?*

How can I not?

Writing a screenplay based on my novel is the opportunity of a lifetime. But my enthusiasm for my career flags when I see my brother's eyes darting like startled jays over his half-eaten cheeseburger.

I consider his string of troubled lab jobs.

Five years earlier, at Metpath, a high-volume lab in New Jersey, Claude confronted a female co-worker who mistook his shyness for a lack of manhood and began taunting him, supported by a chorus of fellow technicians. One day my brother asked her to lower her radio so he could concentrate on his slides. She dared him to make her, stood in front of the radio, a two-hundred-pound challenge to the short, soft-spoken man. On a wave of adrenalin, Claude pushed her aside, then silenced the radio. She grabbed a glass beaker. He held her wrists until security guards separated them. Everyone knew he'd been provoked. But in the end my brother was blamed for acting on the provocation and forced to leave.

"Maybe they found out about Metpath?"

"That would explain the surveillance. But why won't they talk to me about it? I can assure them I'm no danger to anyone. People never know what to make of me. At Einstein they would always give me this contemptuous look when I didn't fit their image. Here's this guy who never says a word and suddenly he comes up with a diagnosis no one else thought of. Some nerve. Who does he think he is?"

"It always seems to play out this way." *I observe.*

"I make them uncomfortable." *He glances around.*

Is it possible that my brother is being scapegoated? It wouldn't be the first time he's been forced to play the victim. I note the pressure-cooker rattle in his voice.

Claude glances at his watch. "I gotta go."

He waves rather than hugs us, then starts off, leaving his food half-eaten.

"Don't worry. He'll be fine." Irving repeats this like a mantra, his voice already on its way back to West Palm and his house within walking distance of the golf course. "I've renewed his prescription for Xanax."

We watch Claude cross Second Avenue, shoulders hunched, hands in his pockets, executing his jerky version of the Lords-of-Flatbush mean-street walk. As Brooklyn boys we had used the walk for protective covering against the Pig Town Italians, Irish Lords from Park Circle, and Chaplains establishing their turf in Bed-Stuy. But that was then. The Lords of Flatbush have since become cops or gym teachers. My brother's predators now wear lab coats and keep scrupulous track of their overtime.

It is a situation Xanax will not address.

What I see in Claude is a petrified piece of his pre-Cambrian self. It fills the shadow creature he has become. At the same time, I remember my brother from earliest childhood: the shock of his innocence and beauty, the clear round eyes of one of Jehovah's choir fallen to earth. I strain to see that golden child in the startled figure disappearing into lunch-hour traffic.

I

Claude in his crib: blue eyes, haloed by golden ringlets. At three years old, my joy at the sight of him is immense. I will never be lonely again. He stares at me. I know what he sees. It is easy because I see through his eyes as well as my own. I recall what it was like to sit in the middle of that playpen, having recently been there, where he is. He will always be one step behind me. I like this idea. But our experiences are not identical. His cheeks glow with the excitement of something that was lacking for me: the sight of another. I jump up and down, smile and wave my hands. I know what he sees. My laughing face staring at him through the bars.

"Say good-bye to your brother."

My father appears. He stands at one end of the crib, grips it with his fingers, and pushes it out of my bedroom. I follow as far as the threshold. Beyond, the hall is dark and smells of Brilliantine, the flowery sheen on my father's dark hair combed back from his high forehead. I can't see my brother, or hear him. But my own voice screaming comes back to me as from afar.

"No! Daddy, please!"

"He'll be in the blue room. You can visit whenever you want." My father's voice is soft but unyielding. His trim mustache shapes itself around his words. "This way you'll both get more sleep."

My father doesn't know what he's doing. He wears his dark wool suit, which is where I locate another odor—nutty peanut butter. The hall smells damp, like the dirt where I dig for night crawlers in Prospect Park. The blue room is at the far end. To reach it, I have to pass the linen closet full of sheets and towels. Ghosts hide there, seep out at night in wisps of smoke between the cracks to take shifting shapes that hover outside my bedroom door or drift into the blue room. They leave behind cold pools of air. First thing in the morning I can feel where they've been. Our father doesn't know this, or what might happen to my brother at night in the blue room all alone.

I throw myself on the bed and pound on the pillow. *Our father doesn't know what he has done. He doesn't know how dangerous it is for my brother to be alone at night in the blue room.* Or that he has taken away my other set of eyes.

I'm always relieved to see Claude at breakfast in the kitchen. Heads resting on identical red cushions, we lie side by side on the floor next to the stove sucking on our bottles until I am three-and-a-half and insist on drinking from a glass. My brother's eyes are closed. He holds his bottle straight up in the air. His cheeks hollow, and he makes a loud sucking noise. He refuses to let go of his bottle until he has drained the last drop from it. At four, he still won't let it go.

And I know why.

My mother nursed me for the first three months of infancy. She tells me this when I crawl into bed with her and ask why Claude won't drink from a glass. She explains that there was no milk in her breasts for Claude, which is why he hugs his bottle. When she kisses me I taste salt on her lips. Her hair against the pillow is the color of her violin. She doesn't smell like my father, but sweet like brown sugar in oatmeal. Her breasts, she whispers, just "dried up."

I wonder why they dried up for Claude and not for me. I try to imagine dried breasts but see only dried pudding skin or brown paper bags that have been blown up and exploded. But hers are so round against my cheek. The way they push against her nightgown makes it clear that they are no longer dry.

Our father moves Claude out of the blue room and into mine when he is four and no longer fits into his crib. He sleeps in the twin bed next to mine. The sound of his breathing comforts me.

This is true four years later, making Sunday morning

rounds with our father. I am grateful for my brother's presence beside me in our new Oldsmobile. It is always cold and dark when we start out, moving between hospitals. First we stop at the Brooklyn Jewish, then the Swedish, before parking in the space reserved for him in front of the Adelphi. Ben is a surgeon, and must visit his patients after he has operated on them to make sure that they don't die like Mr. Middle, who bled to death because no one was around to pack his throat with ice. Our father hardly spoke a word to anyone for weeks after Mr. Middle died, even though our mother said this happened to people who drank too much. Her explanation didn't make our father feel any better.

Claude and I wait for him in the car with the heat on, listening to the radio, hoping no one has died. When someone does, our father returns to the car clutching his overcoat, lips pressed tight, looking straight ahead, never at us. We then drive in silence to the next hospital and the next until we get home and he locks himself in his study. When no patient dies, he walks briskly back to the Olds, then makes puns and asks us about school between stops.

This morning he tells us how much he wants another child, a baby sister for us. His eyes glow. We also would like to have a sister. A beautiful little girl. Surely he can make that happen.

Our father shakes his head sadly.

Why not? We want to know why he and our mother can't have a little girl.

"Your mother didn't want children." He stops at a red light. "She would have preferred to concentrate on her career."

"But she wanted me," I protest. Didn't she nurse me for three months before her breasts dried up?

"One child was workable," he answers. "Claude was a surprise. *I slipped that one in.*"

He says this playfully, so that we all can enjoy the trick he played on our mother. But Claude isn't smiling; he gazes beyond us with a look I recognize from a black-and-white photo, one of several on the antique table in the downstairs hall. When we get home I sit down and study it.

In the photo he is three and I am five. Golden curls lick his face, but the impression of beauty falters around tremulous lips, eyes glazed with invisible tears. I stare boldly at the camera, displaying full rows of baby-teeth. My eyes shine, too, but not with tears. My head tilts toward the photographer. Claude tilts away, as if to avoid an impending blow.

On the same desk, a snapshot taken the summer before shows us in short pants fishing with hand lines for spiny sunfish we call *crappies,* at the edge of a basin in Prospect Park full of floating debris. Claude faces the water, back hunched, eyes fixed on the point where his line disappears. I face the camera shirtless, ribs pushing against a thin covering of skin, more interested in being photographed than catching crappies. I have none of my brother's feel for the bait and how to pay out line, set the hook. My brother loves waiting. I always strike too soon.

I study the photos.

If I was nursed for three months and Claude not at all, then why do I look like a Halloween skeleton, and suffer from allergies and asthma attacks that leave me struggling for breath like a dying crappie? My brother isn't forced to take spoonfuls of "red medicine" from the Gay Clinic in Biloxi, which my parents rush for at the slightest hint of a wheeze.

Claude never cries or complains, just smiles as if that is what he's been sent to earth to do. But how does my brother, who wasn't nursed at all, float through Brooklyn Friends School on a bubble of light, while I who nursed for three months have a permanent seat on the "bad-boy bench" in the front hall? It's clear we are different, even though I believe I can see what he sees, look out at the world through his eyes. I am possessed by the dark, drawn to and scared of it at the same time. His bright curls and round body dispel the shadows that pool in corners of our home, under beds and behind closet doors.

At ten years old, I still fear the shapes which chase me in my dreams up and down the attic stairs. Claude sleeps nearby. Our beds are separated by a night table. When I wake from a nightmare, I crawl into his bed and hug him until I can get to sleep. He never protests. Claude is there to comfort me.

We go to bed early Saturday evenings in order to wake up for Sunday rounds with our father at 6:00 AM. Barring an emergency, we get back in time to turn on the Motorola, get under the covers and hear Bob McNeil address his friend, Froggy the Gremlin: *"Pluck your magic twanger, Froggy."* In addition to *The Bob McNeil Show*, we listen to *Nat King Cole, Yours Truly Johnny Dollar, Gunsmoke, Autolight Theater, The Green Lantern, Boston Blackie*, and *The Shadow.* We delight in *Amos and Andy* and their adventures at The Mystic Knights of the Sea Lodge Hall. When undertaker Digby O'Dell in *The Life of Riley* complains about the toothpaste company that advertises on the walls of his funeral home, "If not satisfied, return the empty box," we joke about it for the next two weeks. We are roused by the sound of *Sergeant Preston of the Yukon* calling out in a deep baritone to his faithful husky: "Mush, King! Mush!"

The radio is an escape from our parents' increasingly harsh arguments. Their fights bewilder and frighten us. Once our mother left the house for two weeks and nobody knew where she was. We can sense tension building under the surface but are shocked when it bursts into the world with the suddenness of a summer storm. This morning we brace ourselves. Our father is talking about having a daughter, how a little girl would bring such joy to our lives. He is so taken with this idea he can't hear the rumble of thunder until it breaks. *"Just who the hell do you think you are?"* Our mother's voice peals from the kitchen. *"I don't take orders from you."*

"If you'll just listen..."

"You always assume the moral high ground. *Bastard! I should expose you for who you really are! Let the whole world know.*"

Our father's fantasy of a third child dissolves in the deluge. His voice shifts from enthusiasm to a soft-spoken appeal. "It was just a thought."

"I know exactly what it was."

"Be reasonable, dear."

"Why should I? Afraid the neighbors will hear us? That's what really scares you, isn't it?" His footsteps follow hers up the stairs, into the study. "I'm going to open the window and yell so everyone can hear me. The whole neighborhood..."

"Charlotte, sweetie, it was just an idea."

We hear the window open behind his desk. It faces the Schillers' house next door. Our mother's voice becomes a roar. "Another kid? How can I feed another mouth on what you give me, *you cheap sonofabitch!*"

"What can I do? Tell me what you want," he begs.

A door slams. She's locked herself in the bedroom. We won't see her the rest of the day. He'll spend the night in his study, a strip of light under the door burning into our bedroom.

Claude and I turn up the volume on the Motorola just as Tonto tells the Lone Ranger he can track rustlers even through the Badlands. This time we know what our mother and father are fighting about. He wants a daughter and she wants to concentrate on being a lawyer. But something is supposed to happen when you track rustlers through the Badlands, a conclusion that includes punishing the bad guys and restoring the herd.

I know something even more important but can't figure out how to say it except in the way I finally do.

"*I understand.*"

Claude's eyes dart like caged parakeets. "Me, too."

"No, you don't."

"I do."

He thinks I mean that I understand why our parents act as they do: it's the question foremost in his mind. Claude hopes that their arguments are like a cold from which they will finally recover. This is Tonto's promise to the masked man.

What I understand exists at the secret heart of the Lone Ranger; things between our mother and father can only get worse. I understand that I am a masked man, alone with this knowledge. But this isn't what I am trying to articulate. I have to track what I want to say, which is why the Lone Ranger needs Tonto. If I set him to the task, he will guide me through the Badlands of my mind. Perhaps we will find it together, behind the bit of sagebrush, rustlers with stolen cattle, or the inevitability of a parental bloodbath—but this is where the Lone Ranger and Tonto part ways. For me what is known, no matter how trivial or grave, is viewed against the backdrop of knowing itself. In this awareness, the watcher watches himself watching. It is an activity that defines the Lone Ranger. I want to explain this to my brother, but can't find the words.

I realized this a year ago, curled under the Steinway watching our mother play her violin. Huddled there, I saw myself in the living room of our house on Lincoln Road, on a street bathed in moonlight, surrounded by quicksilver maples. I could see the Empire Boulevard trolley, Ebbets Field bleachers, Botanical Gardens bounded by the Triumphal Arch in Grand Army Plaza, our father's office on Eastern Parkway, and beyond to the webbed cables of the Brooklyn Bridge. I understood, then, that this way of seeing expanded in ever-growing circles to contain the galaxy and beyond that the entire universe, all of it rising from the point I occupied in that moment under the piano. From this perspective, the shaky condition of our home, so frightening up close, melts into an ever-expanding structure, the meaning of which lies not in the microscopic dissonance of our household but in the grand design that enfolds it.

"I do understand," Claude insists, attempting to force from me a concession which I am unwilling to make.

rue de Bièvre
Paris/April 22ⁿᵈ, 1986

Ten days later, Carol and I, our Maltese, Violet, secure in her flight bag, land at Charles DeGaulle Airport. Lila, a leggy Argentine in her late thirties, meets us at the gate, her long chin and nose crowned by a gamine cap of black hair styled after that of her best friend, Paloma Picasso. In the cab she informs us that the director they've hired feels "our movie" can't be made in Paris, which has no comparable jazz scene. The closest thing to it is the African music scene in Montparnasse, but that would be a different movie. They've decided to explore Sao Paolo, which is closer in spirit to the music and street life of the Lower East Side.

"But Paris is the city of Sidney Bechet, Bud Powell, and Dexter Gordon."

Lila smiles indulgently, then makes small talk until we're installed in an apartment on the fourth floor of rue de Bièvre, overlooking the walled garden of Francois Mitterrand's mistress across the street. Gendarmes in black slickers at either end of the narrow block ensure privacy. Over lunch, her husband Jean, a boyish man with a head of contentious curls, lets me know I'll be flying to Rio with Lila, the director, and his Brazilian starlet girlfriend as soon as he can make the arrangements. Carol will stay in Paris. With the self-assurance of one born to privilege, Jean asks for my passport. Two days later, he informs me that I leave for Rio sometime next week.

The prospect of moving again feeds my worry about Claude. I dial his number, amazed at how easy it is to reach New York directly, and tell him that I'm going to Rio. "That's crazy," he says, then cautions me to be alert, things are not what they seem. When I ask what he means, Claude answers, "Just that." He takes our number at rue de Bièvre, repeats his warning, then hangs up.

Carol tries to be stoic about remaining in Paris with Violet. But our little Maltese mirrors my wife's moods. Watching the dog drag her tail, I know exactly how Carol is feeling. On our afternoon walk, Violet sniffs the ancient stones, but remains constipated and refuses to pee outside.

Strolling in the shadow of Notre Dame, I recount a dream I had the night before. In it, Claude swaggers down a dark Brooklyn street until he turns into a guppy. Carol suggests I call him again.

I dial his number as soon as we get back to the apartment. Someone picks up on the second ring.

"Hello." I hear a pulsating sound, like breath inside a snorkel. "Claude?"

"Paulie, is that you?" A pause, then: "Listen, Paulie. I'm under suspicion."

"What do you mean?"

"I can't go into it on a transatlantic line. It has to do with mugging old ladies. You have to be here to know what I'm talking about."

"Mugging old ladies?"

"That's what they're saying. Don't worry. I know how to handle it." Another pause, then: "Paulie, be careful."

"Careful of what?"

He does a credible imitation of Tony Bennett singing I Wanna Be Around...

> to pick up the pieces
> when somebody breaks your heart
> somebody twice as smart
> as you...

II

Our father is twice as smart as anyone.

At eight and ten, Claude and I know this because of the way people treat him when we walk around the block after dinner. We do this every night, when the weather allows. Our father says it is good for our health and urges us to take deep breaths as we walk.

Our house on Lincoln Road, between Flatbush and Bedford, faces a wall of apartment buildings on the other side of the street. Tonight, at the beginning of summer, lights go on before the sun goes down. As we walk, our father points out that we live in one of the few brick-and-stucco houses on a block lined with wooden Victorians.

Dr. Schiller, his wife, and two sons live in a gray-and-white Victorian next door. They hardly nod when we say hello. Maybe it's because they hear our parents fight when our mother opens the window and screams to the neighbors. I don't care that the Schiller boys avoid us. Danny wears his pants too high. Joel's glasses make him look like an owl. Joel's eyes are too bad for punch ball. Even if Danny could hit the ball, he wears his belt too high to run. Our father wants us to be more like them, to take piano lessons, play chess, and go to Hebrew school.

Two blue-haired spinsters, the Robinsons, live in the beige Victorian on the other side of our driveway where we play ball. They are related to Walter O'Malley, owner of the Brooklyn Dodgers, and never mow their lawn. The grass in front of their house is taller than we are. We play "jungle" in it, chase each other until someone steps in a pile and has to scuff his sneaker on the curb.

Yah, Yah, here he comes.
Claude the Shit Man. Everybody run!

During the summer, the Robinsons run the rowboat rentals in Prospect Park where they dispense tickets from a booth as if they were handing crusts to beggars.

The houses on our block are mostly owned by doctors and lawyers. Around the corner, on Maple Street, the Fabrikant mansion is surrounded by box hedges. Behind them is an expanse of green lawn and a fountain that lights up at night. A gravel driveway arcs around it to the white columned entrance. At the center of the lawn a glass ball on a white pedestal shrinks everything to a point. Rosebushes line a brick wall at the rear. Our father says the Fabrikant family buys and sells diamonds.

On the other side of Bedford Avenue, row houses line treeless streets that lead to Crown Heights. Further east is Brownsville where tough Jews live, the sons of *Murder Inc.* Pigtown, so named because the Italians who settled there raised pigs, belongs to the *Pigtown Tigers*. Their rivals are *The Gremlins,* from Park Circle. The *Irish Lords* control Park Slope. Our father hardly notices the kids on the corners along Flatbush who give us hard looks.

Claude and I would rather walk up Empire Boulevard to Ebbets Field, where "'Dem Bums" will win pennant after pennant, only to lose the World Series. On summer nights like this one, the lights of Ebbets Field flood the sky as Red Barber calls plays over radios heard through open windows above the chirping crickets and blinking fireflies. But it is still postwar Brooklyn. Uncle Irving visits us in uniform. People in our living room whisper about German atrocities.

In his gray Italian suit, our father is as respected on the street as General Eisenhower. Turning the corner from Maple onto Flatbush, a man in a golf cap with deep lines at the corners of his mouth grasps our father's hand in both of his. He speaks in Yiddish. Our father replies in the same tongue. A cab driver, he explains, whose wife was gravely ill but has since recovered. He is grateful because our father adjusted his fee. Mr. Middle, wobbles over, the lapels of his once expensive jacket frayed. His nose and cheeks are red with grog blossoms. He bows elegantly from the waist. When our father returns his bow, Mr. Middle stands a little straighter. An elderly couple wave from the bus stop. The man says something in Italian, to which our father replies in Italian. "Emergency appendectomy on their grandson," he tells us. "A few minutes later the boy would have died." He responds to people in Polish, Russian, German, and French. He identifies them by their procedures; *there goes a tracheotomy, bleeding ulcer, hiatal hernia, kidney stones, breach birth.* His surgical technique for *a twisted umbilicus* has saved countless babies.

Now a bald man with an Ichabod Crane Adam's-apple touches his beret. The man's eyes are darker than my room at night. *Gall bladder*, whispers our father, adding that the man narrowly escaped a Nazi concentration camp called Auschwitz.

"I did that one for free."

He doesn't have to tell us why. We know that our father came from Poland, at the age of six, to escape marauding Cossacks who rode through his village, swords dripping Jewish blood, and that many of our family have died in both the pogroms and the gas chambers. We are greeted by Sam at the deli, Sonny at the candy store, by the pharmacist, and the dry cleaner on the corner. *Maison Charles* reads the sign on the dry cleaner's window, but he, too, is another death-camp survivor.

It is easy to be proud of our father. No one else dresses in silk suits, a handkerchief folded in three perfect pyramids, the largest one in front. His voice is soft, and most people think that he is, too. But he tells us all the time that nothing comes easily. "Success is ninety percent perspiration." He wants us to work as hard as he does. I fear that I will never sweat enough to please him.

By the time I am eleven and Claude nine, the sound of our father's car pulling into the driveway at night makes us want to hide. We relax with him only when he joins us in the blue-room which houses our new television. We watch *Milton Berle* or *I Love Lucy.* I lie on the floor at his feet. My brother nestles on the broad arm of his chair, watching him as much as the TV, warmed by the sight of wrinkles forming at the corners of his eyes just before he emits a rasping sound that we recognize as laughter.

Tonight, while they watch *Amos & Andy*, I sit at the antique table in the downstairs hall staring at a photo of our father holding me, at three, in the Union Temple pool. He is kneeling at the shallow end. I am relaxed in the crook of his arm, my head on his shoulder. My hands rest on the water's surface, trusting him completely. Two years after that picture was taken the same man paces behind me as I hunch over the desk in my bedroom, terrified. I must memorize the alphabet before I am six, he tells me. Every night after dinner he sits me at the desk, and drills me.

"All right, start with A." He mouths the first letter.

"A, B, C, D, E, F...F..."

"What follows F?"

"F...G...H..."

"Keep going."

"I can't."

"Start over again."

"A," I tell him, falter again at F. "I can't..."

"Don't tell me that."

"Sorry."

"Begin again."

I speak the letters, until I draw a blank. After E there is only darkness, as if the world ended there and I have fallen off the edge. Even as I fall, I hear his footsteps behind me. His hand moves with lightning speed.

Crack! Comes the blow to my head. *"Dummkopf!"*

"A, B, C, D..."

"Again." *Crack!*

I see stars. The only thing that comes out is a long wheezing breath. I brace for another blow. But he storms out, convinced my paralysis is disrespect, that I am disobeying one of the commandments God gave Moses. I wonder if God was ever as angry at Moses as my father is at me.

Claude watches it all. When it is over, and I am sure that our father will not return to punish me, I look up to see my brother huddled on his bed. We are ashamed and alone. Like a comforter in the book of Job, he is sure that I must have done something wrong to bring about such a reaction, and angry at me for exposing him to it. He will also make sure that the same thing doesn't happen to him.

Long before I master the alphabet, Claude, who has never suckled a drop of mother's milk, can recite it from A to Z. He learns how to earn our father's praise. My experience is more confusing. Like the God of Moses, our father may not let me into the Promised Land of his approval, but neither will he let me perish. I learn as much at the end of my eleventh year when I come down with "double" pneumonia.

My father in shirtsleeves, sweat glistening on his high forehead, takes my pulse, temperature, checks my lymph glands. Beside him is a nurse in a white uniform. Claude stands in the doorway as I struggle for breath under the oxygen tent. My brother is frightened that I'll die and leave him alone. *Such things happen to bad boys.*

"This medicine will save your life," our father whispers.

He turns me over onto my stomach. His broad palm presses the small of my back. It takes three people to hold me down. I'm pinned like a bug. He jabs the needle into my rear end, pushes the plunger. I fight violently, ripping my pajamas, twisting in the bed sheets even as the thick new "wonder drug" swells my tissue. The horse needle leaves scabs on my behind. I howl like a wounded animal. Claude covers his ears.

rue de Bièvre
Paris/ June 8th, 1986

On the night of my departure for Rio, Carol confides that she may be pregnant, before wishing me bon voyage. I float onto the plane behind the director and his Brazilian starlet girlfriend, heady with this news. Aboard the Air France 747 we eat tournedos, served with a dark Merlot. My headiness turns into confusion. I hear Claude's voice, and find myself singing along: "I wanna be around to pick up the pieces..."

There is one more piece now. We are going to have a baby. But it is unclear to me how this fits in with all the others I am trying to put together. I am not sure any longer how or if the pieces fit. Why do we assume that they must? Maybe the reality is otherwise; certain pieces have no place in the puzzle. Does such a piece constitute a puzzle in itself? What do we call a puzzle without pieces? An anti-puzzle? Will my baby be a girl or a boy? What will we name it? Why should Claude say he is under suspicion for mugging old ladies? He's always had a dry sense of humor. Why am I on my way to Brazil when I've just arrived in France? Is my brother any crazier than my producers, who have brought me from New York to Paris to write a screenplay they now want set in Brazil? Why mugging old ladies?

In the summer of Claude's eighteenth year, he answered a knock at his door of the sixth-floor tenement apartment he shared with a roommate on East 9th Street. Two policemen flashed badges, then arrested them both on charges of rape and sodomy. Their accuser was a blowzy woman across the hall with whom they shared a toilet. They were held overnight at The Tombs. Next morning, Charlotte appeared at the Criminal Court on Center Street to see her eighteen-year-old son and his roommate enter in handcuffs. Wearing sensible pumps and an Eva Gabor wig, she informed the bench that her clients were "good boys" with no prior record. The judge appreciated our mother's appeal and released them in her custody pending trial.

Claude was almost as outraged as he was frightened. Why should that woman target him, of all people? He didn't understand it. He had done nothing. And neither had his roommate.

They both stewed for several weeks in a brew of anger, fear and guilt, until Charlotte received a call from the DA's office that they were dropping the charges if her clients agreed to walk away without making trouble for their office or the police who were simply doing their job. It seems an investigation revealed that their accuser had a history of mental illness, which included a number of false accusations of rape and sodomy. Confronted with her record, she admitted making up the story. My brother and his roommate signed off on the agreement. Charges were dropped, but Claude's night in jail, and his appearance sitting handcuffed in the courtroom, remained hardwired in his mind.

Now, once again, he's under suspicion. But why for mugging little old ladies! It's too early to say. Pieces of the puzzle are missing. Or have no place to go.

We deplane at dusk in Rio. Windows in the terminal frame the sun's last rays on rocks that jut like dragon's teeth from the bay. A customs inspector waves the director, starlet, and Lila through, but asks for my visa. I tell him I've only got what's in the passport. He motions for me to follow him. In an office, under an overhead fan, an official with a Santa Claus beard studies my passport. No visa. Too bad. I can't enter without one.

What about my companions?

France doesn't require visas of Brazilians. The United States does. So, Brazil does the same for US citizens.

An oversight on the part of my producers. Can't something be worked out?

The chief customs man strokes his beard. It's Friday night. Embassies are closed for the weekend. I can fly to Paraguay for a couple of days, get a Brazilian visa there on Monday, or spend the weekend at the Rio airport. I can also return to Paris on the next plane.

I choose the latter. Santa Claus ushers me back into the terminal and wishes me luck. The next plane to Paris leaves in four hours. Pacing before the windows separating me from the lights of Rio, I wander like a ghost among those arriving or departing. In the bookstore, I buy a copy of Colin Wilson's MYSTERIES, and then shamble through the crowd, the Citizen X of Rio airport. Is this what my brother feels like, visaless in the terminal? The only other person in the universe who might know what I'm going through is half-asleep when I call.

"Claude?"

"My God, where are you?"

I explain what's happened, hear heavy breathing from his end, followed by, "Ah ha!"

"Ah ha?"

"You believe that they forgot your visa?"

"What do you mean?"

"I'll talk to you in a couple of days, after you've had a chance to see how the puzzle fits."

He signs off with a few more bars of "I wanna be around..."

Seventeen hours later, I'm back at DeGaulle. I've read up to page two-hundred eighty-seven in MYSTERIES, where mathematician P. D. Ouspensky describes walking a Petrograd street in a state of mystical intensity through which he can see peoples' dreams hovering "like clouds in front of their faces." At 5:00 AM, in a similar state, I crawl up four flights into Carol's arms.

Jean calls on Monday to ask if I'll get a visa and fly back to Brazil. No, I tell him. Lila returns five days later. She loves

Sao Paolo, but doesn't think it right for our film. Carol and I spend the next two weeks getting used to the idea of her pregnancy after a home-test kit proves positive. I work on my screenplay and fantasize sitting with Carol and our child, now a teenager, watching "The Tin Angel," a French cult classic being rerun on TV. One evening, the phone interrupts Robert Mitchum and Jean Simmons in "Baby Face."

"Paulie, the people in my neighborhood are spreading malicious rumors about me."

"What are they saying?"

"No one will tell me. But the charges are libelous and I'm going to see a lawyer."

"Who are you suing?"

"That's the problem. Whoever they are, I'm not going to let them get away with it." *Claude changes the subject.* "Had any further thoughts about Brazil?"

"I never made it out of the airport."

"Ah-ha."

"Nothing mysterious. They forgot to get me a visa."

"And everyone mistakes me for Humphrey Bogart."

"So, I hung around the airport until the next plane left for Paris."

"Did anyone there mention me?"

III

At the age of twelve, I announce to my ten-year-old brother that I need his help in executing a plan, and that only he can do what I require. Claude has always wanted to be my sidekick, but greets the offer with a healthy skepticism based on his past experience with *The Ghost Riders*.

Two years earlier it dawned on me that the world needed saving. I reasoned further that if superheroes did great deeds all the time in comic books and on the radio, why shouldn't we be able to do them in real life?

My buddy Richard, a thin boy with loving-cup ears, agreed that by simply assuming such powers, we might in fact realize them. Claude threw his lot in with us, and endorsed my suggestion that we call ourselves The Wild Geese, after Frankie Lane's tune.

> *My heart goes where the wild goose goes*
> *And my heart knows what the wild goose knows...*

Claude lost heart momentarily when we told him that he was too young to be a full fledged hero, but he agreed to help us make wings and strap them to our backs. These would be no ordinary wings, but ones that could be used as both a weapon and a shield. We soon realized that while this was a good idea, it presented certain problems. Wings have to be made out of something. But what? Sheets tear. Cardboard creases. Metal is too heavy.

And that is how the Ghost Riders were born, inspired by Vaughn Monroe's hit song:

> *Gho-o-o-o-o-o-st Ri-i-i-i-i-ders,*
> *Ghost Riders in-n-n the sky.*

The only requirements for these superheroes were bed sheets.

Claude insisted that he could carry it off, but we prevailed on him, arguing that someone had to make sure things were in place behind the scenes. Where would Batman and Robin be without Alfred the Butler? Who would clean the Bat Cave and keep the Batmobile ready to roll?

"I don't want to be Alfred the Butler."

It was Alfred's job to shine the Bat signal so that everyone in Gotham City would know the mighty duo were abroad. We found a task for my brother that was roughly the equivalent—beating a conga drum nonstop in our bedroom two hours prior to the appearance of the Ghost Riders. Reluctantly, he swore to keep on drumming from the moment we left the house until we returned.

"People will say they heard drumming *that day.*"

At the appointed time, Claude took the conga between his knees and began beating the skin with both hands. Even as Richard and I ran through yards and alleys between Lincoln Road and Maple Street, Claude pounded the drum. Belted into bed sheets, we scaled a brick wall to breach the security of the diamond merchant's grounds, where barking dogs set us running faster than usual across the lawn to burst through the Fabrikants' boxhedges into the street.

"So? What happened?"

Claude regarded the scratches on our arms and legs, our shredded sheets, then slumped over the conga as we confessed that people generally seemed not to notice us. The only direct comment had come from a young couple who watched us streak out of the Fabrikant estate, dogs nipping at our heels.

"Early for Halloween," they'd said.

My brother held up his red, swollen palms. "Find someone else to beat the drum."

* * *

"This is different. Really. I mean it. No drums."

Claude is skeptical.

I confide to my brother that I have fallen in love with

Adele, a skinny girl in bobby socks, who lives in an apartment house across the street. For weeks I have watched her jumping rope and sitting on the stoop, but can't work up the nerve to speak to her. But I have a plan. This will not be a repeat of the Ghost Riders, I promise him. He will be at the center of the action. But he must be willing to play the bad guy. But it only looks like he's the bad guy. In fact, he is the real hero.

"Who will know?"

"Me. I'll know." I ask if Claude has something better to do than be my hero.

He shrugs.

His job, I tell him, is to perch like a gargoyle on the mailbox at the corner of Flatbush and Lincoln. When Adele walks past on her way home from P.S. 92, he must jump from his perch and attack her. Not hurt her. Maybe knock her down.

"I don't know..."

"If you don't do this, I'll never speak to you again." I use this threat only when the seriousness of the occasion leaves no doubt that I will be true to my word. Claude's head hangs in submission. My heart soars.

The following day, I watch from behind a car on the opposite side of the street as my brother mounts the mailbox, struggles to balance himself on the curved roof above the steel maw into which several people very reluctantly post their letters. Adele steps off the Flatbush Avenue bus and approaches the corner, hugging a stack of books. She's clearly prepared to ignore the gargoyle squatting on the mailbox as having nothing to do with her. I hold my breath. Claude hesitates until she is nearly past, then jumps.

Her books fall, papers scatter. But she hardly has time to emit a scream before I bolt across the street, pull him off, then subdue him with a body slam. "You're not supposed to hurt me," he winces.

I pretend to choke him. He lies on the sidewalk stunned, fingers locked to my wrists.

"Let go," I mutter.

"You first."

I wait until he lies motionless before rising to ask if she's all right. She nods. I am surprised by her lack of gratitude, but help her pick up her books and papers. Out of the corner of my eye I watch my brother get to his feet and throw me a withering glance before limping across the street. At that moment, something magical happens. Adele reaches out. I hold both her hand and her books. Strolling thus, I hum Patti Page's recent hit, "You Belong to Me."

Strangely, the next afternoon, Adele and I glance at each other from opposite sides of the street, and it's as though we've never met. My brother glares at me from the porch.

rue de Bièvre
Paris/ July 8th, 1986

"Paulie?"

"You know what time it is?"

"I'm sorry."

"Three in the morning."

"There's something I have to know. Remember when Mom and Dad used to argue? Mom was all for opening windows. Dad was very private. Very guarded. She'd threaten: 'You don't want the neighbors to hear? I'll tell the world.'"

"What about it?"

"But Mom was the one who swore us to silence when she told us secrets. She worried continually about what THEY might think. What THEY might say."

"So?"

"Why would she hang out their dirty laundry, but swear us to secrecy?"

"Mom was full of contradictions."

"What did she yell out the window? WHAT WAS THE INDICTMENT? I need to know."

"She said he was cheap."

"That can't be all of it. I could go to Becker's Deli and charge whatever I wanted, and at the pharmacy. At Sonny's I bought egg-creams on credit. I had more allowance than any other kid on the block. Mom's indictment—he had money hidden under the floorboards. He sure didn't throw money around, like any Depression baby, but he wasn't cheap. There had to be more."

"His sexuality."

"Of course. She suspected everyone. 'Don't go to the men's room by yourselves.' I would ask, WHY? WHY? 'Because you're both adorable boys with round little tushies.' You were two years older, but I was a baby. I JUST DIDN'T GET IT!"

"I know."

"She scared the shit out of me. And then she dressed me up for Halloween assembly at Friends School as a bathing beauty. I was seven. Everyone walked down the aisle in costume. I told her I needed a costume. She said, "Let me do this, Claude. You'll be beautiful."

"She did the same to me."

"Not a pirate, a cowboy, even a ghost but...my God, a BATHING BEAUTY!"

"That was a long time ago."

"And I went along with it. WHAT THE HELL DID I KNOW? She was telling me, 'They'll really like you. Oh, you look beautiful.' I walked down that aisle, a pedophile's fantasy, and Mr. Popinjay, the principal, turned green."

IV

I've noticed how strangers, women as well as men, follow our mother with their eyes. At this morning's assembly in what doubles for the Quaker meeting house on Sundays, lower-grade children seated on benches watch Charlotte glide down the same aisle Claude had walked last Halloween dressed as a bathing beauty. A crimson shawl drapes her long black dress. At the front of the room, she puts down her violin case on a bench and faces the room. Mr. Popinjay, the principal of Brooklyn Friends School, who had turned green at the sight of my brother's "round little tushie" poking out of his bathing suit, takes Charlotte's hand in both of his. My brother, on the fifth-grade bench two rows in front of me, squirms.

This is not the first time our mother has played her violin at our assembly. Her past performances have left an indelible impression. Even my pal Robert, who reads Spinoza in the bathroom, gets a sappy look on his face when Charlotte, beside the grand piano, exposes her neck to the violin. Elbows on knees, the future philosopher watches her raise the bow. When she draws it suddenly across the strings to tune her instrument, his chest heaves.

Renoir and Rubens are Charlotte's favorite painters. After her bath, she used to strike "Rubenesque" poses. I may have been six when I entered my parents' bedroom one morning to find her standing naked in front of our father, still in bed. At first she seemed surprised. Then she began dancing around the frozen figure of my father. Arms above her head she turned in front of the half-open Venetian blinds, a living Renoir, thighs and rear as pink as bubble gum. Her breasts moved like nothing I'd ever seen before. (How could they have ever been dry?)

My father watched her, too, his face pale, the way it got when he trembled before leading a prayer at the Union

Temple seder. She rolled her shoulders forward, then danced back in quick little steps, rose on her tiptoes, arched, her arms reaching out TO ME! Suddenly I saw her as one of those figures she played on her violin, *The Dying Swan*, or *Daphne*, a nymph fleeing the attentions of a god.

At the assembly, she gazes out over this sea of faces at her fingertips: *La Mer*. Claude looks at me, a stricken Bambi: *L'Après-midi d'un Faun*. He knows that in a minute our mother will turn the meeting house into a place where swans die, or a faun conceived by a composer named Claude will appear in throbbing tights to pursue little woodland bathing beauties unprepared for the chase. Charlotte announces that she will play *The Meditation* from *Thaïs*. Her cheek rests against the slender violin. At the first sweep of her bow Robert abandons philosophy. But neither Robert nor my brother understands what they are watching: Charlotte has become *Thaïs*.

As far back as I can remember, my mother disappeared into the living room alone after dinner. Small enough to hide behind the pedals of the Steinway, I would watch her pull the drapes, then remove her violin from its velvet-lined case. I listened to her bow gypsy melodies. Her chin trembling, she played with a longing I couldn't understand. I lay there hardly breathing. What I saw from under the piano seemed more forbidden than the sight of her Rubenesque body dancing like Salome. Here was a nakedness she kept hidden even from herself...*Thaïs*, who now stood in front of the Quaker meeting house playing to mesmerized children. The same Thaïs I have glimpsed in black-and-white photos fronting her all-girl band at the Downtown Athletic Club, or with her trio on a cruise ship, perhaps the one on which she met our father.

***

Sunday morning, two days after Charlotte's performance before the lower-school assembly, our father wakes us at 6:30 AM to go on rounds. It's still dark. He has been in the operating room since 5:00. No one works as hard he does. We agree to keep him company even though we feel like staying in bed. Claude dresses in his sleep. Our father takes out a ring of keys, unlocks the closet next to my bed, takes an envelope from his jacket pocket and puts the money inside. Money. He has many envelopes of cash in the closet, and not, as our mother insists, "under the floor boards." Also in the closet are expensive watches, rings, cufflinks, tieclips, and bracelets. None of which he will wear. He likes linen shirts and silk ties. No jewelry. His olive skin, black hair, hawknose, and mustache make him look like the Sheik of Araby; our Sephardic ancestry, he tells us.

Not only cash and jewelry are locked in his closet, but mysterious memorabilia, some that go back further than 1911 when he left his *shtetl*. Once he put on his old *tefillen*, phylacteries, to show Claude and me how he prayed when he was our age, wrapping the little black boxes around his forehead, arms, and hands. We had laughed at the sight of him bound up that way, like a prisoner or cripple.

At just over five feet tall, he has the chest and arms of a boxer, which he was as a young man. He gave up boxing because it gave him headaches and surgeons have to take care of their hands. His hands are remarkable, not only for their speed, but their dexterity. I've seen him practice knotting and unknotting a silk cord in his pocket or in a matchbox with two fingers of one hand.

"We should start planning your bar mitzvah."

"That's a year away."

"A blink of the eye. You can do it at the Union Temple."

This is the first time he's spoken to me about this since I was kicked out of Hebrew school at the Ocean Avenue Synagogue for lighting a cigarette in the back of the classroom. (*What am I going to do with you?* my father lamented. *Keep this up and you'll end up on the Bowery.*) I can handle it, and tell him as much. The Union Temple is Reform. I won't have to memorize much Hebrew.

Claude sleeps against my shoulder. As we drive downtown to the Brooklyn Jewish Hospital, a sad gray building, he asks me if I remember my grandmother, Pepi, a.k.a Pauline, after whom I am named. It is a question he asks only in the car on Sunday rounds. I shake my head.

"She was a remarkable woman."

Pepi crossed in steerage with her two sons from Hamburg on the *Kaiserin Auguste Victoria*, then kept her family together after her husband, who drank beer by the bucket, left them in a tubercular tenement in Williamsburg. She took in sewing, cleaned the halls, and carried out the garbage. At the thought of her, his eyes fill. His sadness is different than Charlotte's, but also too deep for me to touch. I hate to see his silent tears. He has no eyebrows and only the faintest hint of lashes on his heavy lids.

When he clears his throat, I know that he is about to say something that is hard to get out.

"Your mother...is very unhappy."

"Is she going to leave again?" Claude suddenly wakes up.

"I don't know. I've given her everything. I don't know what else to do."

We don't either. Our mother and father are so different, and war within us as well as outside of us. I am dark-eyed like father but behave like Mom. Claude is blue-eyed like Charlotte's side (hers are hazel), but shy like Dad. I am named after Pepi, by Father, and recognize myself in that name. Claude is named by Mother after great French Claudes, like Debussy and Monet. He hates his name. It reeks to him of water lilies, improbable fauns, and little-boy bathing beauties.

Charlotte has become the protégée of "hanging Judge" Samuel Leibowitz, once the defense lawyer in the famous Scottsboro case. Drawn to her glamour and earthy humor, he has assigned her to a highly visible murder trial, the kind of case on which lawyers build big careers.

34

Our father, on the other hand, insists that he's become surgical chief-of-staff at Brooklyn Jewish Hospital over talented, more aggressive men precisely because he is modest and threatens no one.

"Are you all right?" I ask as we leave the Jewish Hospital.

"I'm just a *little stiff* from Bowling."

His laugh is a shattered exhalation. None of his patients have died this morning. He's grateful for the opportunity to tell his favorite pun one more time. The punch line, we have learned, refers not only to an athletic activity, but a small town in Ohio.

"*Call me anything but late to dinner,*" he smiles on our way to the Adelphi.

Depression humor, our mother calls it.

Charlotte loves Lucille Ball. Two nights ago our mother appeared in the living room after dinner in a strapless gown, holding her violin, hair pulled back in a bun, a stern expression on her face. The minute her cheek rested on the wood, our father's doctor friends and their wives stopped talking. She bowed the first notes of her favorite gypsy lament, *Zigeuner*, and then smiled to reveal a mouth blackened with candy wrappers, except for a single white tooth. After the guests recovered from the shock, everyone but our father applauded.

rue de Bièvre
Paris/ June 9th, 1986

I dream about two brothers strapped into chairs like those on a ride at Luna Park. In matching suspenders, short pants, striped polos, and beanies, they remind me of the Katzenjammer Kids, an old cartoon Claude and I followed in the Sunday papers. Their chairs are fixed to one end of an iron bar extending several feet from a central pole. As the pole turns at an ever-increasing speed, the chairs move contrapuntally up and down like horses on a merry-go-round. I find myself looking out through the eyes of one of the brothers. I can't see anything clearly because of the whirling motion, but have a heightened sense of my interior: my thoughts race, but with great precision. I formulate sentences expressing these thoughts, complete with illuminating metaphors comparing my brother and myself to orbiting moons, dadophori, photons that are particles or waves depending on the position of the observer. Other insights flow from a source buried in my unconscious that organizes perceptions according to its own intention and then sends them to my conscious mind until I recognize something I could not see before. This is my genius, a companion that understands the long-body of experience at a glance. If I listen, it will speak through me. I feel gifted and blessed, as well as powerful.

Suddenly I look out from the body of the other brother. I know this because I can feel the difference right away. Where I had felt light, I now feel heavy. In my former state, my genius could speak through me. Here, I open my mouth to speak but can't. I am dumbfounded. Mute. Weak. Vulnerable. I have no sword or shield, am utterly transparent. Without words everything transpires in unbounded space. Subject melts into object. I remark at this insight, but it instantly dissolves in unbounded space, an undiluted awareness in which pain and joy are married into a single substance that can only be experienced in the Body of Silence. My earlier experience in the Body of Words is as a candle flame to the sun.

I wake with a vibrant sensation in my chest that I can only describe as radiance, a heat that doesn't burn. I suddenly understand that what I thought of as my claim to insight might be as superficial as my dream experience in the Body of Words; but for the message encrypted in the dream by a genius buried below consciousness, I might never have suspected the depth I now locate in the other brother, the Body of Silence.

Nothing seems of greater importance than sharing the message of my dream with Claude. I dial my brother's number. It rings ten times before I hear breath on the other side.

"Who is this?"

"It's me."

"Are you sure?"

I tell him the dream and wait for his response. When none seems forthcoming, I ask him to think about it and let me know if he has anything to say.

"Sure, Paulie. For you nothing is real unless it can be put into words. Even after you've had this dream, felt the world from the Body of Silence, you will try to squeeze something from the Body of Words. You can't help yourself. That's just who you are. Does that sum it up?"

I am wordless.

"Ok, so tell me why Mom dressed us as bathing beauties and then turned us out into that den of pedophiles."

Still struggling to hold onto my dream experience, my response to his question is a confession that leaves me feeling utterly transparent. Charlotte had convinced me that I looked beautiful, and I joined the Halloween parade convinced that this was so. I had experienced my beauty as a kind of power, liked the attention I received, the ohhhs and ahhhs of the spectators. Especially those who said what a pretty girl I might have been.

"Well, you and Mom always were the flashy dressers."

V

"Your mother's a celebrity." Our father spreads the newspaper on the dinner table. "The *Brooklyn Eagle* compares her to Portia in *The Merchant of Venice*, who spoke of mercy as a gentle rain."

"*It is twice blessed.*" I know something about "the quality of mercy." We are reading Shakespeare at school.

"I have to convince a jury of that."

Mom signals Esther in the kitchen to serve our meal. Our Mom hired Esther to help around the house now that she will be busy at court. Only six years older than me, she is a round and (as she calls herself) "teasin' brown" country girl from North Carolina.

"Cheeseburgers, again!" I complain.

"What's wrong with cheeseburgers?" asks Claude.

"I can't afford anything else on what your father gives me."

"Now that you're famous, we can eat steak."

"You expect me to fix gourmet meals for your friends. But when I need you for a State Bar dinner, you're too busy."

"Soon you'll be giving me an allowance." He smiles at Esther, who serves his "chopped steak," a cheeseless burger in disguise.

Esther purses her lips in an exaggerated display of doubt that strikes us funny. Esther, in her own words, "tickles" us. She dips snuff and says things like "look-a-yonder." Claude and I agree that she feels more like a live-in sister than a maid.

"Did you see the *Daily Mirror*?" Our mother passes the paper to Ben.

There is a photo of Charlotte that takes up half the page. Her hair is pulled back in a bun. She looks directly at the camera, her lips set, neither smiling nor frowning. Our father's hands tremble slightly.

"What did the woman do?" Claude wants to know.

"She killed her husband with an ax," our mother answers.

"That's enough." Father closes the paper.

"While he was asleep," Charlotte adds.

"Eat your vegetables, boys," he commands.

Brussels sprouts make Claude fart. Our father calls him *little fartling*. My brother gets a mischievous smile on his face just before he lets one go.

"Why did she kill him in his sleep?" my brother asks.

"Because he beat her regularly for years."

"Paulie punches me all the time."

"In the arm."

"Farting is better than fighting," Claude says.

"Not at dinner," I tell him.

"Why do you want to be her lawyer?" my brother picks up a Brussels sprout with his fingers.

"I don't think she deserves to die."

"Your mother fights for the underdog." This thought comforts our father.

We had always thought of an underdog as a creature who lies at the feet of his master like our boxer, Barney, at our father's feet, farting tirelessly. Once, Mom brought home a woman she found on a Flatbush Avenue doorstep. She bathed the woman, gave her a change of clothes, then let her rest in the bed she shared with our father. When he came home and saw the woman in their bed, Ben was furious. Our mother thundered back at him until he could no longer stand it and locked himself in his study, where he spent the night. This extended our understanding of the word "underdog," as it applied to our father. The definition now includes a woman who buried an ax in her husband's head while he slept.

The phone rings. Our father answers it. Usually, the calls are for him. Since Judge Leibowitz assigned our mother the Martha Hochfeld case, reporters, lawyers, clients and well meaning friends have been phoning nonstop to speak to her.

Especially after the story broke into the headlines. She takes the receiver from him.

"Yes, this is she."

Claude and I know "Hanging Judge" Leibowitz. He is the gray-haired man we visit with Mom in his chambers at the court on Schermerhorn Street, next door to Friends School.

"Why would he assign this case to *me*?" She cradles the phone to her cheek as she does the violin. "Because I've paid my dues. When I defend a prostitute, I go down to the tank and talk to her, get to know her story. I do it all the time. You know what I've discovered? Most of them are women who have been abused, just like my client."

"Must you give interviews at dinner?" our father inquires.

"What are prostitutes?" asks Claude.

"Women who sell themselves to men."

Dad glares at her. She returns his stare. This isn't the way she usually fights with him. Most of the time she'll either yell or break into tears. When the phone rings again, he starts to reach for it, but stops. Mom gets to it before the ringing stops.

"What do prostitutes have in common with *normal* women like those who work at respectable jobs or take care of the home? *You want to know?* Because I or your wife might as easily find herself in the same position if fate had ruled otherwise."

It is a short interview.

"You're going to make people suspect I beat you," says our father.

"Not all wounds are made with a fist."

"Will you plead insanity?"

"Should I? Martha knows what she did. The man broke her arm in three places, blackened her eyes, and used her face as a punching bag. The question is how do I handle a press that wants to make her Lizzie Borden so they can fry her like Joan of Arc?"

"So, unhappy women can kill their husbands and get away with it."

"Thank you, Ben, for your support."

"Watch out for the ax, Dad." I say it before I can stop myself.

"How dare you!" She glares at me.

Claude gives us his *little fartling smile.*

* * *

Neither of us has seen Charlotte since she walked out of the house on Lincoln Road a week before Christmas. We knew things would never be the same after the Martha Hochfeld case. From the moment her client was sentenced to life in prison, until our mother's departure ten days later, our mother's cheeks were glazed with tears.

"You saved her from the electric chair," argued our father.

"For what? A life behind bars?"

The *Daily Mirror* described the way lawyer and client embraced that day in the courtroom before guards led Martha away. "Portia Outraged," read the headline. Our mother told the *Brooklyn Eagle*: "Today, Justice is another abused woman."

It was as if they'd locked our mother up as well.

After that she moved to the attic bedroom, next door to Esther, who brought her meals to the room. Claude was too scared to go upstairs, but I went up one evening with Esther. The room was damp and smelled like face cream. Our mother lay in the dark, propped against the pillows, crying. I hugged her but she couldn't stop. My cheek slipped off of hers. Esther, who was only eighteen herself, led me downstairs.

Claude couldn't believe our mother was going to leave for good. He made her a card with a drawing of children fishing under a rainbow, but she left one day while we were at school before he could give it to her. What could we do to make sure she'd come back? he asked at dinner.

"Nothing," our father replied. The best he could do was assure us that Charlotte would call us once she was settled. As the weeks passed, my brother stopped talking about her. He stopped talking much about anything. When she finally did call, we refused to speak to her. Esther tried to hand me the phone, but I'd waved it away. I couldn't think of anything to say and didn't want to pretend that nothing had changed. We were the only kids at Brooklyn Friends whose mother had left them. Finally, two months before my bar mitzvah, I accepted the receiver.

"I miss you," she whispered.

I couldn't reply, *I miss you too*, but agreed to visit her at the Hotel St. George. I'd been there before to swim in the huge indoor pool with a waterfall at one end. I knew my way around Brooklyn Heights.

I leave my usual dungarees and motorcycle boots on the chair. Instead, I put on a pair of clean black chinos with a belt in the back, a white shirt covered by a red V-neck pullover. A little Dixie Peach to hold my hair down. I don't brush it into a DA, but part it on the left, then push it up in front with my palm to make a pompadour like our father's. My new foreign-intrigue trench coat is perfect for the role of secret agent. I promise Claude to scout the territory and report back. He can go with me next time.

"Maybe." He hands me the card with two boys fishing under a rainbow and the message inside: *Welcome Home, Mom.*

I take the BMT from Prospect Park to Fulton, where I change for the IRT to Pineapple Street. I like the feeling of traveling this way. I watch my reflection in the window, wondering if my mother will be surprised by what she sees; the child she left has become a man.

Inside the hotel, I am surprised at how shabby it has become. The tables in the lobby are scratched, the carpets worn, and the upholstered chairs dusty. Paint peels from the high walls. At the desk, I remember to ask for our mother by her maiden name. I feel as though I am going to visit a distant relative. A dark-suited man gives me a sixth-floor room number.

The paneled elevator stops on six. I wander down a hall lit by bulbs in party-hat shades until I locate room 602. There are no sounds on the other side of the door. I button, then unbutton my trench coat. What if she isn't there? I knock, remembering my reflection in the subway glass. This is what she will see.

The door opens.

A woman stands there in a flimsy black negligee. Her hair is platinum. The small upturned nose bears no resemblance to my mother's bold one, Portia's nose that leaped from the pages of two newspapers. I am about to apologize for mistaking the room when I see a flicker in her eyes, which are chestnut flecked with green.

"Hello, Paulie."

I'd gotten lost in those eyes as a child, feel myself trapped in them now. Thaïs peeks out at me. Not even a nose job can disguise her.

I fall helplessly into her embrace.

Afterwards, I am ashamed.

I wanted to present her with the boy become a man, but that was before I stood speechless before a more dramatic transformation than my own. Instead of the mother I'd known, I find a face I don't recognize, a mask called Charlotte who reminds me more of Jean Harlow in *Hell's Angels* than the Portia who had defended an axe-murderess.

What does that make me?

A twelve-year-old boy in a trench coat.

The following Saturday, Claude accompanies me. He insists on wearing his own beltless trench coat. All the way to the

Hotel St. George I warn him not to expect the mother he's known. He will still see her if he looks into her eyes.

Whatever fears I may have had for Claude vanish. The instant she opens the door his head is buried in her chest. Afterward, Claude and I change into bathing suits and go down to swim in the pool. My brother is happy, slipping around on the mosaic tiles, imitating a midget doing a back stroke under the simulated waterfall. Back upstairs, we are shocked to find a freckled man with a Friar Tuck fringe of red hair in our mother's room. He sticks out his hand: "Hi, boys. Call me Derf. That's Fred, backwards."

Claude can't hide his disappointment. We aren't going to have our new blonde mother to ourselves. But we go out for dinner, steaks, the way my brother likes them, rare, with fried onion rings. He eats as if he hasn't had anything for days, and ends with a banana split. We learn that Derf is a dentist who can make his face look like a box by pulling down the skin under his jaw.

"Be square," he tells us in the hotel lobby, before disappearing into the night. We change into pajamas and crawl into a pullout couch facing the TV. Neither of us are surprised to learn six weeks later that Charlotte has married him and moved to Forest Hills.

rue de Bièvre
Paris/ July 16th, 1986

Après Bastille day.
Jean and Lila invite Carol and me to screen the French director's films. What we see leaves us dumbstruck. The silence becomes even more oppressive when the lights go on. Lila stares at the floor. My wife fidgets. At last Jean says,

"We may have made a mistake. But we went through the list of available French directors carefully. Tavernier just finished Round Midnight *and wasn't interested in another film about jazz. Truffaut would have been ideal, but he's dead." Jean pulls out the list. "Can you think of anyone?"*

"What about Daniel Vigne?" I try a long shot, recalling how much I admired The Return of Martin Guerre.

Jean shrugs. "I'll call him in the morning."

Lila phones the following week to say that Vigne likes my book. A few days later, we arrive for dinner at Le Boucherie to meet a small man in a blue sport jacket, open shirt, and chinos. His curly black hair graying at the temples frames a broad face. His eyes burn into me when we shake hands. He recalls following John Coltrane and Elvin Jones with a camera through the south of France in the early 70s. His love of jazz is second only to his love of opera. He hums Berlioz's Les Nuits d' Eté. *My wife, who trained as an opera singer, joins in. Together they segue into Canteloube's "Songs of the Auvergne." Do I like Betty Carter? McCoy Tyner? New York is the only place to shoot this film, n'est-ce pas? Raising money won't be a problem after his latest movie starring Gérard Depardieu, Sigourney Weaver, and Dr. Ruth Westheimer opens this September at the Paris Theater in New York. A real American comedy. It will make him bankable in Hollywood. We'll talk further after he finishes reading my scenario. The Director disappears after dessert with my screenplay tucked under his arm.*

Returning to our apartment on rue de Bièvre, we are both ready to take a deep breath and relax until we hear from Vigne. We are a couple twice blessed, pregnant with a movie and a child. It occurs to me that I haven't shared the news of Carol's pregnancy with Claude. I want to do so. I am sure he will be delighted by the fact he's about to become an uncle. Perhaps it will replace his current obsessions.

I try his number only to hear a message that his telephone has been disconnected. As of this moment, he is truly the Body of Silence.

I panic. Has Claude defaulted on his bill? Ripped the jack from the wall? Sealed himself off against his accusers? I review our recent phone calls. There were the old ladies he'd been accused of mugging, and someone was spreading libelous gossip about him. Perhaps that he had once paraded down the aisle of the meeting house at Brooklyn Friends School as a bathing beauty?

WHAT WAS THE INDICTMENT?

I pace wildly, wondering what has happened to him, trying to figure out my next move.

VI

I mean it when I promise Claude to make him the best second baseman known to man. There'll be no one like him in the Ice Cream League, where we play baseball with a team of neighborhood kids, the Jaguars, organized by the father of a boy my age, Artie, whom I had known only casually. For the last two years, the Jaguars have been the center of my life. Claude has just started to play with the team this year. My promise to make him a Jaguar hero takes him by surprise. He regards me with suspicion, even as hope darts in his eyes like an impossibly blue hummingbird.

"We've got to work at it every day," I tell him.

"Sure." My brother shrugs.

For an hour every day after school Claude meets me in the alley where I pepper him with grounders.

The idea came to me when my career as starting pitcher for the Jaguars hit the skids. Batters seldom touched my fast ball, but I beaned as many batters as I struck out. When our benevolent coach, Mr. Bookbinder, shifts me from the mound to shortstop, I figure grooming Claude at second base might pay off for us both. Brooklyn Dodger scouts are always hanging around the Parade Grounds looking for talent. How can they miss us!

For six months I drill him with every kind of hop, slider, skidder, and bad bounce. When his spirit sags I remind him that with my help his glove will soon become a miraculous fielding machine. One day, he'll thank me. "Forget Tinker to Evers to Chance, or Reese to Robinson to Hodges," I call out. "It's Pines to Pines, the pride of the Jaguars."

At twelve, Claude is coming into his baseball prime while I am slightly over the hill at fourteen. This, I tell myself, is why I am sitting in Becker's Deli, watching our teammates paste each other with French fries. Danny, the waiter, in a white shirt and black bow tie, stands watch at the rear. Even so, Artie flicks a piece of coleslaw at Yagamitza, our catcher. Joey Suarez and his cousin Juan Montero spray mustard on a kosher dog, then on each other's hands. A year ago, they danced to *ha-va-nagila* at my bar mitzvah reception in the Hotel Granada ballroom. No one cared that there were no girls. The Jaguars, pride of the Parade Grounds, were happy dancing with each other.

When I started throwing him grounders, Claude wanted nothing more than to be a Jaguar. I kept my promise. He now has the glove of a god. But things have changed for me, too. As deeply as I once felt about hitting one over the fence or executing a clean double play, I'm suddenly more interested in shooting pool at Louie's, or picking up a cutie with Bad Bill at the Patio Theater. I've spent at least as much time this summer drinking Southern Comfort with guys who used to give me hard looks as playing baseball. *But here, for a moment, in Becker's deli, I remember how good it feels to be a Jaguar.*

This morning, we arrived early at the Parade Grounds, before the diamonds filled up. Instead of waiting for one to empty, a bunch of older guys challenged us to play for ours. What started out as Jaguar practice turned into a pick-up game. Claude was at the Grand Army Plaza library finishing a report on Poland. Even without the best second baseman known to man, the impossible happened: we beat these older guys. It was just one of those days when everything went right. When it was over, I invited the Jaguars to a victory celebration at the deli, on me.

Walking down Flatbush, shouting and backslapping, I dared to dream again of baseball possibilities, when it hit me: *Pines-to-Pines would never be. Girls and adventure called out too strongly. I will not be able to stay with Claude, and he will not be able to follow me where I'm going. There's no place for a second baseman in a pool room, not even one who can field grounders with his teeth.*

No matter how painful it may be, I am ready to move on.

Frankie Lane said it best; it is as undeniable as the call of the wild goose in my heart.

It is different for my brother. He tries to hold on forever, as he did with his upright bottle. He hoards food, shirts, toys, baseball cards, and fishing tackle. In the same way, he holds on to our father by being *a good boy*.

"Claude understands *frugality*," says Ben, remembering the other Ben, from Boston, who made a name for himself handing out such advice.

More than anything, my brother holds on to money.

Claude squirrels his allowance in a cabinet by his bed just the way our father stuffs envelopes full of cash into his closet. I can't save a dime. I stay out till all hours of the night, and I come home with bad grades.

"I don't understand you!" Our father shakes his head. *"Do you want to end up on the Bowery?"*

My brother worries that he'll have to save me later in life when I'm huddling with the other bums around a garbage-can fire under the Third Avenue El. If I learned to be frugal, I might avoid the Bowery. It is simply a matter of impulse control. This is why he has agreed to my suggestion that we pool our allowances. We will buy something special at the end of the year. To this end, for the last six months, I have turned two dollars a week over to Claude, who has matched the amount.

Following my revelation at the corner of Lincoln and Flatbush that my Jaguar days are over, I detour home to raid the savings. This is more than a victory celebration. It is a wake. A funeral. A silent goodbye. There are six packets of ten one-dollar bills wrapped neatly in rubber bands. The issue of money, how much or whose it is, melts into insignificance. On the wings of a transcendent impulse, I take it all.

Back at the deli, I watch Pappy, our power-hitter-center-fielder order two more specials. Yagamitza, "the human wall," calls out for onion rings and another Cel-ray tonic. Danny turns his back to put in the order. A ruffled fry whizzes by my ear. I'll miss these guys. Claude has games ahead of him, brilliant moments at second base. He doesn't need me. He can do this on his own.

Potato and kasha knishes, pastrami on rye, corned beef on kaiser roll with Russian dressing, club sandwiches and baked beans washed down with Dr. Brown's or Coke are my parting Jaguar gifts. I'm filled with a sadness and exhilaration larger than anything known to frugal souls...

My brother's face appears at the window, his nose pressed to the glass like a Tyrolean mushroom. I raise my deli club with Russian dressing. His eyes are on fire. His hair electrified. Jaguars wave and call out, glad to see him.

Claude takes a step inside, but stops in the doorway, unable to advance any further, his body shaking, speechless.

"Wanna bite?" I say.

Our mother starts showing up after school. At the end of the day we can never tell when we'll find her in the front hall sitting on the bench where I have lately been logging more time for bad behavior than usual. Today I spent an hour there for talking back to the math teacher, Mr. Engelhard. He singles out a kid in every grade to bully. In 9th grade, I'm it. I wear my hair long and look different from the other kids: a perfect victim.

"Mr. Pines, is there something going on in that excuse for a brain? Why don't you come to the board and show us how to solve for X."

"X equals fuck you!" I told him.

I've been sitting on the hall bench since first grade, humiliated by countless lines of kids filing past on their way to the cafeteria, library, gym. I was here through lunch. Now, at the end of the day, we find Mom in my spot, hands folded in her lap like a repentant child.

Where everyone can see her.

Her presence reminds everyone that our parents are divorced. I can hear the unspoken question in the minds of my classmates: What desperate acts in this unscripted version of life do her appearances signify? How different she looks from the woman who enchanted the assembly with her violin. Even if they don't say anything, it's clear that there is something fishy about the New Charlotte. When Claude shows up, we leave the bench-of-humiliation behind.

We no longer visit Judge Leibowitz next door at the courthouse after school. Instead, our mother takes us shopping at Mays or A. & S. Claude chooses striped polo shirts, long-sleeved navy-blue flannels. She lets me buy the clothes our father won't, black shirts with silver threads, lavender dress shirts with rolling "Mr. B." collars. At a store on Fulton Street I find apricot pegged pants with double saddle-stitching and a five-inch rise above the belt loops. A perfect fit. Our mother is delighted. My brother cringes. I wear the pants out. Claude refuses to meet my eyes.

A visit to Schrafft's, across the street, marks the final phase of our outing. The art-deco ice cream parlor is a monument to matronly elegance. Today we are the only people here. It is really tomb-like. We walk on white tile floors, past a marble ice cream counter, to tables set with linen napkins and paper doilies. The waitress wears a white apron and a lace collar over her black dress. Claude orders his usual hot turkey sandwich. I get a burger, our mother, a watercress sandwich. After we are served, the New Charlotte again reviews the terms of the divorce.

"Your father was determined to fight me all the way. He told me he'd let you boys go *over his dead body*. I would have had to drag you both through court. Better to let him have his way. Besides, I knew that he'd provide for you in a way that I can't."

Charlotte's voice sinks to a whisper when the waitress comes to see if we need anything, then moves on. Our mother shifts into a higher gear.

"The only woman Ben ever loved was his mother. A real *Momma's boy*. She let him lie in bed, read, and eat apples while she took in sewing, cleaned the halls and toilets. His brothers had to work. She made them promise to pay for your father's medical school. And they did."

Claude stuffs the last of his hot turkey into his mouth, before demolishing the gravy dam he's constructed in his mashed potatoes. I wonder if she thinks of my brother as a *momma's boy* because of the way he escapes into his food, and finish my burger.

"During the Depression he sold apples on the street. It scarred him for life. No matter how wealthy your father becomes, he'll always be cheap."

Even though Claude put away a cafeteria lunch as well two hours earlier, he orders a banana split. For me a scoop of chocolate with fudge and crushed pineapple will do. Our mother orders coffee. The waitress gives us a smile as white as her apron.

"Your father was also humiliated by his size," her voice rises. "Ben wears lifts in his shoes. Once he had to stand on a box to operate."

Her words are like her dance. She is Salome shedding veils that hide something freakish, the Man/Woman at Luna Park, with one pink nipple held by a net.

A part of me wants to protest, defend our father's honor. *My father's humiliation is my own.* I, too, am smaller than my friends and hide that pain by playing the tough-guy with my leather jacket, motorcycle boots, long DA, and dark stare. I wish the man she calls Ben were tougher, could hold his own like Alan Ladd in *Shane.* They say Ladd had to stand on a box to kiss his leading ladies. Short-statured George Raft makes women swoon when he flips that silver dollar and talks out of the side of his face. Our mother would never speak disrespectfully to James Cagney in *Public Enemy* or Edward G. Robinson in *Little Caesar.* Digging into my ice cream sundae, I want to be a scrappy little Jew like John Garfield in *Body and Soul,* a boxer who can go twelve rounds, shower, and then play a Rachmaninoff piano concerto.

Claude's face is full of whipped cream. He's already as tall as I am and will probably pass me by. Being short doesn't seem to bother him. I search myself for the grit of a Bugsy Siegel. Before I can find it, my mother's lips have spoken the most feared word in the English language, one that makes me tremble as I might before *Godzilla* or *King Kong*. It falls from her lips like nitroglycerin.

"And there is, of course, the issue of your father's *latent* homosexuality. There are so many of them. And not all *latent*."

According to our mother, even active homosexuals are often hard to recognize. But they can pick each other out in a crowd and band together, like communists. Many are quite charming. Take Wallace, for instance, our father's best friend, who is a crony of Leonard Bernstein's.

Wallace, I point out, is happily married to June and has three kids.

"Many *latents* have wives and children. But they usually treat their wives like servants, as if women were there to *worship their little weenies*."

I instinctively cross my legs. My brother appears to be fishing for crappies in his half-empty ice cream boat.

"Claudie, you remember I taught you that there are men who like to touch plump little boys."

"Like Mr. Popinjay," Claude cites the principal who has made passes at bad boys like Barrett and Mark, never the good ones.

"You have to be careful. Homosexuals know just how..." Before Charlotte can finish, she bursts into tears. "I know how angry you are at me for leaving. But I couldn't live at Lincoln Road another day. *If I hadn't left, I would've died.*"

The three of us stare at our soiled doilies, a signal to our waitress that we're ready for the check. We walk our mother to the subway. Claude no longer cares that I am wearing apricot pants. At the entrance to the IND line that will take her through a series of tunnels to Forest Hills, Charlotte

makes us promise never to discuss what she's just confided.
We promise. Our mother hugs us before descending into the
underworld.

rue de Bièvre
Paris/ July 17th, 1986

*I spend a sleepless night, worrying about my brother, chasing
obsessive fantasies from my mind's eye: Claude perched on
the Brooklyn Bridge, decomposing in the darkness of his
room on West 75th Street, jumping onto the subway tracks of
the IND as a train to Forest Hills pulls in. From the living-
room window of our apartment, I watch sunrise set fire to
the red tiles of Parisian rooftops. Suddenly a light goes on
inside of me as well.*

Of course! Why didn't I think of it earlier?

*I phone Wallace and June in Rye. If Claude isn't with
them, they are likely to know where he is. June answers. It's
been a while since I've spoken to either of them, and I hear
myself stammer an apologetic hello.*

Claude is there.

*My brother and "Le Chat" have moved to Highcliff at
their invitation, June informs me. The New York apartment,
that "basement hole-in-the-ground," was no good for Claude.*

*"He needs to take stock of himself in a supportive
environment."*

*I picture June's guppy mouth as she talks from the
luxurious Tudor mansion surrounded by ancient shade trees.
Inside, Wallace's curvilinear chairs in teak and bleached
rosewood, abstract paintings that echo cabinets inset with
cane and turquoise leather dance above exotic carpets*

floating on hardwood floors. A wall of windows looks out on Long Island Sound, punctuated by small islands. Gulls cry.

Highcliff has been a refuge for Claude since our father died, a second home where he enjoys the company of celebrities such as Rita Moreno and Steve Gordon, author of the movie Arthur.

"You may have bitten off more than you think," I tell her.

"We won't pamper him. Claude will have to carry his own weight—wash the dishes, clean his room, help with the chores."

I wonder how chores work in a house with a maid and groundskeeper, but think better of asking. "Can I speak to him?"

"He's down at the dock, fishing." I can hear the twinkle in June's eyes. "I'll tell him you called when he comes up for dinner."

VII

In late March, 1955, our father brings Betty home for dinner. We have been alerted to this unusual event at breakfast when he also tells us that the woman he met recently at a cocktail party is an elementary school teacher from Queens. Nothing he has said prepares us for the woman who follows our father into the house.

Betty is twice as tall and half his age. He has to reach up to help her out of her plain cloth coat. We are struck by the size of her round head, crowned by puffy blond hair, on a long body with spaghetti-thin arms and legs. At the dinner table she asks us in a breathy voice about school, what we like to do most and with whom, then makes an exaggerated display of listening to our responses. When I tell her I am reading Wordsworth and learning to hustle eight-ball at Louie's, her face breaks into a gleaming smile. *Little Bo-peep*. On the couch that evening, skirt flared over bony knees, Betty holds our father's hand and addresses him in baby-talk. *Rebecca of Sunnybrook Farm*. They are composing their very own fairy tale in which Snow White ends up with Bashful.

We are speechless at bedtime when he asks, "Well, boys, what do you think of her?"

"Why can't he fall in love with Miss Smith?" Claude mumbles before turning out the light. He wants Dad to marry his secretary whose eyes bathe us in motherly concern whenever we show up at the office. But our father has shown no interest in Miss Smith or in any other woman since our mother left. There was Edna, a Texas oil widow, who wore flowery hats, had loose skin under her chin. She would stare adoringly at Dad over dinner. When he decided against moving to Lubbock, Edna simply dropped away.

We are most disturbed by Betty's effect on him. When our father gazes at her, sparks fly from his flinty eyes. She inspires a lightness of spirit in him we haven't seen in years, maybe never. He makes bad puns. There is a spring in his step...and the suggestion of something a little out of control. He wonders aloud, "Who would have thought this could happen to me?"

"I don't trust her," says Claude.

I remind him of what our father was like before he met Betty, how he'd withdraw to his study after supper and that would be the last we'd see of him until the following afternoon. Does he remember the heaviness of Dad's basset-eyes? We had both begun to stoop under the weight of our father's melancholy. Claude would shuffle down the hall after his father refused his invitation to watch TV.

My brother sees that Betty makes our father happy. On the eve of his bar mitzvah at Union Temple, Claude agrees to give her the benefit of the doubt, but not without a dubious tilt of his head. He is so delighted to be the center of attention that he even allows her to kiss his forehead after the ceremony. At the reception, my brother stands proudly beside Ben in front of two large chopped liver swans on the buffet in our dining room. Counting his booty at the end of the evening, Claude is surprised to find that he now owns twenty traveling alarm clocks.

"What's the message? Wake up and get out of town?"

A month later our father marries Betty, after assuring us that things will turn out for the best.

The first thing Betty does is fire Esther.

We cry and beg our father to keep the woman who has been a mother/sister to us, who has sheltered us in her big brown arms, reassured us that as long as we stuck together, the three of us, everything would be all right.

"Betty has a right to a fresh start," he insists.

"What about us?" pleads Claude.

Before she leaves, Esther makes Claude and me promise to look after each other. A solemn oath, she calls it, and we have to raise our right hands and swear this to her before she goes. "Whatever happens, you boys have each other."

Betty hires Estella, a Cuban who speaks no English. Our father likes the idea that we'll have to learn Spanish. Estella has skin the color of pecans and a gold tooth that glitters when she smiles. We don't blame her for the loss of Esther. Perched on the edge of my bed, Claude, Estella, and I watch Castro make his triumphal entry into Havana, the three of us shouting, *Viva Fidel!*

"She's a gold digger," Charlotte announces at Schraffts.
"Gold digger?"
"Betty's after his money," I explain to Claude.
"How do you know?" His cheeks color.
"You're a bar mitzvah boy, old enough to deal with the truth."
"He has twenty traveling alarm clocks," I put in.
"Your father is sending her to Columbia University for her masters in education, financing her nursery school, and building her an art collection worth *godknowshowmuch*. I couldn't get five bucks out of him to pay the butcher."
It's a mystery to me how our mother knows so much about all this, especially their art collection. It's as if she snuck in and saw it when no one else was home, but that's impossible. I suddenly understand why Betty insisted on firing Esther, and what Ben meant by giving her a fresh start. Esther had been our mother's eyes and ears.
"Betty drags him to Park-Bernet to bid on Utrillos. The man I knew couldn't tell a Utrillo from a Petrillo."
Our father makes sure we know the names of painters he buys. There are two in the blue room by Utrillo, a Monet in the study, and a new landscape by Pissarro in the hall. Downstairs, in the living room, I am haunted by Iness's red sun going down behind a hayfield. Their latest acquisitions are a bronze casting of Rodin's *Balzac* and portraits in huge gilt frames of two men in George Washington collars, after the style of Godfrey Kneller.
We don't tell our mother that our father has begun to

entertain again at the house, as he did when she lived there. His friends are quickly won over by this young wife who seems so anxious to please. When Dad and Betty dress to go out, he sings like Perry Como. They have a box at the Met and go to the ballet at the City Center. Sometimes we tag along for dinner at the Brass Rail or the Spindletop. But it is usually under protest. Her teased straw hair towering over his small head crowned by thinning hair is too hard to take.

For him, his marriage to Betty is even more remarkable than his success as a physician. He wonders aloud: "Who would have thought that a poor Jewish boy from Williamsburg would bag such a radiant *shiksa*?"

***

Weekends with the New Charlotte in Forest Hills are a relief from life in Brooklyn. That house on Lincoln Road is dark, occluded by tall trees, awnings, other apartment houses across the street. Our mother's one-bedroom apartment with a large sunken living room is on the sixth floor. Light pours in through the topmost branches of the trees outside. Our mother and Fred, the painless dentist, take us out for steak dinners at the Four Posters, then to Jahn's in Jamaica, where Claude and I face off with their infamous "Tall In The Saddle," eight scoops of ice cream, syrup, and other delights like crushed pineapple and sprinkles in a glass so tall we have to eat it standing up.

At the Forest Hills Cinema we watch Alistair Sim in *The Bells of St. Trinian's*, Satyajit Ray's *Pather Panjali*, and Federico Fellini's *La Strada*. I recall the rape scene in *Rocco and His Brothers* while having sex for the first time with a fireman's daughter behind a bush by the bridle path in Prospect Park. She has bad teeth and lets me do whatever I want to her. I'm almost fifteen and troubled that what should have rung my bell echoes instead like a hole in my heart.

Claude slinks around the Brooklyn house in sullen defiance of Betty, who orders him around in her sweetest voice: *get me a Kleenex, would you be a good boy and see if my glasses are on the table downstairs, do me a favor and run to the French Cleaners for the dress I have to wear this evening.* My brother knows there'll be no end to her grinding him into submission.

"I'm sorry," he replies. "Do it yourself."

We both can't wait to take the train to Forest Hills where every other weekend we are greeted at the door by Derf (Fred, backward) in a red fright-wig and an apron full of rubber-foam breasts. Spike Jones plays "My Old Flame," punctuated by foghorns and whoopee cushions on the hifi in the living room. If we bring a friend, we warn him that *Derfy-diddle* is hypersensitive. Any reference to his baldness, wigs, and apron must be avoided. Free for a moment from his struggle with Betty, my brother laughs as though the world will come to an end when he stops.

The New Charlotte has replaced more than a nose. Instead of playing her violin now stashed in a closet, she is painting a mural in the dining alcove. Poplar trees around a pond reflecting lacy clouds bounce back at the diners from a mirrored wall in the sunken living room. Claude and I sleep on a Castro convertible daybed between the mural and the mirror. The living room ends in floor-length silver lamé drapes behind a golden sectional around a clover-shaped glass coffee table with brass legs. Three Moorish globes with braided pull-cords hang at the far end. The whole ensemble floats on a flowery cream and red Karistan carpet.

The New Charlotte has replaced her Brooklyn criminal law practice with one out of her home specializing in matrimonial cases. The tabloid Portia pleading for the victims of an unresponsive system has vanished along with a bit of nasal cartilage. The New Charlotte doesn't want that kind of heartbreak.

The Old Charlotte was a Democrat. The new one is a Republican hoping to rise in borough politics. "I may not become a judge, but I'm going to be a guest on the radio," she tells us after meeting talk-show host Barry Grey at a Republican Club dinner.

Back at Lincoln Road, we mark the day and hour of her debut as a radio personality, lie in bed at dusk with the radio on. Betty's footsteps pad up and down the stairs. Our mother's voice comes over the air waves. "I try to teach my women clients lessons. What I've had to learn myself."

"That takes a degree of psychological astuteness," says Barry Grey.

"Not only women, but men also have to learn self-reliance. You'd be surprised how many men think the aim of marriage is to find someone to depend on."

"Not me," laughs Grey. "What do you tell them?"

"I quote Ralph Waldo Emerson, 'Two human beings are like globes, which can touch only at a single point...'"

The following weekend Claude is distraught. Our father has yelled at him for speaking abusively to Betty. He complains about it to the New Charlotte, who has also left her antifemale Jewish roots to embrace Christian Science.

"Be alert to *error*," she tells him in the vocabulary of her new faith. "Just remember, you are God's perfect child."

Nestled in our beds at Lincoln Road, we listen to the host introduce her as *an authority on self-reliance in and out of marriage*.

The phones ring with call-in questions. The New Charlotte tells Barry Grey, "Becoming one's own person in this culture is a difficult proposition."

"I agree." Grey responds admiringly. "Some couples have their fangs sunk so deeply in each other's throats that if they separated they'd both bleed to death."

"It's a good thing I got a cash settlement from him." Charlotte tells us the next day at Schrafft's. "At least that's protected."

Our waitress gives us her best Mary Baker Eddy smile. More and more, Schrafft's takes on the aura of a Christian Science Reading Room.

"Just see it as *error*," Charlotte tells us. "Error can't harm you. The truth is that you are God's perfect children."

Claude isn't convinced. If error can't harm us, then why does he feel trapped like a rat in his own house?

"I suppose I'd better tell you." Charlotte licks her lips. "God's perfect children deserve to know the truth."

"Especially one with twenty traveling alarm clocks."

Claude kicks me.

"Betty's nothing more than a high-priced call girl."

Our mother's colorfully beringed fingers tap her paper doily until we are served and the coast is clear, then she strips off yet another veil to reveal the secret of our father's new wife.

"Your father met Betty through Colonel Bligh, whose penthouse parties are well known to those in the loop. The Colonel invites a select group of men to meet carefully picked women."

I remember meeting Colonel Bligh, with our father. His jowls were stubbly and his beach-ball stomach had tested the limits of his Bermuda shorts.

"Can anyone go to these parties?" my brother wants to know.

"You have to be invited." Charlotte nods knowingly. "And it's very expensive. Russian vodka, beluga caviar, the works."

"Dad said he's in public relations," my brother volunteers.

"Is he a real colonel?" Claude's eyes widen.

"Only in Kentucky," answers our mother.

We had crossed the bridge into Manhattan with our father one summer afternoon two years ago to meet the Colonel Bligh—maybe two years ago before Betty came on the scene. On the way to the lower-East-Side penthouse, we drove through the Bowery, under the Third Avenue El where, according to our father, I would one day find myself.

The Colonel's penthouse sat on a rooftop surrounded by taller buildings. The flagstone terrace outside the large living room received just enough light to nourish a small garden built into variously shaped boxes along the parapet. Claude and I cooled ourselves under a garden hose while the host served drinks to our father and several other men reclining on chaise lounges. The colonel was a fat man, a Sydney Greenstreet look-alike with multiple chins that wobbled when he talked out of one side of his mouth while chewing a cigar in the other. I wondered then what it was about him that excited my father's admiration. *Now, I knew. It was his ability to bring young women on-the-make to parties where they met lonely, affluent men like my father.*

"That's the real story," Charlotte dabbed her lips with her napkin.

We nod. Another veil has been peeled away. And what we've found behind it is not nearly as mysterious as the Man/ Woman at Luna Park with one pink nipple. Our father was introduced to Betty by a pimp who called himself a Colonel. The leggy blonde who wears plaid skirts and penny loafers and looks down at the top of my father's head as she speaks to him in baby talk had been one of many fillies in the fat man's stable. Claude and I take this information back to Lincoln Road with us on the Flatbush Avenue bus. Along with the admonition of the Mother Church: *We are God's perfect children.*

My brother is not comforted by the news of his perfection. No matter how often he hears it, the experience of being one of God's perfect children is annihilated by what happens to him at home. Increasingly, he is being called to account for behaviors toward Betty that he might harbor in fantasy but utterly denies expressing in daily life.

Even so, I am surprised one day after school when I find our father backing Claude into a corner by the linen closet in the upstairs hallway, his voice breaking with anger.

"What do you mean speaking to her that way?"

"I didn't..."

"You called her a bitch. Told her to go to hell."

"No."

"Don't lie to me." Our father bends over my cringing brother. He's taught us not to lie. Claude never does. He really believes that lying about something is worse than the original offense. My brother protests, but his voice quivers, frightened by Ben's escalating anger and lightning-fast hands. The blows can come at any second. A fearsome flurry. Not always hard, but with a speed that will leave him helpless, off balance, gasping for air.

"She says you muttered it under your breath."

"That's not true." Claude stands up straight.

"I won't tolerate that kind of talk." Our father's shoulders sag, his voice trails off, uncertain of what he had just been so sure of. He disappears into his study, only to return to our bedroom ten minutes later. We are sitting on our beds, puzzling out the reason our father refused to consider Claude's side of the story. Leaning against my dresser, he appears calm now, and his tone is earnest, almost imploring.

"We need to cooperate with each other to make this family work. If Betty asks you to do something for her, do it with grace."

I tell him we will make an effort, and then ask if I can be honest with him.

"All right. What's on your mind?"

"If you didn't have a penny to your name, the only ones who would be here with you are Claude and I."

He is quiet for a minute, taking in his sons as we face him in this moment that has opened for us. There is no rancor in his voice when he turns to Claude. "Do you agree?"

"Yes, I do." My brother's head bobs like a spring toy.

"Time will tell," he sighs.

rue de Bièvre
Paris/ August 1st, 1986

Jean, in prep-school tweeds, and Lila, wearing a black, backless evening dress, hair gelled à la Paloma, take Carol and me to dinner at their favorite bistro, where they inform us that Vigne wants to write his own screenplay. I'm out, it seems.

"Well, let him run with it," says Jean. "He feels that you wrote the book, now let him write the movie."

The last thing I expected was to be fired by the man I fought to hire. I force a smile, but feel betrayed. After dinner, I leave Carol at rue de Bièvre and walk blindly through the streets until the first yellow rays lick the sky. Carol finds me later on the couch, drunk on Bailey's Irish Cream, the only booze in the apartment. "He read your script as a formality." She strokes my hair. "He never intended to work with you. Daniel Vigne does it all himself. He's an auteur."

My brother's words come back to me.

They've broken my heart. The fact he is not around at the moment to pick up the pieces becomes moot when he calls me later that day to let me know that several cars had him under surveillance as he drove up to Rye from the city last night. One of the drivers stared at him when they were stopped at a light. Claude stared back. Just as the light turned green, the guy rolled down his window and threatened to drive him off the road next time.

There's no humor in his voice. I ask if he's allowed for the possibility that none of this was directed at him, and that the man next to him might have rolled down his window to ask directions.

"You had to be there."

"Claude, think about it. Look at the number of people you've involved in this surveillance. Why would anyone spend more money and resources on you than the FBI, CIA, and Interpol do to apprehend the Jackal?"

"Why did they fly you to Brazil without a visa?" He draws a deep breath and lets it out. *"I know it sounds classic, but what can I say? They've worn me down. They're winning."*

"You'd have to be the most important man in the world."

"Et tu, Paulie."

VIII

For my fifteenth birthday, Charlotte gives me Emerson's *Essays*. Last year it had been *Autobiography of a Yogi*. At eleven, Gibran's *The Prophet*, from which she read a passage stating that children were not the property of their parents but honored guests in the household. Ever since I can remember, our mother has tried to enlist me as a companion on her journey of self-discovery.

The morning after my birthday dinner, Charlotte takes us to visit her guru, Yogi Vithaldis, who numbers Yehudi Menuhin among his followers. He is a man of indeterminate age, draped in a white robe. We stretch out on mats on his balcony above the traffic on West 23rd Street.

"Imagine you are floating in a clear sky...weightless. You can see in all directions and there is only peace. Peace. Peace."

When we have relaxed, he starts with the easiest posture first, the Corpse, followed by the Cobra, the Lion, and a shoulder stand that hurts my back. Our mother has no trouble folding herself into the Plough. My brother strains. His feet come within striking distance of the floor behind his head. He farts.

"Ah," says Charlotte, "The winds of Kashmir."

After our yoga session, we take the train to Union Square, and then walk to Weiser's Bookstore on lower Broadway, specializing in the occult. We descend to the basement where the familiar face of the owner, a small man with a white goatee, greets us like old friends. He seems to have read everything on the shelves. I discover *The Secret Teaching of All Times*, by Manly Palmer Hall, and *The Complete Alchemical Writings of Paracelsus*, in two volumes. Claude trails me. He would much rather be sitting in front of a hot turkey sandwich than floundering in these stacks. No blue Krishna astride a holy elephant or Pythagorean gnosis by way of California-based Rosacrucians can illuminate his reality. If astral projection worked, he would long ago have found an alternative to hiding out with twenty traveling alarm clocks in his room after school, where he retreats to avoid Betty, who is increasingly adept at drawing him into a dispute which she will later use to trigger an argument with our father.

Claude stands with his hands in his pockets watching Charlotte thumb through *Isis Unveiled*. I see him shift his weight from foot to foot and realize the absurdity of all this for him. How can my brother contemplate *satori, chesid, karma,* or *ma'at,* conceive of *the pearl of wisdom in the lotus of compassion* when his father refuses to believe in his innocence?

Betty, a tactical genius in this kind of warfare, treats me with disarming kindness. Perhaps she realizes that it isn't necessary to expend effort dividing me from my father. I am doing a good job of that on my own. Maybe she has calculated that any attachment I feel toward her will separate me from Claude. Last week she took me with her to the Greenwich Village art show. She gave me a copy of e. e. cummings' *tulips & chimneys* for my birthday. I am a divided man. Worse. I have deserted Claude again, as I did at the end of my time as a Jaguar. He can no more follow me into the esoteric worlds of poetry and the occult than he can into Louie's pool room. These worlds frighten him. He stands alone at the door to a chamber of books he can't read. I might as well be seated at Becker's Deli spending his money to celebrate a triumph in which he has no part.

We take the subway back to Forest Hills. Our mother has prepared boiled beef flanken, one of the few things she cooks. My brother looks forward to this. But his heart sinks when we sit on the sectional beneath the Moorish lamps where Charlotte reads from her favorite poet, Lord Byron. I resonate to his lines filled with a sonorous rebellion:

Still there are many pangs that pursue me,
They may crush but never contemn,
They may torture but shall not subdue me,
'Tis of thee that I think, not of them...

I am drawn to the poet whose incestuous love for his sister Augusta burns in the lamp of his verses. I am, like him, a fugitive, except my deformity is not as visible as a club foot. I too am pitted against a hostile world armed only with the power of an aching heart. Charlotte passes me the book. I know she sees in me the club-footed poet with the face of an angel. *Does this make me a momma's boy?* No. I am a Byronic figure who makes "his suffering tributary to his will."

My brother would rather be fishing for crappies. He counts the minutes to the boiled beef. For him, mother's meat has taken the place of mother's milk. Seated at the dinner table, color returns to his cheeks. After ice cream sundaes Charlotte brings out a bottle of Moët, and a bouquet of crystal glasses. She lights the candles, fills each glass, and then toasts my liberation from Brooklyn Friends School. A few days before my birthday, Mr. Popinjay, the principal, called my father and me into his office to deliver a message concerning my future at the school. In a voice that rose to a pitiful crescendo he informed Ben: *We've decided not to invite him back.* My father and I received the news in shock, and continue to be speechless around this issue.

My mother greets the news in her own way.

"To your freedom," Charlotte raises her crystal glass.

Claude hesitates. He will be alone there.

Six months after my liberation celebration, I am sitting with my father on the bench in front of another principal's office. Old Bullethead, at Erasmus Hall High School, bears no resemblance to Mr. Popinjay. There are no carnations in his buttonhole. Just a massive torso in shirtsleeves rolled above thick forearms made more menacing by the shiny bald dome that comes to a point. He dwarfs my father who has risen to shake his hand.

"Thank you, Doctor, for taking time out of your busy schedule."

We sit in straight back chairs. Bullethead tells us that he has been a cop and a trolleycar conductor and understands boys in motorcycle boots with ducks-ass hair welded in place by Dixie Peach. There are quite a few of us walking up Flatbush to Church Avenue every morning to the walled fortress spanning several city blocks. Erasmus boils over with students in two overlapping sessions, out of which a small stream of elite students are siphoned from the raging river of Irish Lords, Pig Town Tigers, Gremlins, and Chaplains into the top tier. I fall into the lower one, a *Blackboard Jungle* minus Glenn Ford and Sidney Poitier. Three days a week I take in the triple-feature cowboy movies at the Majestic Theater on Fulton Street instead of going to school.

"Your son is an incorrigible truant."

My father's knuckles turn white. He's blinded by shame. He can't see how scared I am of becoming what he has foreseen, a Bowery bum.

"He's been absent a third of the semester."

"I'm passing all my courses."

"It doesn't matter if he passes or fails, Doctor." The big man in shirtsleeves ignores me. "The law requires daily attendance until he's sixteen."

"What do you suggest?"

"You're welcome to educate your son privately. If you choose not to, he'll be sent to a place that deals with incorrigible problems."

Tears well in my father's eyes; the threat of incarceration eclipses even that of the Bowery.

"I don't mean to be disrespectful, but it's my experience that boys like your son rebel because they hate their fathers."

I want him to tell the man to shut up. I recall James Dean

in *Rebel without a Cause* throwing his father to the floor while yelling that he loves him. I want to do the same. Instead, I leave him welded to his chair.

Claude watches me pack. He wants to know where I'm going.

"Parkside Avenue. Stew's parents are in Miami for the month."

"Don't leave me with her."

"You'll be all right."

My brother stares at me, unconvinced. His only ally is Barney, our sad-eyed boxer. Betty's assaults are escalating. Yesterday she accused Claude of spitting in her face when asked to run an errand. She claims that he goes through her drawers and steals money from her purse. Betty has boxed our father in. Either Claude is guilty or she is lying. Unable to entertain the latter, our father comes down on my brother.

"Take me with you."

"I can't."

Claude's plea weighs me down. I want to be free like Charlie McGee, a seventeen-year-old orphan who lives in a basement room beneath the Tollgate Tavern. McGee has done time upstate in Hawthorn, where I will go if Bullethead has his way. Maybe I'll break my teeth like Charlie on the "mystery meat."

"What if Stew's parents come back?"

I can live on the street like Charlie. There are the early morning milk deliveries, boxes of prune and apple Danish in front of the Rexall pharmacy. As a pin boy at Louie's I can always earn a buck.

"Don't go, Paulie."

I have to. My fantasies are fed by Harold Robbins's *A Stone for Danny Fisher* and Mickey Spillane's *I, The Jury*. Claude identifies with "Noodles the Shiv" in *The Amboy Dukes*. Especially when thinking about Betty. Noodles would skin her alive. Mike Hammer might hold Betty in a lover's embrace as he pumps a round into her stomach, whispering, *"It was you or me, Baby."*

But Claude has no friends like Noodles. The idea that I do fills him with dread. He knows "Bad Bill," and Stew, son of a Jewish prize-fighter whose apartment bedroom is plastered with posters of Manolete, Dominguín, and the Brooklyn matador Sidney Franklin.

I shut the suitcase. Claude follows me downstairs.

My brother stands at the front door, his head peeking out of a scarf like a small child or an old lady in a *babushka*. I break out laughing at the sight of him. It hurts so much we laugh ourselves silly.

At first, I think that my father will come for me. I expect to find him waiting in front of the building on Parkside. In my fantasy, he begs me to come home, tells me how much Ben misses me. But as the days pass into weeks, I realize my father will not come to take me home. Claude calls nightly from the pay phone in Sonny's candy store. "He doesn't look well, Paulie. You should see the circles under his eyes. His voice cracks when he asks about you."

"What does he say?"

"He wants to know if you're all right."

No matter how much my father misses me, he will die rather than ask me to return. I think about him more and more, feel him inside like a second self. A month after leaving, I head home.

It's dusk when I turn the corner onto Lincoln, try the front door, which is usually locked, find it open, then push the beveled glass of the heavy inner door. The hallway is illuminated by an art-deco lamp on a small desk at the rear. It doesn't throw much light. But our father loves to tinker with the wiring that runs through its base, a ceramic sculpture of Leda and the swan. Now, he stands in front of it, back lit, as if he's been waiting here for me all along. I rush into his arms and burst into tears. He holds me and strokes my head. Claude, the watcher, crouches on the landing midway up the stairs.

rue de Bièvre
Rye/Paris/ August 10th, 1986

Paulie, it's me. I'm calling from a pay phone at Pergament's in Rye. Two men at the sales counter were eyeing me. One of them said loud enough for anyone within fifteen feet to hear, "We've got him under surveillance, but we don't have enough evidence to make an arrest." This morning at the bank two lawyer-types in line behind me said, "We made the bust on the lower East Side but moved too slowly uptown. Things work differently on the upper West Side."

I know they were referring to me. They're mad about my move. They thought they had me pinned down on 75th Street, but I fooled them.

Don't give me that stuff about my perception being distorted. And don't play analyst!

You want to know who is pursuing me?

It started over a year ago at Metpath, and still I don't know who is behind it, or why.

Does that sound questionable?

I know. You've made the point before. Why would anyone spend more money and resources pursuing me than the FBI does on catching Public Enemy Number One? Or Carlos the Jackal?

You love that question, don'tcha? Admit it. It's a stunner. Really. I have no answer for that one. But I don't care what you think.

You think I'm crazy?

Of course you do. Of course you do. You'd be crazy not to.

Ok. I'll be Monty Hall. Let's make a deal. If I find the answer to your question, you'll eat crow. If I can't by this time next year, call out the men in the white suits. Until then, I am going to treat this as real.

I'm angry, Paulie. I'm tired of trying to convince people. I'm under a lot of pressure, and I'm tired of this conversation.

The good news is that the Sound is boiling with mossbunker. Those little oily fish, what a thing—the bait running before the catch. When the bait comes in, can the blues be far behind? My persecutors are out here too, in rental boats. They're also on the party boats out of Montauk and Sheepshead Bay, drinking beer and calling me names. They're trying to provoke me, Paulie. They give me the finger and scratch their balls. I don't pay attention. I'm too busy pulling in mossbunker. I just cast out my lure and reel. Come back and fish with me, Paulie. Remember who's got the blues.

IX

I am always running away from my brother. He knows that I'll be leaving at the end of the summer for Cherry Lawn, a co-ed boarding school in Darien, Connecticut. Because I will miss the wildness of the Brooklyn streets, I agree to steal a car with the Hump, one of several guys I know from the Glen Ranch section, near Canarsie. Instead of hanging out at home with Claude, I will drive a hot car to visit the Hump's hot girl, Rosie, vacationing with her parents at a bungalow colony in the Catskills. How a gorgeous girl like Rosie can settle for a beefy guy with a soprano voice and wild black cowlicks is beyond me. But I consider our adventure a valedictory gesture, a last glimpse in the rearview mirror at what might have otherwise been a life outside the law.

Claude pulls out his babushka, offers me money for transportation to the Catskills, but there is no dissuading me. Hump swears that Rosie has many good-looking friends at her bungalow colony in White Lake. She is herself a beauty. I can't understand how a moon-faced boy with a cowlick has won her heart.

On a hot June night, while our father and Betty cruise toward Bermuda, I leave Claude to rendezvous with the Hump at a diner on Nostrand Avenue. I have fifty bucks in my pocket made setting pins at Louie's. Our scheme is simple. We stash our bags in bushes outside the diner, then walk to a neighborhood of houses with postage stamp lawns. Hump assures me that at this hour everyone is sitting in front of the TV.

Everything is as he described. There's just enough light from the street lamps to see what we're doing, but enough tree cover to keep us in shadow. Neither of us has jumped a car, though we know the theory. Suddenly, we realize that we've forgotten a *slim Jim*, and have nothing with us to jimmy a door, much less take apart an ignition. We search for open doors. Halfway down the second street, the Hump finds a Chevy with keys still in it. I wait for him to get into the driver's seat but he can't drive a stick shift. I walk around and slide behind the wheel.

The engine turns over right away. I stomp the clutch and throw it into first. The Chevy sputters, then bucks down the street to a red light, where I stop without stalling. The Hump is bouncing up and down in the passenger seat singing, "In the Still of the Night." When the light turns green, I bring my foot up on the clutch to make a lurching right onto Coney Island Avenue, careful to avoid the trolley tracks. No sooner do I complete the turn, than a siren sounds behind us. Revolving red and white lights rake the car. The Hump is really jumping up and down now, but he's no longer singing.

"What'll we do? What'll we do?"

The Chevy bucks to the corner. I hang another right and jerk to a stop in the shadow of an old oak bordering an overgrown lot. I throw the door open and dive into the undergrowth. I hear the Hump behind me and crawl on my elbows as fast as I can until I stop in the middle of the lot. Hidden by tall grass, I whisper his name. Once. Twice. No answer. I'm alone on my belly in the weeds. I recall chasing my brother, the Shit Man, through tall grass like this around the Rogers's house next door. A voice in my head screams: *It's every man for himself.*

Red and white lights flash behind me. There is more than one patrol car. A voice booms over a bullhorn: *Surrender and no one will get hurt.* Unamplified voices repeat the message. They are still at the curb. If they catch me, there'll be no Cherry Lawn School in my future. Only reform school, where Bullethead thinks I belong.

I crawl until I'm stopped by a six-foot storm fence. I hurl myself over the top, hardly aware of the cut-wire ends, then run through an alley toward the street on the other side of the block. I cross it, cut through another alley, make a left at the corner away from the Avenue thinking that it's only a matter of time before a patrol car spots me. I keep to the darker streets of two-family homes and small apartment buildings until I notice a red neon sign advertising car and limousine rentals over one of the buildings. I descend to the bottom of a long driveway to the garage. Five men in undershirts around a card table look at me strangely when I ask to rent a limo with one-way glass. Their hesitation ends when I put a twenty on the table beside their nickel-and-dime pot. One of the players grabs it, puts on a black jacket and cap on a rack in the corner, leads me to a black limo and opens the door for me.

Exiting the garage, my limousine turns left on the one-way. I prepare myself for questions, but the driver just turns on the radio. Eddy Fisher sings, "Oh, My Papa." I get the shakes. What would my father say if I were caught?

> *Oh, my papa, to me he was so wonderful*
> *Oh, my papa, to me he was so good*
> *No one could be, so gentle and so lovable*
> *Oh, my papa, he always understood.*

Prowl cars are banked at the intersection. I slump down. A cop waves us past without a word. When we finally pull up at the diner, the driver opens the door for me, smiles knowingly when he says he hopes that I've enjoyed the ride.

The Hump, sweaty and dirt stained, is already waiting in a booth at the rear. "What took you so long?" he asks.

Our gear is behind the hedge where we left it. The Hump tells me we can take the subway to the Port Authority and grab a Trailways bus to White Lake.

A week later, Claude greets me at the door. He is breathless with worry but can't conceal his joy at the sight of me. Why haven't I called? Our father and Betty have been home for three days. There's going to be hell to pay, as if there aren't enough problems already. I show him the wound on my right ankle I received playing "chicken" with a motor boat on White Lake, recount our close call with the hot car. My brother's face alternates between horror and fascination as I describe bungalow girls armored with big hair, except for Rosie, who makes my heart ache. Claude shakes his head. My father never asks where I've been. They both know that I'll soon be safe at Cherry Lawn, in Darien, a bastion of suburban America made famous for its silent anti-Semitism by Gregory Peck in the movie *Gentlemen's Agreement.*

***

At the boarding school on Brookside Road I discover bright but abandoned kids whose parents can afford to send them here. I room with Joe, son of a recently deceased Toronto gambler with mob connections, and Ed, from Montreal, a handsome boy with a speech impediment and the reflexes of a prizefighter. Paulette and Roger are the tow-headed children of a rabbi and his wife, both deceased. Norma is a willowy flamenco dancer, an army brat who comes here from a convent school in Spain. Then, there are the celebrity children: Dan, son of black-listed actor, J. Edward Bromberg; Jimmy, son of actress Gwen Verdon; and Dal, who looks like his father, John Forsythe. Finally, there are those whose parents scrape by financially but simply can't handle their children like gaminish Susie, Ted, whose eyebrow crawls like a caterpillar across his forehead, or darkly philosophical Dick with a large Adam's apple.

I say little to anyone. I wear motorcycle boots and long hair, the uniform of the outcast. I am James Dean, with roots in Lord Byron. My real dialogue is with the landscape. I take solitary walks, explore old cemeteries, and lie among the wild flowers in open fields gazing at the sky. I think of Brooklyn, now and then, but it seems far away and I have no wish to go back. Not even to see Claude, who is alone in a bad place. Sometimes I sit by the pond with Ted and plot our course to Rapa, a South Sea island where women outnumber men ten to one. Perhaps I will take Claude to make up for all the times I've abandoned him.

In the Manor House library I pick up Freud's *Future of an Illusion* and Horney's *The Neurotic Personality of Our Time*. In the fetal warmth of the basement below, I talk with Joan, my intellectual soul-mate, about the intelligence in dreams and my intuition that Einstein's cosmological space-time interfaces with psychological space-time. The discovery that I can use my mind fills me with an elation I have only glimpsed before. I am a wet chick burst from its shell.

On a spring day at the end of my junior year, I sit on a rock by a stream and open Perry Miller's *American Puritans* to a sermon by Theodore Parker. Suddenly, I am spinning faster and faster, I feel myself elevated to the treetops and beyond. I've been sucked out of my flesh and rise without resistance. When the spinning stops, I flow into bound-lessness; like Emerson's "floating eyeball," I see in all directions at the same time. I contain and am contained by the whole, aware of every prism in the dewdrops. Well-being floods me. I hear myself think, *everything is as it should be.* And know it is true, beyond paradox or contradiction.

I'm not sure how long I remain in this state; it could be seconds, minutes, or hours. I return to my body seated on the rock. The stream bubbles in front of me. My book is open on my lap to the page I've been reading. I get up. Everything glows. I won't say a word about what has happened. I leave the woods knowing that for the rest of my life this experience will serve as a reference at the silent center of my being.

In my weekly phone call, I describe life at Cherry Lawn to Claude. I want him to come up here with me. But he declines, no matter how bad things are in Brooklyn. The more I do this, the more he pushes me away; it's as if my expanding world seals him more tightly into his narrow one.

Claude's life has become a battle in which he is increasingly helpless to counter Betty's strategies. She knows how to outflank him, whatever move he makes. He can ask when they're having dinner, and she'll twist the question into something insubordinate. Claude dares not even acknowledge a question with a simple Yes or No. But failure to respond is read as insolence. Our father considers any form of disrespect for Betty to be directed at him.

My brother offers only token protest when confronted. It's easier to take the blame and punishment, whatever it may be. Fortunately, he isn't without his own means of retaliation. He searches out Betty's hidden vodka, empties the bottles. He's discovered most of her hiding places: in the linen closet, the towel drawer, behind the silver platters in the china closet, at the bottom of the laundry bin. Even better, he can sense when a bottle has been moved, and find its new nest.

"The beauty of this is that she can't openly accuse me of this."

Claude complains of sleeping long hours, that he has difficulty waking up, and is regularly absent from school. Mostly on Mondays. He hates Mondays. His grades are still good and his behavior exemplary. But no one seems to notice that he is slow to make friends, and doesn't brush his teeth or change his socks for weeks.

When I arrive home unannounced on my winter break, I enter the house and immediately hear the sounds of struggle coming from upstairs. Claude's frightened protests rise like bubbles bursting above the froth of our father's anger. I drop my bags and race to the top of the stairs in time to see Ben bent over my brother cowering against the blue room's door.

"I wouldn't turn down my radio, so she slapped me. Honest, I didn't say or do a thing to her."

"Liar!" Our father raises his hand.

"No, no," I step between them. "That's enough."

"Get out of my way."

Determined not to let him strike Claude, I grab my father's wrists, first one, then the other. His eyes grow wide in shock. He attempts to free his hands but I hold on. Ben's feet begin to move. At first I think he is trying to get away, but soon realize he is kicking me. His shoes striking my shins are painful for a second, but quickly become meaningless. The resistance slowly seeps out of his wrists and arms.

"It's over," I tell him. "Don't you ever raise your hand to Claude or me again."

He is spent.

I let go.

Pale as plaster, our father turns and walks away.

rue de Bièvre
Paris/ August 15th, 1986

Yesterday we went to the Church on St. Louis to listen to a medieval ensemble sing the works of Schütz and Bouzignac, early baroque composers. Last night, Claude called from Highcliff. He said only, "Don't worry about me. Just watch what you eat and keep in shape. Take long walks along the Seine."

Then he hung up.

I dreamed that I was walking along the Seine with Carol and Claude. He was joking about my failure as a screenwriter. I took his hand playfully and bit down on his fingers. As I did so I realized that I was doing it too hard and wounding him—perhaps even severing the fingers from his hand. He didn't say anything until I was through, and then he began to complain about how much his hand hurt him and held out this stump. I felt guilty for disfiguring him, a deep, dark guilt such as I hadn't felt since we were kids and I took his money to treat the Jaguars at Becker's Deli; or earlier, for those times I had reacted to his defiance of my wishes with explosive anger, like the time I threw a hard ball at him so fast it hit him in his stomach. I could hear the air escape from his lungs on impact. When he doubled over, I doubled over, too, as though I had been hit. I couldn't breathe either. Tears filled my eyes, driven by a sense that I had done something beyond atonement. I felt it without understanding that what I did to my brother, I did to myself. In the dream I rush to wrap his hand in bandages, praying that it will heal, that he will regrow fingers.

This morning, I wake in a sweat. Standing at the window, I look out over the red-tile rooftops of Paris, then down at the empty walled garden belonging to Mitterrand's mistress. I have done all I can here. On the other side of the Atlantic my brother is trying to recall the exact terms of our mother's indictment of our father even as he is being pursued by tormentors of various shapes and sizes, including little old ladies brandishing open pocketbooks. I think of him and feel helpless. My hand hurts when I open and close my fingers.

It is time to go home.

X

Before spring break in my senior year at Cherry Lawn, Claude calls to say that Betty has poisoned Barney. I think he is joking and chuckle at his black humor, before I realize that he is serious. "Dad and I were bending over his body. When I look up, she stares me straight in the eye and smiles. Barney is twitching like he's been plugged into a light socket, foaming at the mouth, and...*she smiles!*"

If what he's telling me is true, I can't begin to comprehend the impact it will have on him, or the implication for us all. Ever since Betty's been in the house, Barney has stayed close to my brother. Locked in his bedroom fortress, Claude and the boxer have lived like survivors on a life raft. For years Ben, too, has drawn comfort from Barney's sloppy jowls and flatulence.

Our father was off on Sunday morning rounds. Claude had gotten up earlier than usual. From the bedroom he saw Betty playing with Barney in the backyard. That seemed unusual. She never liked the dog. My brother closed the blinds and went back to sleep. An hour later, he went downstairs to the kitchen and found Barney sprawled on the linoleum, his paws at an angle, jowls flat on the floor. A tired dog, he thought, then noticed Barney's legs twitching. At first he thought the dog was dreaming. Foam appeared on his jowls.

"I tried to wake him, but he didn't respond. Next thing I knew Barney was having convulsions. I cried for help. Nobody came. I knew right away *that she had poisoned him.*"

Ben returned from the hospital, felt for a heart beat, put two fingers on the boxer's femoral artery, pulled back his lids and studied Barney's eyes...*they'd gone white, Paulie*...then shook his head.

"That's when I saw her in the doorway, arms crossed over

her flat chest, smiling. You know she didn't want to take Barney to the new Sutton Place apartment."

Well over a year ago, our father put the Lincoln Road house up for sale so that he and Betty could purchase a cooperative on fashionable Sutton Place. Betty argued that Barney, who belonged to the Brooklyn past, wasn't appropriate for their new life in Manhattan. But Ben found it harder to fire a pet than he had a maid. He encouraged Betty to buy a dog of her own. She did, a miniature white poodle that clung to her, yapping hysterically when anyone drew near.

But that didn't end the dispute.

Betty vowed that Barney would never leave his scent at Sutton Place. She also knew how much her husband loved the dog.

"So she poisoned him."

"Where's your proof?" I asked.

"The box of rat poison in the pantry. We don't have rats."

When the spasms stopped, our father wrapped Barney in a rug and carried him into the unheated garage. Claude spent the rest of that day and night with the corpse; he skipped school on Monday, refusing to come into the house for breakfast. Finally, garbage men carted the corpse away.

"The rat poison was on the shelf below the Ken'l Ration. His bowl was clean. I mean, spotless. He usually left a ring of Ken'l Ration below the lip of the bowl but *somebody scrubbed* it."

"That's still not conclusive..."

"Paulie, her message is perfectly clear. I can't be sure that my hamburger tonight won't be laced with rat poison. I probably couldn't taste it in Brussels sprouts."

Claude knows our father won't believe him, but after some thought, confides his suspicion to Wallace. Our father's friend is dismissive. Claude asks about the possibility of an autopsy, but Wallace concludes it is too late. The body has already been burned. He suggests that the problem lies in

Claude's refusal to accept his father's new wife. Does he have any idea what it would mean if Betty were capable of such an act! The evidence is entirely circumstantial. Any D.A. will say as much. Besides, how can Betty have done what Claude claims and a brilliant doctor like Ben fail to suspect it?

"The big question," Claude says.

The following week, my brother informs me: "I asked Dad about the rat poison. He said that there are rats in the basement. He bought it himself. And he admitted that Barney might have been poisoned, but most likely by something he picked up on the street, maybe even while I was walking him."

"He might be right."

"Absolutely not. *Barney didn't forage.* Someone poisoned him. It wasn't me. Or Dad. You're at Cherry Lawn."

"Come here with me."

"How can I leave him alone with her?"

"What good can you do by staying there?"

"She knows that I know."

Glens Falls, NY
August 27, 1986

In late summer Carol and I return to upstate New York. Eyelids heavy with jet lag, I drive to Rye the following day. Turning off the New England Thruway at the Playland exit, I thread a street of exquisitely edged lawns and topiary hedges then make a right onto a dead-end road. I navigate by memory. It's been fifteen years since I laid eyes on the metal plaque set in one of two stone pillars that mark the entrance to Highcliff.

White stucco walls at the end of a circular driveway glow

in the afternoon sun. I steer past a four-car garage to park in front of a vegetable garden beside my brother's Subaru Brat, a mini-pickup, acned with rust. The house, too, has seen better days. I note window frames in need of repair, fluking paint, and fissures in the walls. Beyond, sailboats wait for wind as outboards trace white lines on the water. Gulls circle Manursing Island, their cries like unanswered prayers.

I last saw Wallace and June in the early 70s. I knew through Claude that the Lion of Contemporary Furniture, inventor of the sectional sofa, had been forced to sell his business. Financially, he'd emerged intact.

I bumped into them one day on Cooper Square. His blond mane had thinned to wisps of silver. He complained of migraines and depression. June, on the other hand, spoke animatedly about her husband's activities; since his "retirement," he'd discovered the computer, rediscovered his old watercolors, evolved a theory on the development of language, and was contemplating a career in education...

The door is open. June sits alone at the island counter in the middle of an outsized kitchen, sipping coffee as she scans The Sunday Times Book Review. *After her obligatory hug and stiff-upper-lip smile, she tells me that I'll find Claude down at the dock.*

I exit through the kitchen to the deck, down a steep hill, past the pool and over the seawall bordering the sound to a wooden pier. My brother is a backlit silhouette at the end of a slip where the Jewel, a forty-foot Viking with teak decks once moored. It's easy to imagine that nothing has changed since Claude and I hooked our first crappies with hand lines in Prospect Park. Our best moments together have been spent waiting for a strike at the end of our lines, trolling for billfish in the Gulf Stream, or at the rails of the Chief out of Sheepshead Bay. I still admire the way my brother casts, sets the drag, and reels at precisely the right speed. He turns as my shoes touch the planks.

"It's the man from Rio."

"Rio airport."

I hug him, careful not to hook myself on his rig. He casts again, a large yellow plug pegged to a quarter-ounce shot keeps the lure floating just below the surface.

"You hear any interesting conversation on the plane?"

"No, I read a book."

"What book?

"MYSTERIES, by Colin Wilson."

"Life is full of mysteries," Claude reels. "Look out there. It's a fisherman's wet dream."

The Sound is bubbles with blues and the baitfish. He hands me the rod. I cast, let the lure float, then something hits. I turn off the clicker and reel. The rod bends almost in half as the fish dives. I play it, holding fast to see what the monster on the other end of the 20-lb. test line will do next. The tension remains steady. I start reeling again. There's a quick move to the left, then the right. Suddenly, the resistance stops. I crank faster.

"Reel!" Claude commands.

A silver streak hurtles toward us. Just as it closes, the sun hits the dorsal surface of a huge bluefish. He shimmies like quicksilver before breaking the beaded water. The line goes limp. I pull up a frayed end where the line has snapped below the sinker. Claude's homemade super plug will rust out of the big blue in time. I hand back the rod.

"You've lost my best lure."

"You can get another."

"Forget the lure. It's Wallace I'm worried about. He's been depressed. Only electroshock works for him."

"Jesus!"

"It's not like the old days when they fried your brain. Today they give you a series of light shocks to targeted areas. True, they still can't predict the long-term effects." Claude casts a new plug twenty feet directly in front of him. "I don't know why, but I cheer him up. As long as..." He winds, then

stops and sets the drag. "Why don't you go back up and talk to Wallace and June? I need to concentrate."

Claude's attention is fixed on the water. There's still so much I want to ask him, but that will have to wait. I've satisfied myself that he isn't in any immediate danger. For now, our conversation is over.

I re-enter the kitchen from the deck, find Wallace holding a glass under the icemaker in the refrigerator door. A graying ghost in a blue terry-cloth robe, his smoky mane rises wildly above uneven sideburns. The nails of his once elegant hands are long and nicotine-stained. He speaks with an exaggerated emphasis on key words that signals one accustomed to commanding the attention of others, though he now commands little more than his icemaker.

"Hello, kiddy. Get yourself a soda or coffee and sit down."

I join Wallace and June in a booth tucked into the dining alcove.

"I know you think this is the right move for Claude... "

"Better than that apartment," Wallace interrupts me.

"He can be as private as he wants," declares June. "But we're here if he needs us."

No doubt my brother's apartment had been a lair, but it was his own. I am concerned that he'll stop seeing the therapist in Manhattan I found for him before I went to Paris. It occurs to me that June has invited Claude to Highcliff as a distraction for Wallace, whose depression is a weight on her. I tell them, "For the moment Claude feels safe here, away from what he thinks are his pursuers in New York, but who can say for how much longer? Sooner or later what he's running from there will find him here."

"Nonsense," replies the pioneer of the slabside desk and the waterfall edge.

XI

"You can't be serious," Wallace tilts his head.

A week after my graduation from Cherry Lawn, Claude sits on the front porch at Lincoln Road, trying once again to persuade Wallace that Betty poisoned Barney. My brother repeats his concern for our father's safety. Wallace is more than a decade younger than Ben and so bridges a generation as well as a communication gap. He may be our father's best friend, though Ben functions as his mentor. Wallace, in turn, is like a golden son; an artist whose business is flourishing, he has set the mode in contemporary furniture design. There are even legends about him, like the one in which he traded his Cadillac to Picasso for one of the Spaniard's paintings.

Wallace inclines his leonine head as if smelling odors beyond normal perception. His full lips purse and smoky blue eyes stare into the middle distance. Finally, he concedes that he can't totally reject my brother's case, and certainly not his fears, but still doesn't believe Betty could have poisoned Barney. But, he repeats, *but*...even if what Claude says is true, how can *he* intervene? What do we think Ben would say if Wallace were to warn him that his wife may be homicidal?

"There's another point I want you to consider. It may not have occurred to you boys, but it's an important one. Betty makes your father happy in bed."

My brother recoils. I too feel off balance. This simple statement carries incredible weight. Wallace has a unique intimacy with our father, who undoubtedly confides in him.

"Imagine what it's like," he continues, "for the first time in his life, your father feels sexually fulfilled. After years of frustration and rejection, he's discovered what it's like to make love to someone who enjoys making love to him."

And this, I think, from the man whose friendship with Leonard Bernstein our mother has cited to implicate both Wallace and our father in the shadow world of *latency*.

Wallace's implication is also clear: after Charlotte, Betty might be a source of sexual healing.

Charlotte points out that our father's gratitude for Betty's favors is bounded only by his means. He has underwritten her master's in education at Columbia, bought her a building in Queens to house her private nursery school, continues to build a collection of paintings and sculpture at her direction, gifted her with a co-op in the Hamptons and, now, another at 25 Sutton Place South, overlooking Cannon Point, in Manhattan, all in her name.

The Sutton Place co-op features a kitchen, a living room/ dining room facing the East River, two bedrooms and two bathrooms on the 12th floor of a pink brick building above the FDR at 55th Street. Ben had customized bookcases built into the smaller room to serve as a study. Betty put two couches with rubber foam cushions there for us to sleep on. Her message is clear: the space Claude or I occupy at Sutton Place is provisional.

A week after their move, I hitch down from Boston, where I am in my freshman semester at Boston University, to find Ben alone in his study, face drawn, pouches under his eyes. One of the couches is made into a bed. Ben shakes his head mournfully as he tells me that my brother has been gone for two days. At first, he assumed Claude was at Charlotte's. When his son didn't come back or call after the first night, Ben picked up the phone and spoke to his ex-wife for the first time in years; he learned that she'd neither seen nor heard from Claude. Now, he's priming himself to phone the police.

"Sit tight," I tell him. "I know where he is."

I ride the BMT to Prospect Park Station, walk down the hill, past Louie's pool room, then wait in front of Don Pallini's Dance Studio for the light to change at the intersection of Lincoln and Flatbush. Dusk is falling. Lights flicker in apartment buildings across the street. Our old house is dark, except for a glow in the master bedroom. The place should be empty, pending the closing still a week away. I try the front door. It's locked. So I enter through a basement window in back, as I did whenever I came home after curfew to find myself locked out. That window has been jimmied so many times it gives to my touch.

I drop into the furnace room, noting no sign of rats, or even the scampering feet of mice. I find Claude upstairs in the master bedroom, his face streaked with dried tears. He sits on the floor hugging his knees. For the longest time I sit beside him in silence. Finally, I tell him what he has so many times told me, that our father is worried. We have to go home.

"Where is that?"

"To...Manhattan."

"That's not home."

I reply that *this* is no longer home either. The new owners will be moving in at the end of the week.

"I can't live there. I don't even have a real room."

"Before you know it you'll be leaving for college. Then it won't matter."

The phone is still hooked up. I dial our father's new number, tell him that Claude and I are at Lincoln Road. We'll take the subway back.

"Wait, I'll pick you up."

"That's not necessary."

"I'll be there in a few minutes."

We're outside on the porch steps when he pulls into the driveway. He gets out of the black Cadillac, pauses in front of the hedges to gaze at us, the house, at us again, then approaches. We come down the steps to meet him. When we are standing face to face, our father puts his arms around us both and holds us there. I suspect he is feeling what we feel, sad and orphaned. His hands tighten on our shoulders as he pulls us close. We remain together this way, in front of the gray stucco house, its lidless windows staring back at us for the last time.

September 1st, 1986
Rye, NY
Labor Day

I drive to Highcliff a second time, arriving as twilight softens the outlines of the giant elms. Sails billow on the horizon. June and Wallace are having cocktails on the deck with three of their four sons, up for a Sunday visit. Claude appears, fresh from a shower, wearing pressed chinos and a crisp white polo shirt, holding a bottle of Heineken. He embraces each of the boys, all stamped with their father's broad nose and full lips. The absent son, the oldest, who has a stormy relationship with his father, chooses to live in North Carolina. The others, still unfledged, remain within an hour's drive, returning regularly to the nest. In Claude, also unfledged, they recognize a kinship. My brother has made their nest his own.

Claude follows his first Heineken with a second, then a third, fortifying himself for dinner with his former girlfriend, Michaela, now his stockbroker, living in nearby Mamaroneck.

On our way I ask if he remembers the time I packed my bags to leave Lincoln Road and he begged me not to leave?

"How did you feel when I left?"

"You're missing the point, Paulie. It wasn't about how I felt...."

"Really?"

"I cried. You were shocked, didn't believe anyone could feel that way about you."

"What else?"

"I always feared that you would hurt yourself. Plus, I didn't want to be alone. I didn't make friends easily. I lived through you and your friends. Eventually I found a few

buddies at Brooklyn Friends, but they were like me, little guys with not much going for them."

"You had Lenny on Lefferts Avenue..."

"Meaner than a junkyard dog. I did the best I could. I let you do things to me which were hurtful."

"Like?"

"Stealing my allowance to feed the Jaguars, forcing me to field grounders day after day."

"I'm sorry."

"That's okay, Paulie." He pats my knee. "We're all mixed bags. As Shakespeare said, If we were all held to account which one of us would escape whipping."

We meet Michaela at a family-style seafood restaurant. She's no longer the slim colleen I had met on West 75th Street, but still has a ready laugh and dancing freckles. I wonder if she's as protective of all her clients as she is of Claude. My brother finishes two piña coladas before dinner. Halfway through a third, he tells us that time is running out at Eastcliff. He plans to relocate but isn't sure where.

Michaela suggests New Hampshire.

"How can I live in a place where the license plates say, Live Free or Die? I've been trying to live free all my life without much success. I don't like the other option. There's no way I can live in Missouri either, where the license plates say, Show me. Show me. Show who? Show what?"

On the drive back, Claude repeats that at Wallace's everyone looks at him strangely. The kids are suspicious of him, maybe frightened that Wallace will leave Claude something in his will. June, too. "I've heard nice things about Burlington. Maybe I can come up to see you next weekend and check out Vermont." He doesn't know for sure, but suspects that Vermont has an acceptable motto on its license plate.

XII

My first semester grades at my father's *alma mater,* Boston University, are a disaster, except for the Spanish literature course, *El Siglo de Oro.* I placed into the advanced course thanks to years of bilingual conversation at the dinner table. I'm bored at BU. Harvard, on the other hand, calls out to me. Through my Cherry Lawn friend Joan at Radcliffe, I audit courses given by Paul Tillich on the pre-Socratics, Archibald MacLeish on Li Po. I hear Robert Frost at Harvard, and e. e. cummings at Boston College. cummings wears his shirts open the way a Byronic poet should. Frost croaks. I haunt Widener Library and attend open lectures by David Riesman, Eric Fromm, and Reinhold Neibuhr. It is 1959, and the world of ideas is as palpable to me as the taste of my new meerschaum pipe.

I write poetry which I read aloud at the Za-Zen, a little coffee house off the Fenway. Small tables line both walls of the narrow room, broken only by an upright piano. I am part of a community of poets and a talented prose writer named Russell Banks who lives with his southern wife and baby daughter on the Fenway. I am haunted by the Beats. I discovered the City Lights edition of *Howl* in my senior year at Cherry Lawn, and now I devour Kerouac's *On the Road* and Ferlinghetti's *Coney Island of the Mind.* I determine that by the end of the school year I will join these writers in San Francisco. In my heart I am one of them.

To finance my plan, I find a job four nights a week cleaning the second floor of the Lahey Clinic on Commonwealth Avenue. This includes polishing the floors, emptying used Kotex trash in the women's bathroom, and swabbing four toilets. My supervisor, an Armenian from Chelsea, takes pride in showing me how to clean a toilet until I can see my face in the bowl. By the end of the semester I've saved close to a thousand dollars, enough for a one-way ticket with something left over to hold me until I find a job.

This isn't a frivolous decision, I tell my father at the end of the year. I want a fresh start on the west coast and have no plans to return to New York in the foreseeable future. I'll find a job; then, after a year to satisfy the residence requirement, enroll at San Francisco State.

Ben seems relieved; one boy fewer to worry about. Betty wishes me luck and offers to drive me to the airport, then remembers a previous engagement. It's Claude I hate to leave again. His eyes tug at me as I press forward. Not that he purposely tries to hold me back. He means it when he says he hopes I find what I'm looking for in San Francisco. The physics of our situation leaves us no choice but to tear the threads of our connection.

On the glittering sidewalk of Cannon Point, the doorman hails a cab. Ben pats my head. I throw my duffel into the back seat of the waiting taxi. I tell Claude that he can visit me on the coast, promise I will call, then kiss his cheek. I know how his days will be spent, alone in his temporary room counting the months until he goes off to college. I wonder where that will be, and if he will now be able to leave our father alone with a woman capable of spiking the Brussels sprouts with rat poison. As I pull away, my father and brother stand arm-in-arm.

By the time I arrive in San Francisco in June 1960, the people I've come to find have gone. Pierre DeLattre has closed the Spaghetti Mission, but the Co-existence Bagel Shop is still a hip North Beach bar, and there is the City Lights Book Store. In the basement of City Lights, there is an exhibition of Kenneth Patchen's watercolors, which he is selling to pay his medical bills for a long, terminal illness. The visionary who wrote *Journals of Albion Moonlight* is dying broke.

I find a room at a boarding house on the corner of Fillmore and McAllister. Work is another story. San

Francisco, I discover, is a union town. Failing to qualify for any other job, I "shape up" at the Farm Labor Board on McAllister. By 5:30 AM, the crew I'm in is trucked to Brentwood, where I spend the day picking apricots for thirteen cents a bucket or twenty-two cents a crate. I eat as many as I pack. By the end of the week it's clear I can't pick apricots fast enough to make a living. Fortunately, I am offered a job painting rooms at my boarding house.

When I'm not painting, or walking the city, I write poems. Eventually I collect enough of them to drop off a manuscript at City Lights. Two weeks later, Lawrence Ferlinghetti descends from his upstairs office to hand me back the manila envelope without a word. In my room I take out a note that reads, "Keep writing. You have not yet found your voice."

I do manage to publish a poem in a midwestern literary journal, *The American Weave.* It's entitled "The End," which asks the question: *What will you do/ when the road falls flat/ over the edge of the horizon/ and the prudent word/ is placed before your feet/ like a carpet of thorns?* The answer comes obliquely, in flashes of memory: my father and brother waving goodbye to me at Sutton Place, Ben bent over his desk, Claude curled up like a fetus in the empty house on Lincoln Road.

I call home. My brother assures me that he is having the best summer of his life as a laboratory technician at the Adelphi Hospital, which our father visits daily to take him to lunch. Even so, I am haunted by dreams: *Claude in a lab coat brandishing pipettes of blood and urine asks if I've found what I'm looking for, my father, ghostly pale behind him.*

At the beginning of August I receive a letter from Claude telling me about his latest encounter with Betty. He came home from work to find her watching TV in the study. He asked if she'd leave so he could change his clothes. "In a few minutes," she told him. When Claude returned, he nearly stumbled over the live end of the television cord.

"She'd unplugged the set, cut the wire, and then plugged it in again. It couldn't have been more premeditated. I showed Dad, but he thought I did it myself to build a case against her."

A few days later, I hitch a ride with a salesman who drops me at a diner on the other side of the Donner Pass. I sleep in a derelict car in the back. Next morning, I ride a truck hauling produce through the Nevada desert. Outside of Pocatello, three guys and a girl in a beat-up Chrysler pick me up. They are bail-jumpers from Yakima who have left an interstate trail of robberies in their wake. I don't find this out until the marshal pulls us over in Laramie, where I pass the night in jail before I can convince the FBI agent that I'm not a member of their gang. After two weeks on the road, I walk into the apartment at Sutton Place, my duffel over my shoulder.

My father greets me in the study. He doesn't ask me why I've returned, or what I plan to do. I don't know myself, except that I find myself staring at the television cord Claude told me had been severed and plugged in again. It's fixed, and safely in the socket. For two months I have escaped the horror beneath the surface of our lives, only to be drawn back into it.

Claude, he tells me, is on his way to Quebec City with two of my Cherry Lawn friends. Betty will be away for a few days supervising renovations at her nursery school. What do I think about spending a weekend with him in Westhampton? I feel his loneliness as if it is my own.

The next morning we leave for the beach-front co-op he bought at Betty's urging. It's the first time in years that we've spent time alone together. From the moment we set out, we share a new assumption of intimacy that requires no words. We lie on the beach watching sandpipers race the surf. Gulls spin overhead as children tease long-tailed kites higher and higher into a cloudless sky.

The following morning Ben complains he's been up all night, the surf pounding in his head. Headaches like this one assault him with increasing frequency. He'd hoped coming here would bring him some relief. But last night the waves crashing in his head kept him sleepless. We return to Sutton Place that afternoon. Ben collapses on the floor. I call his friend Phil Politin, head of psychiatry at Columbia Presbyterian. In fifteen minutes medics are at the door with a gurney. A few days later he's diagnosed with brain cancer.

I reach Claude at the Chateau Frontenac in Quebec City and tell him what has happened. I hear him crumble. He flies back the next day from Montreal.

After a biopsy and a series of tests to determine the nature, location, and size of the tumor, it's clear surgery is the only option. Suddenly, for all of us, *The road falls flat over the edge of the horizon.*

"What will you boys do?" our father asks from his hospital bed.

Claude won't stay alone with Betty at Sutton Place. He'll alternate between Highcliff, Wallace's new home in Rye, and Charlotte's apartment in Forest Hills. I already have a room at the Hotel Albert, on University Place, where Nathanael West once worked as a night clerk while writing *Miss Lonelyhearts*. The voices of raucous abstract expressionist painters drift out of the old Cedar Bar at night as I walk by.

Ben doesn't argue with me when I suggest that something more permanent has to be done with Claude by the end of the summer. He agrees to send him to Cherry Lawn for his senior year. I phone Roger Strasser, the director, and explain the situation. He loses no time in arranging for my brother's admittance. Our father writes a check covering the tuition, with enough extra money to keep me at the Hotel Albert for six months.

Standing in front of the train in Grand Central, Claude clutches my worn copy of *Catcher In The Rye*, the only comfort I can give him. There's no sign of the boy who once heard fish whispering at the other end of his line. The din inside of him, like the one in this station, is too loud. He will ride through the tunnel staring at his own reflection until the train emerges on the El through the South Bronx, eye-level with tenement windows, before traveling through the suburban countryside, past Rye, where Wallace lives. I can hear the conductor calling out the stops: Rowayton, Stamford, Darien. He will then take a taxi up Overbrook Road to the gates of his new home full of strangers.

While he unpacks, I'll walk past the Cedar Bar, to the San Remo, or meet Bard Dupont at the Kettle of Fish, on MacDougal, where Maxwell Bodenheim used to drink. Bard has also just come east from San Francisco with a group who now live on East 3rd Street. I've become friendly with several of them, including folk singer Mark Spoolstra. And another folkie among these refugees, a sullen kid originally from Minnesota.

My brother hugs me. I promise to keep him posted on our father's condition. Meanwhile, he'll walk autumnal grounds with kids like himself, castoffs, adrift in the world. As the train pulls out, he presses his face against the glass. I hope he finds something of himself in Holden Caulfield, Salinger's boarding school kid determined to survive an adult world full of "phonies" unaware of their own condition. I watch the train disappear, knowing he must inevitably ponder the question central to all catchers in the rye: *Where do ducks in winter go?*

***

"I know what I'm doing." Our father looks at us from the hospital bed. The bandages have been removed from his stubbly head to reveal the angry smile of a raised, V-shaped cicatrix surrounded by radiation burns.

"You can't go back to Sutton Place," I plead.

"There's no telling what she'll do to you," protests Claude

My brother has been wandering the halls of Columbia Presbyterian Hospital with me since Thanksgiving, when Ben went into surgery to remove the carcinoma. Ten hours under the knife. We were forbidden to see him for several days. When we finally did, our knees went weak. His face staring out of the bandages was bruised and swollen, as if he'd been mugged. At Claude's Christmas break, Ben is still ashen, able to walk only short distances with the help of a cane, but ready for release.

"Please. We can check into a hotel. Paul and I will stay with you."

"I understand why you're worried." His tone is conciliatory.

"Think about what she did to Barney, the live wire she left plugged into the wall," my brother warns.

"Listen to him," growls our Uncle Sig. "This woman will stop at nothing."

A former head of the State Liquor Authority under LaGuardia, our father's oldest brother chews his cigar and paces like a battery-driven toy. He's been cool toward Betty since her departure from the hospital on the day that Ben's operation coincided with the disappearance of our father's new will.

"I don't know who's crazier. How can you be so blind?" I plead.

"Time will tell." He repeats his mantra.

I wheel him out of the hospital in the receding winter light. Claude and I exact his promise that he'll call us at my apartment on East 9th Street and Avenue B, a sixth floor walk-up with a bathtub in the kitchen and a toilet in the hall. The rent is thirty dollars a month split between me and two other guys. Claude sleeps on a mattress on the floor.

"I'll call if I need you." Our father trembles as I help him into a cab.

We ride with him to Sutton Place where the doorman is waiting with a wheelchair, but Ben insists on using his cane.

Braced on the doorman's arm, he wobbles toward Betty, who waits for him at the other end of the canopied entrance.

"Remember," I yell. "We're close by."

At 10:00 PM the phone rings. In a broken whisper my father begs us to come right away. We catch a cab on 14th, and then take the FDR uptown. Soon we're banging on the door at Sutton Place. I hear his cane scraping the floor. He opens the door still in pajamas, an overcoat around his shoulders, then takes two steps back and collapses on an Empire love seat in the hall.

Betty stares out from the kitchen, arms crossed, her white poodle yapping at her feet. I start for their bedroom to get Ben's things. She steps out to block my way. I push past her. In the bathroom I notice his glasses on the floor, lenses shattered. A rolled towel lies against the door beside a fallen broom. I pick up the glasses. They're useless. I drop them on the tiles, then ask if there's anything else he needs.

"I want to leave. Right now."

"Don't forget your codeine." Her grin is lit by a childish cruelty that becomes maniacal in an adult. Her kind of predator has no equivalent in the wild.

In the elevator, we brace his trembling body between us. Outside, the night doorman hails a cab. I direct our driver to an apartment hotel on West 86th owned by one of Charlotte's old boyfriends where our old maid Esther works. Here we can get a room by the week.

"What happened?" asks Claude.

"I never knew such evil existed in the world," he whispers.

"Did she hurt you?" I demand.

Every time he opens his mouth to speak, his chest heaves and he has to catch his breath. Finally, as we enter Central Park at 86th, the words come haltingly. He'd gone to the bathroom, fallen, and couldn't get up. When she came in, he reached out to her. But instead of helping him up, she stood over our father and ridiculed him. Look at the big-shot doctor on the floor like a baby. A whimpering, helpless piece of shit. Where were all his big-shot friends when he needed them?

"Did she hurt you?" I feel his arm twitch.

She presented him with a document, and asked him to sign it. A new will. One she'd drawn. When he refused, she started cooing and stroking his wounded head, and asked him again to sign the document. He refused. Betty grabbed a towel and tried to smother him. He fought back, pushed her away. She rolled up the towel and hit him with it, until he managed to grab the end. She left and returned with the broom. He caught that, too. By this time, she was enraged, spewing profanity like one possessed. She attempted to kick his head. He fended her off, grabbing an ankle and holding on until she promised to leave him alone. I see black and blue marks on his wrists and palms, examine his swollen index finger.

"I'm all right," he insists.

She left him on the floor "to think things over," but let him know she'd be back. He crawled to the living room phone, and called us. When she found him, he warned her that his sons were on the way.

We sit in stunned silence, three monkeys whose hands have just been wrenched from their mouths, eyes, and ears.

"You were right all along," he whispers. "Your father is a horse's ass. A real horse's ass."

Claude kisses his father's head. "No, you're not, Dad."

"Time will tell," Ben mutters, eyes full of tears.

Paul Pines

Glens Falls, NY
September 12th, 1986

I return home after my third visit to Highcliff. Our little red cape in a cul-de-sac called Greenway Circle is hidden from Aviation Mall by a thin line of trees. It is smaller than my old Manhattan penthouse, but has a yard and lawn. It feels like a sanctuary—something I recall from my early days in Brooklyn, only warmer, a spot of time as it was before the tyranny of time. Inside, I play back a message from Amos Poe. I recognize the name as one of two screen writers Jean planned to contact for our project. Poe, the author of Alphabet City, *and Guy Gallo, who adapted Malcolm Lowry's* Under the Volcano, *were both chosen by Daniel Vigne. The French film maker's last words to me haunt my random moments; standing in front of Shakespeare & Co. he said: "I don't want you. I want someone else like you."*

Poe compliments me over the phone on my novel. "I'm too busy to take on anything else, but after reading The Tin Angel, *I've decided to do it." He considers this an opportunity to redeem himself after* Alphabet City. *I wish him well and am relieved I no longer live in "Alphabet City," but in the time-warp town of Glens Falls, where I am now confronted with the problem of how to make a living. I learned how to hustle in the demimonde tending bar, managing jazz musicians (not a real living there), passing an illicit drug now and then. Life between Avenues A, B, and C had been the last stand of a truly bohemian existence. But my life has changed since that time.*

I am now a family man with a baby on the way and a brother trapped in a madness that frightens and confuses us both. I want it to just go away so I can concentrate on reinventing myself at the midway point in life which Dante and Longfellow call the "dark wood."

On the first weekend in October, Vigne's "authentic" American comedy starring Dr. Ruth Westheimer, Sigourney

Weaver, and the tireless Gérard Depardieu previews at the Paris Theater on 57th Street. The Director had been *convinced that this film, on the heels of* Martin Guerre, *would make him the toast of Hollywood. Instead, doors slam shut. The film runs two days after its premiere before being put back in the can, forever. In the blink of an eye, Daniel Vigne is unbankable.*

When I tell Claude about this, he answers that he has no time for show business. What can the limelight mean to a man who can't even leave his room? Over the phone he declares that he is tired of being scared. It's time for a little self-assertion.

"I have problems with that. Dad taught me to respect him, not to talk back. With Mom there was so much guilt in the air that I didn't dare let her know I was pissed off. She'd lash out or go into her darting eyes and litanies. In your case, I always had the feeling that if I outshone you, it would hurt you too badly. Remember when we were kids singing and someone said, 'The little one has got a good voice,' and you locked yourself in the bathroom? I felt so guilty. You were sickly, and I was scared you were going to die in an oxygen tent."

"But you're able to talk about it now."

"And it's probably affecting my neurons."

He concludes by saying he will try to visit me soon. He is determined to get out of his room at Highcliff. The last time he remembers being this scared was just before going to college.

I try to sound encouraging. Even if it means that he is determined to bring his madness to my doorstep; I imagine him driving his Brat up the Northway to Exit 18 on his way to what Vance Packard in 1972 cited as a town exceptional for its stability in "a nation of strangers," and Look Magazine *in a celebrated wartime issue labeled "Hometown USA," where Bob & Ray located both their "The Slow Talkers of America," and the flagship branch of their notorious "House of Toast."*

XIII

A few days after Claude leaves for Cherry Lawn, my father and I check out of our room in the hotel on 86th where we had hunkered down. I have hired a male nurse from the rolls at Columbia Presbyterian and bought three tickets to Miami. On the flight down, I am haunted by the fear that Betty will find us and make Ben's last days a nightmare. When we arrive at Miami Airport, I am eased by the tropical breezes rustling in the palms. My most pleasant childhood memories are here—where we swam and baked in the sun, and our father showed us how to pump the rod when fighting a bill fish.

It takes her two weeks to find us. Betty bursts into our room at the Singapore Hotel waving her arms and sobbing about how worried she's been. "I've missed you so, sweetheart."

I stand in front of her and say that she isn't welcome.

"Let him tell me that," she challenges. "I want to hear it from his lips."

I let her pass.

She approaches the hospital bed where my father lies naked under a sheet like an infant in a crib. She leans over the rails and coos in baby talk that she knows how much he loves her and that she loves him and now she'll never again leave his side.

My father's face turns white. After raising himself on one elbow, his voice is so weak as to be almost inaudible. "*I don't want to see you.*"

"You don't mean that."

"Yes, I do."

"Tell me you don't love me."

"I...don't...love you." He meets her eyes. "And I don't want you here."

Betty storms out, but checks into the hotel. She makes no further attempt to see my father. Instead, she busies herself charging clothes, *objets d'art*, whatever catches her eye. I watch her parade through the lobby carrying packages or sipping screwdrivers by the pool. In a quandary, I call Sig, who flies down immediately. Sig is the first-born who's run interference for two brothers. Charlotte always disliked his cigar chewing coarseness. But I can't think of anyone I'd rather see at this time. The day after his arrival, Betty and Sig confront each other by the pool. He calls her a bitch and demands she fly back to New York on the next possible flight. She smiles, but refuses to let him pass, attempting to draw him into a public display of violence that will allow her to file a complaint against him and take him to court. Sig bites down on his cigar; then, after considering his options, throws her into the pool fully dressed. Betty screams, but no one comes to her aid. The few guests on lounge chairs smile at what they mistake for a joke. After another week of trading hostile glances with Sig, Betty flies back to New York.

I sit by Ben's bed, push his wheelchair to the beach at night when he feels strongest. Sitting by the shuffleboard court we watch the moon come up. In a soft voice, he expresses regret that he hasn't led a simpler life in the country with his sons. The moon trail on the ocean extends like a golden carpet across the sand to the foot of his wheelchair. I imagine pushing him up it until we both melt into the Milky Way.

A few days later he asks me to call the Brooklyn Jewish Hospital, where he is still Surgical Chief of Staff, to reserve a bed. An ambulance takes us to Miami Airport. Another meets us at LaGuardia. In the hospital lobby he whispers, "Whatever happens, always remember, I loved you both."

I call Claude at Cherry Lawn to let him know our father won't live much longer. I picture him by the phone in the dormitory hall, and know that he has reached the limit of his ability to deal with pain. He is seventeen years old. I am nineteen. I am sure that this was one of the last thoughts in our father's mind. I repeat Ben's last words spoken to me before an orderly wheeled him away forever: *Whatever happens...*

"Gotta go," my brother says.

PART 2

REASONING WITH THE FURIES

I

The obituary in the *NY Times*, December 22, 1960, announces the death of Bernard Pines, at fifty-five, and notes that he had been Chief of Surgery at the Brooklyn Jewish Hospital, Adelphi and Swedish Hospitals, and the Brooklyn Hebrew Home and Hospital for the Aged, in addition to functioning as clinical professor of anatomy at the Downstate College of Medicine. He had been a fellow of the American College of Surgeons, and a diplomate and fellow of the International College of Surgeons and a member of the New York Society of Clinical Pathology.

I fail to recognize my father in this description—the terrifying, then pitiful man whose accomplishments had failed to protect him and his sons from the woman who had led him like a child into the secret world of his own sexuality, probably at the cost of his life.

My father chose to die alone. His friends at the Brooklyn Jewish, according to his instructions, kept him incommunicado that last week of his life. He knew they wouldn't let him linger. He died a fallen lord in what had once been his kingdom, and was buried forty-eight hours later, in keeping with Jewish tradition, in the Mt. Lebanon Cemetery in Brooklyn.

A month after his burial, I ride the elevator to the apartment on Sutton Place. I'm accompanied by our lawyer and a young cop. Betty opens the door, her newly coiffed poodle at her heels. She holds him on a thin red leash as if he might otherwise launch a devastating attack. Behind her is a gray-haired man in pinstripes, her lawyer. The attorneys greet each other cordially. Betty retreats to the living room, lights a cigarette, and picks up a fashion magazine. I don't know why, but I'm scared. Not of any immanent threat, but the resonance of every thing that has taken place here, most prominently the terrible events that led to our flight from this spot with our wounded father, hovers in the air like the paralyzed note of a struck bell.

Betty flashes a gorgon smile. I walk to the study, lest she turn me to stone. My father had planned to write a will to replace the "lost one." None was found among his belongings. Our best guess is that Betty destroyed that one, too. Assets for distribution don't include the co-ops in South Hampton and Sutton Place, and the nursery school property in Queens, which are in Betty's name. Also escaping inventory is any "hidden cash," Ben's library of first editions, and the art collection which includes an Iness, several Pissarros, Whistlers and Utrillos

Our clothes are stuffed in the closet. I throw a pair of boots into my empty suitcase. One or two of my brother's favorite shirts. My Boston University jacket. The drawers beneath the bookcases are full of photos, letters, menus, and matchbooks. Everywhere I see the artifacts of our lives, objects representing moments that belong to Claude and me. It is all very confusing. I don't know what, or how much of anything I can claim. I touch a snapshot of our father seated in his Brooklyn study, book in hand, Barney at his feet. The lawyer nods. I see Claude's bar mitzvah portrait; he is wearing a dark suit and tie. I put these in my jacket pocket.

"Take your time," says my attorney.

I am anxious to be gone. Clearly, anything I take will be a tiny piece of the whole, a reminder of what had been. And haven't I always prided myself on my ability to let go when it seemed time to do so. In front of me are books that lined the shelves of Lincoln Road. Leather-bound sets of Harvard Classics, first editions. There isn't enough time to go through them. Momentarily I consider claiming the whole library. But how would I transport it, and where? I pick two of our father's prized books, ones he encouraged me to read, Will Durant's *The Story of Philosophy*, and *The Diary of Samuel Pepys*.

The rest, in Hamlet's words, is "alms for oblivion." Neither Claude nor I will come back here again.

On my way out, I notice that Rodin's *Balzac*, a Utrillo, and the Pissarros, too, are gone. Betty follows my eyes, her blond hair like a straw helmet, still holding her little white dog. It's not fair to hate an animal as much as I hate this one. I should inventory the art and antiques in the living room, but I'm sure that anything of value is no longer in the apartment.

"Finished?" asks the cop.

"I believe so." My lawyer inclines his head at me.

The two attorneys shake hands again at the door.

I don't look back. I understand the moment Alice James describes at the conclusion of her *Diary*, when she is diagnosed with terminal cancer. It's a relief to finally be in fact what I've felt to be in spirit for so long: homeless.

For Claude, this is pure sorrow.

October 10th, 1986
Rye/Glens Falls, NY

"It's not safe here. I thought it would be, but I was wrong."

"What's happening?"

Claude is lying in bed on the third floor at Highcliff. Even as we speak, voices from boats on the Sound come over the water. He thinks he recognizes some of them. Earlier, he went down to the garden to listen more closely. One of the voices was female. It reminded him of a woman he worked with long ago at Babies' Hospital.

"She invited me over for dinner a couple of times but I ate and ran, didn't want to get involved. Maybe she's behind what's happening to me. But why? I never did anything to

her! Well, if it is, I'm going to sue her for libel. You have to watch out for the 'Bettys' of this world."

I tell him it makes no sense that a lady lab technician might mobilize such forces.

"No one believed me back then either. Did you know that Dad finally admitted to Wallace that he thought Betty poisoned Barney?"

"When?"

"In the hospital, just before the operation."

"And he still went back to her!"

"He was too good a clinician not to know. I believe that if Betty had thought she could get away with it, she would have poisoned us, too. But she knew Dad would have ordered autopsies and a toxological report. You wanted me to come up to Cherry Lawn?"

"I wanted you out of there."

"How could I leave him alone with her, knowing what I knew? I had a feeling, but I couldn't prove anything. Dad was in over his head, and I was helpless."

I tell him that he should be working this out in therapy.

He protests. Why should he spend time talking about his past when he is being pursued in the present?

What he needs is intensive treatment. His current therapy is a bandage on a gaping wound, I tell him.

"If I thought I was crazy I'd commit myself. Maybe I should do it just to get some peace. And spend all my money."

"What good is your money doing you when you can't even leave your room?"

"It's blackmail. I don't like being blackmailed."

"I'm not blackmailing you. I'm reasoning with you. Where can you go?"

"I can always wait it out."

"You're forty-four years old. Are you going to sit in your room until you're sixty-four before you come out?"

II

I know every worn stair of the six flights to my railroad flat in Alphabet City. The boiler is always broken. We use the gas stove to heat the kitchen. One roommate has moved, which leaves only the darkly philosophical Dick, a Cherry Lawn refugee whose claims to fame are his stamp collection and his *schlong*. For a small guy, he carries a huge burden. Once we went to the St. Mark's Baths, thinking it a place where old-world men *schvitz*, play cards, and beat each other with bay leaves. Thirty seconds after Dick removed his towel the shower filled with ogling men. We left before the frost was off the pumpkin.

We have learned how to survive in meager circumstances. On cold days we visit the home-furnishing department at various stores. Dick likes to sit in a plush chair at Macy's, reading a book or newspaper. I have a favorite recliner at Gimbel's. We browse in bookstores, though we have no money to buy books. But I can't resist boosting a paperback that calls out to me at The Eighth Street: George Orwell's *Down and Out in Paris and London*. I read it with fascination, but am finally forced to conclude that compared to our experience, Orwell seems benign. He writes about smoking out roaches so they move to the apartment next door. We have bedbugs thin enough to fit into a seam, and impossible to get rid of. They raise huge welts that can become infected. My roommate's skinny body looks like death-by-a-thousand-cuts.

We've pooled our money. Before it runs out, Dick sells his valuable stamp collection to Gimbel's. The first thing he buys is a pool table. The sales contract states that Gimbel's will deliver and install it in the desired location. When the delivery crew discovers that our tenement stairs are too narrow to maneuver the heavy table up six flights, Dick stands firm. The department store is forced to hire piano-movers with a hoist. They take out a window frame, winch the pool table up the front of the building, and swing it in from the roof.

We can only shoot from three sides.

Our budget is limited. We allow ourselves a bowl of cabbage soup and two pieces of pumpernickel a day at Leshko's. Twenty-five cents buys enough *kapusta* to fill a shrunken stomach. But this money soon runs out. Whitey, who owns a bar by the bus stop at 10th, watches me put down my last fifteen cents for a draft beer. After serving me, he disappears into the rear and returns with a plate of cold cuts which he places in front of me. He's seen enough hunger in his life to recognize the signs. I don't know how to thank him. He turns away so I won't have to.

The Israelis who run The Little Rose on Avenue C give us their chicken hearts instead of throwing them away. They invite us to bring a pot for their day-old soup. But Dick is sick a lot now. I think he has malnutrition. I know he is anemic. I am glad that Claude is at Cherry Lawn and can go back for seconds and thirds in the dining room, take hot showers, sleep in a cozy dorm without bedbugs: a distant memory for Dick and me. We don't discuss it, but know that our situation is dire.

On a cold February morning, hands stuffed in the pockets of my trench coat, head down against the wind, I walk uptown from 9th and B to the New York State Employment Agency off Times Square. The guy I spoke to a month ago looks up from his desk, then back at his newspaper. Half an hour later, I am still sitting in front of him, teeth chattering from my long walk up here. He tells me again what he told me before. There are no jobs. The economy is brutal. "And you have no skills or degrees beyond high school."

"But I'm hungry." He stares. I repeat. "I'm cold, broke and hungry. Since my father died in December I've lived from hand to mouth. A bowl of soup a day. Now I can't even afford that. I'll do *anything*."

He can't be much older than I am. Maybe he knows that I won't leave until he finds something for me. I'll sit in the hall, on the stairs, in front of the building until I freeze to death or he finds me a job.

"You can type?"

"Very fast."

He riffles through his files, stops, takes out a piece of paper, then dials a number. The conversation lasts less than a minute.

"Go right now. It's the Sheraton East Hotel on Park Avenue, next to the Waldorf. They're expecting you."

He hands me a sheet of paper with an address and a job description that reads: *secretary to the chef!*

I locate the kitchen entrance on 51st Street, at the end of a long driveway, push through a swinging door into the chatter of pots and pans, knives on cutting boards, sizzling meat, and the voices of men in white jackets adrift on the smell of cumin, cardamom, and coriander. A moon-faced man with gray hair escaping from his Pillsbury Doughboy hat introduces himself as Monsieur Dupan, then directs me to an office looking out on the great kitchen, where he sits at a desk, folding and unfolding his hands.

"Your duties as secretary to the chef—actually, to several chefs—involve typing menus on that," he points to an old Royal by the desk.

"Yes, sir."

"And any other bookkeeping tasks like...I'll tell you as we go. Right now, we've more important things to do."

He rises abruptly. I follow him into the kitchen determined to master whatever task he puts in front of me. He hands me a plate, then leads me around the various stations, filling it.

"You like lamb? The veal roast is delicious. Yes, scalloped potatoes, and some white asparagus, our *specialité*, with a sauce *béarnaise*?"

Monsieur Dupan doesn't wait for me to answer. His tongs

dart here and there until there's no room on my plate. I require a second plate for a roll and salad. Back in the office he clears a space on the desk for the linen napkin and utensils in his hand.

"Now, take off your coat and eat."

He picks up the book that drops out of my coat pocket. I first taste the veal roast, then the asparagus, trying not to wolf them down. He examines Franz Cumont's *Astrology and Religion Among the Greeks and Romans.*

"Ah, Persephone in the underworld," he says, knowingly.

"I was born with a silver spoon." I refuse to become the object of pity.

M. Dupan summons the other chefs to his office, introduces them to his new secretary, and instructs the saucier to make sure my *viands* are sauced, the chef in charge of *poissons* to show me where the shrimp and lobster are kept, and the vegetable chef to make sure I eat *legumes* daily. My new boss charges the Dutch pastry chef to let me sample his bread pudding and *crème brûlée*. Nothing is to be served from his station until I have sampled it and given my okay.

"How else can we expect him to type our menus?"

Glens Falls, NY
Labor Day, 1986

Claude arrives at my doorstep in Glens Falls at the beginning of Labor Day weekend on his way to Burlington, Vermont, the first stop in search of a place with an acceptable license-plate motto. We lunch on the deck of the Shoreline Restaurant overlooking Lake George. The Minnehaha and the Mohican, sightseeing steamboats with high stacks and calliope whistles, pull in and out of their slips at the southern end of the lake, next to the Million Dollar Beach. Tourists buzz past on jet skis. Parasailors float in a cloudless sky like puffs of red, yellow, and blue smoke. Claude starts to describe how he has lain awake all week listening to Chat snore beside him on the pillow...until the beehive of noise and activity around us makes it impossible for him to go on.

I pay the bill.

Claude follows me home in his Brat.

For the next two days he sleeps. In the middle of a conversation his eyes close and his head bobs on his chest. He dozes in the back seat of the car, in front of the TV, in the lounge chair on the deck. It appears unlikely he'll ever get to Burlington. At the end of the second week we pack him into Carol's Toyota and set out for Vermont.

Snaking north along the lake on 9N, Claude snores uninterruptedly to Ticonderoga, thirty-two miles away. He stirs briefly crossing the Port Henry Bridge at the southern end of Lake Champlain. Hunger wakes him for lunch in Middlebury. We eat at a converted mill above the stream. My brother finds the town "too college."

Burlington hugs the shore of Lake Champlain, which lies like a fallen mirror at the bottom of a sloping hill. Part of downtown is closed to cars. As we search for a parking space, Carol points out the purple outlines of the Adirondack High Peaks in the distance. We stroll the pedestrian promenade, stopping to explore boutiques and bistros, browse in bookstores, and drink cappuccino at a waterside cafe. The crowd is too young, Claude complains. Too trendy. No matter what the license plate reads, he can't live here.

My brother snores all the way back to Glens Falls, where he wakes long enough to make it into bed. I try to rouse him for dinner. He blinks and says, "I think I'll pass." Later, while Carol and I are watching Casablanca *in the living room, he shuffles by. I mention the plate of barbecued chicken in the fridge. I needn't worry about him, he snaps. He can take care of himself. I ask if he's angry. No, he shakes his head, sorry if he sounded that way.*

"I'm under a lot of pressure," he tells us through a mouthful of barbecue. "Every time I finish a conversation with Wallace and June, I hear it repeated by strangers at Pathmark. Before I left, Wallace started talking about the increase in serial murders in the United States." My brother's face softens when he says, "Wallace knows I'm a suspect and is trying to protect me."

Carol excuses herself to go to bed. I want to follow her, but Claude is just warming up. For the first time, he tells me exactly what he'd experienced during his last days on West 75th Street.

"One day I went outside to find strangers glaring at me. At the corner of Columbus, I noticed these smiling old ladies with open pocketbooks." Attempting to lure him into unspeakable acts, they spread the lips of their purses like vulvas. He'd run back home and turned on the TV only to discover the morning talk shows were discussing him. In a deceptively conversational way, Bryant Gumbel aired his suspicion that Claude had committed a heinous crime, the nature of which the TV host refused to reveal. "Every night I heard whispering under my window. Finally, I called Wallace and June."

But he's no longer safe at Highcliff. Strangers in town are taunting him. Old ladies have started trolling their purses through the town parking lot like mossbunkers, the oily live bait we use to catch blues.

"You think I'm delusional, don't you?"

His question stops me. If I challenge him, I risk his anger. If I humor him, I might lose his trust.

"Yes," I tell him. "Most of the time."

"Of course," he nods. "I'd think so, too, if I weren't living it."

The accusations had started at University Hospital, but continued when he left the lab. "I knew they suspected me of something. But what do I have to do with little old ladies? Paulie, don't you get it? They think that I'm the Manhattan

Creeper!" I hold my breath. Claude's humor is often dark, verging on the grotesque. But now he's deadly serious. "Watchers are everywhere."

He falls back against the blue velour easy chair. I carry his empty plate to the kitchen. By the time I return, the Manhattan Creeper is fast asleep.

III

Tonight we are celebrating Claude's graduation from Cherry Lawn with a dinner at the Czardas, a Hungarian restaurant on the upper West Side. Wallace tips the strolling violinist, who interrupts us in the middle of our *paprikash* to announce, "This is for Clode." I admire the irony of his choice, a sugary version of a tune made popular by Eartha Kitt, "Allez-vous-en," which means "*go away.*"

My brother smiles sheepishly at the attention. His mood, elevated by a martini, is further enhanced by our mother's stated desire "to make a home for her boys", which she announces over dessert.

"We'll live as a family. I've put in a request for a three-bedroom apartment on Queens Boulevard. It should be ready by the end of the month. Until then, you can both sleep on the pull-out in the living room."

Claude and I return to East 9th Street that night, pack, then arrive as instructed at her Forest Hills apartment the following afternoon. Fred stows our gear in the hall closet. Charlotte has prepared a pot-roast supper, Claude's favorite. Before dinner, my brother drinks two Beefeater martinis.

By candlelight, Charlotte assures us that the new apartment will be ready earlier than anticipated. They simply have to throw on a coat of paint. I imagine sun streaming through windows that sit evenly in their sills and don't rattle in the wind, spotless white walls with no flaking plaster or rats lurking behind exposed lathing, hot water day and night. The hall toilets in our tenement walk-up receive no heat even in the dead of winter. We must wear our overcoats to use them. Paradise is a bathroom where you can shit without freezing to the seat.

Fred wakes us the following morning. Standing at the foot of the Castro, his pale face turns an alarming shade of red. "Your mother has something to tell you," he says.

Charlotte enters on cue, stops at the steps leading down to the sunken living room. In a frowzy housecoat, *sans* makeup, eyes almost swollen shut, her message is brief. This apartment has been her sanctuary for over a decade. The pain of giving it up is more than she can bear. Since there isn't room for us to live here on a permanent basis, we will have to leave. As much as she'd like to help us, she can't go through with the move.

"Sorry," she says, before retreating to her bedroom.

I'm speechless. It's as though I've just witnessed a performance in a tragedy by Aeschylus or Eugene O'Neill about a family curse unfolding over generations. Claude stares after her, then at me. It's not that he doesn't know what's just happened, but I can see in his eyes that he would like me to explain it to him. I shrug and sing:

> *Allez-vous-en, allez-vous-en, go away*
> *I have no time for you today...*

My brother's body moves even more slowly. He brushes his teeth and combs his hair at the bathroom mirror like a blind man. I want to be out as fast as possible. Why should either of us be surprised. No matter how much Charlotte wants to, she'll never be a homemaker. I kick myself for thinking otherwise. I am surprised at myself. Claude moves like a zombie.

As we stand in the hall, waiting for the elevator, Charlotte squints through the peephole. When the car arrives, she steps into the hall. Her words slip past the closing elevator door. She has tried to do the right thing. Our father beat her down when she was too sick to fight him. No one will ever know the truth. There will always be those who judge her harshly. *"But they don't understand!"* Our mother's cry follows us down. *"I'm always the one who always gets left holding the bag!"*

***

The pool table takes up most of our living room. There is just enough space under it for Claude's mattress. He's lived with us on 9th Street all summer while holding down a job in the mailroom at Atlantic Cement, where people talk about his bright future. He's even forgiven Charlotte. Oddly, I'm the one who can't bring myself to talk to her.

Claude goes to Forest Hills for dinner and martinis several times a week. I watch as he puts on brown slacks to go with a yellow shirt and departs. He'll return with a Beefeater glow, then go to sleep. Not a word about what they did, or talked about. During my days of near starvation, I'd have wasted away to nothing before asking my mother for help. He savors the illusion of a mother who provides for him. I am jealous of the possibility that in some way she really does. The fact that he really lives with me on Avenue Boo goes unappreciated.

I find my home in books.

In San Francisco I learned that Kenneth Rexroth spent a year holed up in his apartment reading. I resolve to do the same. My shelves on 9th Street are packed. Books fill the wall above the pool table. Tonight, I put on a tape of the *Black Orpheus* sound track and prepare to read. But when I face my wall of books, I'm suddenly stunned by the power of Charlotte's presence. She is here in the titles on my shelves: Manly Palmer Hall, A.E. Waite, P. D. Ouspensky, Sri Maharshi, Ramakrishna, and Aurobindo are just a few of the authors I have met through her.

I do not long to be at her table eating pot roast. She never fed that hunger in me. It was her curiosity that fed me. I feel the same hunger for words on the page that I did as a starving person for my daily bowl of soup. I have devoured the historical writings as well as the fiction of H.G. Wells, and the man whose style he compared to "an elephant straining to give birth to a pea," Henry James. Even as Claude sips Beefeater with Charlotte beneath the Moorish lamps, it occurs to me that my hunger for books is an expression of my hunger for mother. The gaudy esoterica of Alistair Crowley, *Papus on the Tarot*, Gareth Knight's *Kabala*, and Gurdjieff's *Beelzebub* glow like saloon neon. I reach for Attar's *Conference of the Birds*. The Sufi mystic, named after his trade as a perfume maker, wrote magically about birds in search of the source of wonder. I open randomly in their journey to locate myself here and now:

> *After the Valley of Unity comes the Valley of Astonishment*
> *and Bewilderment, where one is prey to sadness and*
> *dejection.*
> *Their sighs are like swords, and each breath a bitter sigh...*

I read it over again, then lie in bed listening to the summer evening sounds outside. Kids play bongos in the courtyard of the public school across the street. The smell of hot roof tar drifts in.

In September, Claude goes off to Antioch College, in Yellow Springs, Ohio. We manage to get an advance from our father's estate to cover his tuition, as well as my own at Bard College, in Annandale-on-Hudson. As much as I love Bard, Claude hates Antioch.

"The students are pretentious and the atmosphere arty."

He leaves at the end of his first year.

Our mother encourages him to apply to Tulane, in New Orleans, where she fell in love for the first time as a young musician playing cruise ships. Over their tête-à-têtes she evokes for Claude images of wrought-iron balconies, sunsets laced with Spanish moss, sexy high-yallers with parasols. My brother talks to me about strolling the French Quarter, eating gumbo at Antoine's and *beignets* at the Café du Monde.

I'm not surprised when last minute doubts assail him at Idlewild as we stare at the Delta plane on the tarmac from our plastic seats in the terminal waiting room.

"I don't know about this."

"You'll be fine." Charlotte pats his hand.

It's the first time I've seen her since she kicked us out of her apartment.

"Maybe this isn't such a good idea." Sweat beads my brother's forehead.

Charlotte says, "I know just the thing."

We follow her to the nearest bar. The lunch crowd is gathering but we find a table. In honor of Claude's journey to the land of sour mash, she orders three shots of Wild Turkey, straight up. We drink two rounds. Between shots she sings:

> *What a dance do they do*
> *Baby, I'm just telling you,*
> *Hey, hey, Uncle Fudd,*
> *It's a treat to beat your feet*
> *on the Mississippi mud...*

We stagger to the gate. Claude looks from me to our mother.

"I dunno," he says.

Charlotte sings the refrain of what has now become his de facto theme song: *It's a treat to beat your feet on the Mississippi mud.*

My brother walks to the plane like a condemned man disappearing down the green mile. A week later, he stands at the door of my walk-up on Avenue B.

"All I could smell was stale beer from frat houses. And everywhere these football players with brush cuts...I felt like one of the Seven Jewish Dwarfs.

"No obliging octoroons?"

"Peroxide blondes in Gucci loafers and hot Corvettes. I couldn't find any Mississippi mud." He puts down his valise. "So I beat my feet to the bus station."

I have a dorm room at Bard, but return on weekends and vacations to Avenue Boo. My classmates spend breaks in Europe or at their homes on Park Avenue and Oyster Bay. I frequent bars like Stanley's, The Annex, and Slugg's Saloon, a great jazz room on 3rd and Avenue C. While most of my fellow Bardians are negotiating with their parents for auto insurance, I am navigating junkies in the hallway, no heat in the pipes and roach infestations. I am comforted by the fact that these aren't so bad on a part-time basis.

I don't tell Claude how different I feel even among the mavericks that Bard attracts. I love its ivy-covered buildings, classrooms looking out on the quad, the pool perched on a hillside over a rushing stream, but I move in that landscape like a Fresh Air kid, unable to forget that only a year ago I was hustling chicken hearts and day-old soup.

Glens Falls, NY
September 6th, 1986

At 9:15 AM, I find Claude on the deck in a lounge chair, clutching a mug of coffee. I suggest that he do some deep breathing with me. His head snaps up. I repeat my offer. He glares.
    "What's wrong?"
    "You're overbearing, Paulie. Always have been. You think you know everything." He sips his coffee. "I'm sorry. I know I'm hurting people."
    "Maybe we should talk to Jeff Hoffman."
    "Why should we do that?"
    "Because of what he's been through."
    I remind Claude that ten years ago our childhood friend from Brooklyn jumped out the window of his fifth-floor Ocean

*Parkway apartment, convinced that the Mafia had taken out
a contract on his life. He landed in a tree, spent two years in
an experimental program at Columbia Presbyterian, and had
since become a psychotherapist.*

*"Maybe." Claude leaves without another word, returning
a few minutes later transformed by his metal-detecting gear.
"We'll finish the discussion about Jeff another time. Now I
want to go to City Park."*

"What are you looking for?"

"The usual: jewelry, old coins, Colonial treasures."

*The spectacle of my brother in a leather apron and head
phones, hooked up to a scanning device, creeping over the
earth like a prosthetically enhanced insect, embarrasses me.
Claude senses this. He no longer invites me to tag along but
seems content to probe the earth alone. At 1:00 PM he calls
from a phone in front of Crandall Library. There's nothing to
be found in any of the local parks, no coins, jewelry, or
anything of historical significance. He might as well head
back to Rye, but first would like to prove that everything he's
told me is real. Can I meet him at Aviation Mall, by the Sears
entrance, in fifteen minutes?*

*Claude is already there when I arrive. We enter by the
washing machines and then stroll to the electronics section,
where we price TVs and VCRs. From there, we explore home
furnishings, athletic equipment, and men's shoes. I ask if he's
noticed any suspicious activity. He shakes his head. We move
on to house paint, drill sets, jockey shorts, and hooded sweat-
shirts. Finally, in front of women's lingerie, my brother
heaves a sigh.*

"Of course, it never happens when I'm with someone."

*But the activity has made us hungry. We stop at a coffee
shop with faux Tiffany fixtures featuring a strange local
young man in his mid-twenties who accompanies himself on
the Hammond organ backed up by a drum machine. I often
come to sip coffee and listen to him perform. This afternoon
he sits at the keyboard in his trademark red shirt and black*

bow-tie. His pleasure at doing what he loves usually picks up my mood. I hope he'll have the same effect on Claude.

We order muffins and coffee at the counter. The performer nods from his platform behind our server. He's even more animated than usual, singing Willie Nelson's "On The Road Again." It turns out to be the last number of the set.

"How you doing?" I greet him when he makes his rounds.

"Fine." The musician flashes an asymmetrical smile, which suddenly turns into a grimace.

"What's wrong?" I ask.

"No disrespect," he shakes his head. "But I don't know if I can trust two guys in black shirts."

"He's right." Claude smiles. "You and I are both wearing black shirts." The performer gives us a satisfied salute, then returns to the Hammond. "That was well observed." My brother's tone is admiring. "He may have a touch of CP, but he's not an idiot."

IV

My British Literature professor, Paris Leary, has arranged a public concert reading of a play I've written based on life with Betty at Lincoln Road. Claude, who insisted on transferring to Bard to continue his education under my brotherly wing, is scandalized. Cherry Lawn worked for him because I had already left. Neither of us anticipated the consequences of his arrival at Bard while I am still very much in residence.

"You can't do this to me," my brother insists in the coffee shop. "I don't want people knowing about my private life."

I want to tell him I understand what a betrayal this feels like to him, certainly as great as any of my past betrayals.

"I can't do anything about it."

"Yes, you can."

"The actors have been cast and the announcements have gone out."

"I don't care."

"It's my debut as a playwright."

"If you go through with this, I won't speak to you again."

"This isn't only about you."

"Or you!" Claude storms out.

The reading takes place two weeks later to a full house. For two hours student actors portray Betty's abuse of my brother, family arguments at dinner, and my heroic confrontation with our father to save Claude from a beating. I have been after something mythic, a tragedy worthy of Sophocles, or Arthur Miller. I have my doubts about what I have done. It seems thin to me, even trite. But at the end, the audience applauds. Paris Leary dabs his eyes and pats me on the back. Classmates and faculty congratulate me, speak of my budding talent, and predict future triumphs.

Claude isn't among them.

What has been an artistic exorcism for me is a public

humiliation to him. The shame of it follows him everywhere on campus. When he enters a classroom, people ask him for further details. What happened to Betty and our father? Strangers at Adolph's bar down the road want to know how it feels to live through a version of *Gaslight*.

I hope that it will help Claude to understand what it means to have been *gaslighted*. The merits of my play aside, it can only help him to know that most of his childhood he has been gaslighted in the truest Hitchcockian tradition. But when I next see him coming out of the cafeteria, he passes me as if I were invisible.

Claude transfers to Columbia General Studies at the end of his sophomore year, and takes an apartment on Riverside Drive. A year later, we still haven't spoken. I am a ghost to him. When I talk now and then to Charlotte, she tells me only that my brother is doing well.

I can't say the same.

After my graduation from Bard, I enroll for a masters in literature at NYU. Six weeks into the semester, my academic life is a crucifixion. Before each class I fill a Chock-Full-O'-Nuts coffee container with a Danish fruit wine I call Cherry Wobbly, which I order by the case. A small coffee container holds enough Wobbly to get me through the lecture on Irish literature by Professor Greene, who talks about Synge and O'Casey as if they were old friends. Enduring the woman who bludgeons me with *Beowulf* requires a medium container. *Ancient Greek Literature in Translation* is an extra large Wobbly experience. What drove the ancients to remorseless acts of cruelty and devotion remains unperceived by our teacher. Tonight we are dealing with Tragedy. I drink a prophylactic container of Wobbly before class to make sure I am prepared.

The lecture hall is shaped like an amphitheater; seats in descending tiers form a semicircle around the lecturer who paces in front of his podium. A middle-aged man with a salt-

and-pepper brush cut and Colgate smile, he has no doubt about his ability to illuminate Aeschylus's *Oresteia*. My fellow students fill the rows, talking animatedly to each other. I take my usual aisle seat midway up the slope. We open our text to *The Eumenides*, the last play of the trilogy, in which the Furies, who have pursued Orestes for the murder of his adulterous mother, turn into the Sweet Ones upon his acquittal by the first jury in Western civilization that has been convened on the Hill of Ares.

I celebrate an end to the curse on the House of Atreus. Even though Orestes has his mother's blood on his hands, he is sentenced to the equivalent of "time served," which is to say, half the jury determines he has suffered enough for an act that was foreordained by the circumstances into which he was born. Athene, of no woman born, breaks the tie by siding with Orestes for avenging his father's death.

I toast the newly acquitted boy...but the professor's words ruffle my benevolent buzz. He doesn't appreciate the relentlessness of the Furies, their great age, older even than the gods. *He is too happy.* He waves his arms like a newly crowned Heavyweight. He would have us believe the Furies are vanquished once and for all.

"Tragedy doesn't stop because the play is over!" I mumble.

Sure, we are relieved when the jury frees Orestes knowing in our hearts what a terrible thing it is to have our mother's blood on our hands. Even so, we know the cycle will begin again; another Orestes, in another time and place, will be pursued by the same Furies, blinded by his act, certain he could have acted in no other way.

> For there will come one to avenge us, born to slay his mother and wreak death for his father's blood.

And that guy in the crew neck behaves as if he were at a pep rally.

Go, Orestes!

"Excuse me," I raise my hand.

"Yes, the young man up there."

"So, do you think Orestes will forget what he's done?"

"Do you?"

"This is not a *Krishen* work of redemption," I slur, then read from the book in my hand. "'And when the black and mortal blood of man has fallen to the ground, who can sing it back again?'"

"You think that there is no such thing as redemption for the Greeks?"

"Not like being washed in the blood of the lamb."

"What about the transformation of the Furies into the Sweet Ones?"

All eyes turn toward me.

"Where is my Areopagus? Or yours?" I challenge him.

"That's a different question." The teacher smiles, aware that in the process of vanquishing one set of Furies, he may have unsuspectingly unleashed another.

"Is it?"

I make a sweeping gesture. My hand brushes the Chock-Full-O'Nuts cup off the edge of the desk. The loosely fitted top comes off. Cherry Wobbly runs down the aisle. I realize that this is my Areopagus and my fellow Athenians are judging me even as I zip up my blue windbreaker and pick up my books. The odor of sweet wine pursues me down the aisle and out of the program at NYU.

Glens Falls, NY
December 29th, 1986

Ten days after the birth of our daughter Charlotte, Irving's daughter, our cousin Jo, who lives in Rye, calls to congratulate us. Also to let us know that Claude has decided not to drive up to see our baby, who weighs nine pounds and has laughing eyes.

"He's not in good shape," Jo says. "We drove to the Alexanders' in White Plains this morning. He thinks people from New Jersey are following him. When we parked, he took out opera glasses to search the lot for Jersey plates. He suspects they may be people from Metpath."

"He's been penetrated," declares Jeff, whose delusion incorporated his own crucifixion. If anyone understands how paranoia works, he does. "You know how the object of a voodoo curse reacts when he receives a doll with a needle through its heart? He withers and dies. The power isn't in the doll or the person who cursed him. The power that kills is in the victim. Claude has been penetrated that way." Jeff wants to know when I became aware of my brother's problem.

I'm not sure how to answer the question. Claude's years of struggle with Betty were terrible, but I thought he'd moved past them. Then there was his string of lab jobs, difficulties with co-workers. I had never really put it together. I'm shocked by the evidence of my own denial.

Delusion, Jeff continues, is an extreme version of distorted perceptions common to all of us. Given enough fear, anger, and depression, those extreme distortions seem real. The world often confirms this by responding to certain cues. People on the street, in parking lots and department stores, really might stare and whisper in response to odd or provocative behaviors.

"Claude probably has been the object of taunting or surveillance at the labs because of his conviction that people are doing that to him."

I tell Jeff that Claude has been seeing a therapist.

"Therapy isn't enough. Your brother has to be medicated." Jeff is emphatic. He reminds me that even after two years as an inpatient at Columbia Presbyterian, he'd be back inside without his Trilafon. "In my delusion, there was a contract on my life. I'd been found guilty. I had to be taken away in a straitjacket. Claude is still only under suspicion."

"Why little old ladies?"

Jeff sighs then asks: "What do you think?"

I recall our mother, Charlotte, the way she had appeared without makeup on the morning she asked us to leave her Forest Hills apartment after promising to make a home for us: a little old lady.

V

"Mom told me you dropped out of NYU."

"Now I'm with SIU."

"Is that a college?"

"The Seafarer's International Union on Atlantic Avenue."

"What about school?"

"I'm better off at sea. I work in the galley of a freighter out of Mobile, an old C-2 that should've been retired after the last war. We're tied up in Brooklyn for the night to take on cargo. I thought I'd call."

I explain that the unions have opened their books to fill the demand created by the war in Vietnam. I'm one of the new boys working old boats. It's been almost two years since we've spoken, enough time, perhaps, for Claude to forgive me for what I did to him at Bard.

I tell him about my three months in the Gulf of Mexico on a tin can that heats up so much one can't walk barefoot on her deck plates; about the bars in Beaumont where there are more homicides committed by irate husbands than in all the rest of Texas, including Houston, aka Murder City, where the police are meaner than in L.A.

"We leave in the morning for Southampton, Le Havre, Rotterdam, Bremerhaven, and Bremen. God knows, one winter storm on the North Atlantic and I may wish I were back in the Gulf. How are you doing?"

Fine, Claude says. His final year as a pre-med student at Columbia General Studies is demanding, especially chemistry, but he's up to the challenge. "Funny you should call now. Ted's in town."

Our Cherry Lawn friend has been working on Swedish-Norwegian ships. I'm curious how his experience compares to mine. It's been many years since we sat by the pond together talking about the South Seas.

136

"He's coming over with some Thai *ganja*. Would you like to join us?"

"Tonight?"

"*Carpe diem*. You can also meet my girlfriend."

"I'd like that," I answer, trying not to betray surprise.

My suspicion that Claude has done quite well without his older brother in his life is confirmed by the sight of him at the door of his third-floor apartment in a renovated brownstone off 78th Street. In pressed chinos and button-down plaid shirt, he is trim and alert. He meets my eyes, but stiffens when I hug him.

The living room has a decorative fireplace, high ceilings, and parquet floors. Everything is neat, no papers on the tables, books on the floor, ashes in the ashtrays. His girlfriend, Michaela, flashes gray-green eyes under coppery hair. Her broad-cheeked smile is warm. They met at Columbia, she explains, where she is also finishing her senior year. She touches my brother's hand with an easy familiarity.

Ted shambles in a few minutes later, a pack of Luckies rolled into a sleeve of his T-shirt. His dark eyes under a thick, unbroken eyebrow are heavy lidded. He is already stoned. Sitting around Claude's coffee table, Ted rolls a joint, then recounts jumping ship in Bangkok, where he spent three months with his girlfriend, Doy, in her jungle village.

As he narrates a tale of his journey into and return from the depths of the Asian jungle, we are joined by our sense of life's mystery, the possibility of a plan beneath the seeming randomness of events, a fate tailored to each of us.

"I sail at six in the morning," I tell them. "I have to leave."

"Winter on the North Sea is a bitch." Ted smiles knowingly.

"Take care of yourself," says Claude before closing the door.

In August 1964, after a month in San Francisco hanging around the old NMU Union Hall on Drum Street, I ship out aboard the *S.S. Esparta*, a United Fruit banana boat bound for Vietnam. Her refrigerated holds are full of perishable cargo including turkeys for the officers' Thanksgiving mess.

After nearly two weeks on rough seas that make the North Atlantic in winter look like a swimming pool, we approach the Philippines. When the hatches are finally released and the crew stretches their legs on the open deck, I am surprised to see the little white bird who hitched a ride with us from the dock at Alameda still circling over head. For some reason, I am reminded of Claude.

It has been more than a year since I last saw my brother. Although we have exchanged letters and phone calls, I am not sure deep down that he has forgiven me. Fortunately, the history of my betrayals is not the most important thing going on at the moment in my brother's life. He is doing well in school. Michaela has grounded him. She has taught Claude to use deodorant and change his socks. Then why is it that a white bird hugging a storm-tossed ship in the middle of the ocean reminds me of Claude, when I am the one knocking around the high seas on a tin can and he is the one applying to medical schools?

VI

The S.S. Esparta
Saigon, South Vietnam
12/16/64

Dear Claude,

We anchored for the weekend a mile from the hamlet of Qui
Nohn, in the boonies north of Saigon. On Saturday morning,
I convinced Charlie, another Wiper, to jump ship with me
until Sunday. We were to sail on Monday. We needed the R &
R, but I also wanted to see a local doctor about the venereal
gift I received from a Teagirl in Danang that has been
unresponsive to antibiotics. A bum-boat took us to the beach
for a box of Marlboros. From there we walked a mile to town,
rented a room with two cots and a bidet, then found a barber
shop on the main square. Both of us needed a shave and the
luxury of hot lather was irresistible.

You've heard of wolves in a hen house? We were hens in the
wolves' lair. Two men in white smocks pinned sheets around
our necks. The first stroke of the razor pulled off flesh just
below my ear. Blood flowed. Before I could protest, my
barber dragged the blade from the base of my neck to the tip
of my chin. It dawned on me that one didn't argue with a
blade at your throat. A glance at Charlie in the mirror told
me he had reached the same conclusion. We understood why
the military had restricted seamen. Qui Nohn is a VC enclave.
We were being shaved by men who wore black pajamas at
night when they would simply cut our throats. As it was, they
took the opportunity to play with us. Charlie and I emerged
looking like two scoops of cherry vanilla ice cream. But not
before we left them a tip.

I found a local doctor who held my urine specimen to the sun then assured me he could treat my disease with an herbal remedy he had to order. I asked if he could have it by tomorrow. He said he would try. But when I returned on Sunday, his office was closed. Two days later, a medic in Cam Rahn Bay diagnosed my infection as "Saigon Rose," for which, he said, they had no cure. The disease would burrow inside to eventually kill me. The bos'n told us that the VC use VD as a weapon, that there's a secret compound where guys wheel their balls around in wheelbarrows.

By now you must be applying to medical schools. I hope Michaela is taking good care of you and that you're changing your Odor Eaters once a week. I don't know who the person is coming home dressed like your brother, carrying his wallet, answering to his name, but if he rings your doorbell, make no mistake: he is not the brother you have known.

Sincerely,
Saigon Rose

Glens Falls/Rye NY
January 30, 1987

"I'd like to come up this weekend. There are things best said in person." This is a statement, not a request. Claude hangs up as soon as he has let me know he is on his way.

My brother arrives on Friday afternoon in pressed chinos and a new hooded parka, carrying a camera which he says is useful to document and discourage the Watchers. We go to Ellie's Deli, a dark room in downtown Glens Falls highlighted by a long counter displaying cold cuts and pickled vegetables.

Watchers, he insists, anticipate his every move. At a Thruway rest stop he heard a man declare, "So much trouble over one little guy."

"I should be looking for another career," Claude bites into his corned beef on rye. "But there's not enough left of me to hold down a job in a pepper factory."

"What are you going to do?"

"That's what I'm trying to figure out."

My brother pulls out an issue of Treasure Hunter, *a slick magazine with photos of men wearing head sets and leather aprons scouring the ground with small satellite dishes. I open to an article about pirate booty buried on islands along the Maine coast, another about panning for gold in the Swift River.*

"You're going to pan for gold in Maine?"

"Portland's expensive. People speak highly of Camden. I'll drive around and see."

What about his Watchers? Won't they pursue him? They've already followed him to Rye.

"At least I'm taking them to nice places."

VII

I have fallen asleep in one world to awaken in another. When I left for Vietnam, lower Second Avenue was a grim strip of dying Yiddish theaters and kosher restaurants. On Thanksgiving '65 I return to pulsing black lights, Peter Max posters flanked by lava lamps, flower children in tie-dyes trailing long hair, patchouli oil, and the best macrobiotic meals anywhere at the Paradox on East 6th Street. At the Fillmore East, Timothy Leary preaches the mysteries of LSD, and Janis Joplin urges us to "Come on!"

I move from my old walk-up in Alphabet City to a rent-controlled penthouse ten stories above Second Avenue between 3rd and 4th. It is a wood-and-tarpaper shack that resembles a tugboat. I wake to sunrise behind Con Ed stacks in Long Island City. The wind wails through my penthouse as the boiler labors to push up the steam. It takes an hour to fill the tub. Saigon Rose, like my water pressure, comes and goes; symptoms range from periodic discharge to malarial chills and fever. At the Navy clinic in Seattle I was told that there was nothing they could do. Claude convinces me to see Uncle Irving.

"Treat it like a nose cold, kid." My uncle imitates George Raft.

I have resolved to settle down and lead a "normal life." Wallace once offered to find work for me at United Artists through a VP whose life my father saved. I tell him that I am ready for a real job. He congratulates me.

Claude's life, on the other hand, is now full of uncertainty. His applications to medical schools have all been rejected. "I've moved around too much," he explains. "They smell instability." His relationship with Michaela has crumbled. I press him for an explanation over coffee at the Market Diner.

"We're still friends," he says.

My brother keeps me at arm's length.

We see nothing of each other through the spring: Mr. Uptown and Mr. Downtown. A week before Independence Day, he calls to describe a recent interview at Boston University. "I braced myself with a martini. Just one. The interviewer was a nice man in a gray suit. But I knew it was over when his nostrils began to quiver."

"Not a good sign."

"Unless he considers the smell of gin an asset."

His interviewer doesn't. He is politely rejected. But this has no impact on Claude's weekly trips to Forest Hills, where he and Charlotte comfort each other with Beefeaters. I am delighted when he calls with news of his acceptance at the Université Libre in Brussels.

"Have you told Irv?"

"Not yet."

Our uncle had urged Claude to apply after meeting an American third-year medical student on a cruise ship going home for the holidays. Subsequently, Claude learned that David, one of the few friends he had retained from Bard, had also been accepted there.

"Maybe you'll discover a cure for Saigon Rose."

"Maybe," he replies.

In his first letter on 10/7/66, Claude complains about the trench coat I picked out for him at Barney's. ("It's you," I told him. "Mr. Continental.")

I should have held out for one with a belt. From the back I look like a parachute. I billow crossing the Grande Place. People stare over coffee at the Roi d'Espagne. I'll be all right. David reminds me that we're in a country whose chief claim to fame, besides lace and chocolate, is the statue of a boy pissing in a bird bath.

I dive into my new life as a budding young movie executive at United Artists, surfacing long enough to write him on Transamerica stationery.

> I find myself in palatial offices on Broadway overlooking the Latin Quarter night club. My title is Assistant to the Head of Production Publicity. I wear a suit and tie. They tell me I'm on a "fast track," but most of the time I sit around with the radio contacts— or take rewrite assignments from Sam and Walter, who've been here since year one.

Claude answers in mid-October. I read his letter on the way back from a meeting with Don Kirshner about a new rock group he is packaging "to fill the vacuum left by the Beatles."

> When I registered at the University I was given the choice of studying medicine in French or Flemish. David threatened to take his courses in Flemish just to be different. "Imagine performing a stomach resection in the language of Rubens!"

Two months into the New Year, I send him news from my Asian alter ego:

> I descend every morning from my penthouse to sing the praises of Dick Van Dyke, making a comeback in *Chitty-Chitty-Bang-Bang* or to chaperone Lauren Hutton, a model making her acting debut. Last week I entertained Trevor Howard at Trader Vic's in the Plaza for lunch, then went to the airport to pick up Steve McQueen, who jumped out of the limo blocks away from the Hotel Pierre. The thought of hyping his new film, *The Thomas Crown Affair*, is too much for him to handle. I haven't seen him since. After a few *mai tais*, Trevor Howard confessed that he'd rather be in his

cork-lined room at home listening to big-band jazz
than flacking *The Battle of Britain*. Over the week end
I paraded in front of the Electric Circus in a Blue
Meanie costume to publicize the Beatles' cartoon,
Yellow Submarine, except for a few hours on Friday
night when I made sure Terrence Stamp and Gail
Hunnicutt had a full flask of tequila for the premiere of
The Charge of the Light Brigade. What more could a
guy want? Then why does this dream job in the
celebrity fast lane feel like a life sentence to triviality?
Your brother, Saigon Rose

Glens Falls/Rye NY
May, 5th, 1987

Claude stops at Glens Falls on his way to Maine, his pickup
loaded with gear. Carol, I, and our Poose (short for Papoose),
take him to Pizza Hut. Halfway through the Pan Pizza
Supreme, my brother drops his slice to focus on the salad
bar.
  "Big women, with lots of testosterone," he mutters.
  We pack what's left and leave.
  Claude insists on staying at my studio in the Hotel
Madden on South Street, a strip lined with diners and bars
around an OTB parlor. Next morning he follows me in the
Brat to the elegant Queensbury Hotel on the other side of
City Park, where a huge painting of a scene from James
Fennimore Cooper's Last of the Mohicans *dominates the*
lobby; Natty Bumpo and his Native sidekick, Chingachacook,
face each other in what is locally known as Cooper's Cave at
the foot of the Falls for which the town is named. In the
restaurant, Claude peers through bloodshot eyes. He hasn't
slept. Someone outside his window kept yelling, "Come out
and I'll kill you!"

"I want you to know for the record that I haven't done anything to anyone." He orders French toast. "If something happens, if they try to run me off the road—it's no accident. I know what time it is, my name, and that it looks like rain."

He is sinking in quicksand out of my reach. I throw him the only line I can think of: another invitation to hang around and get to know his niece.

"I can't relate to babies," he replies. "When she's older and has a mind, I'll be more comfortable with her."

Before getting into the Brat, for the first time in years he tells me he loves me. I want to hold him there until the scales drop from his eyes, but my embrace is short-lived. Claude climbs into the cab, then starts the engine.

"Listen, at the shrink's I said some things about you. I was angry, but that's the place to express it, isn't it? If I hurt you, I'm sorry."

"Take care of yourself." I grip his hand.

"Don't worry." He smiles.

Claude calls three days later. His trip to Maine had proved a disaster. Watchers followed him in cars, tailgating, passing perilously on the right, challenging him at high speeds, frustrating him at low ones. The more outrageous drivers tried to push him off the highway. He returned to Rye on back roads.

"I'm not going to take this lying down. Maybe I'll consult a lawyer. Somebody has to pay. If I don't find out who's behind this, I could really become psychotic."

A few days later, Claude tells me that his therapist Dr. M. has put him on medication, but won't tell me what it is. My brother remains convinced that he is the object of a conspiracy.

"I know what I know. There are people all around me. I know what I see. They're all wearing shoes."

VIII

My secretary at United Artists interrupts my meeting with two "former professional bank robbers" I have hired to verify the authenticity of our breakout bank robbery film, *The Thomas Crown Affair*. As soon as I pick up the phone, I hear the terror in my mother's voice.

"I've left Fred."

"What?"

"I'm at Margaret's apartment. Around the corner from Carnegie Hall. Can you come here?"

I am surprised by the call. We haven't spoken much since I returned from Vietnam over a year ago. Only for a moment before Claude left for Brussels.

"I haven't wanted to burden you, but these last few years with Fred have been hell...humiliation, violence...sexual demands." Her voice gives way to tears. "I need you."

I tell the former bank robbers to return tomorrow, and my secretary that I will be gone for the day, then walk quickly up Broadway to the address on 56th Street. After identifying myself to the doorman, I take the elevator to the seventh floor. Even before I ring the bell I hear a bolt release, a chain slide out of its track. Margaret, a faded blond whose steely eyes witnessed "the bloody streets of Budapest," pulls me inside.

My mother stands in the living room wearing an old housecoat, hugging herself as if she were freezing. Her face is bloodless. Mascara pools in creases under her eyes.

"Just let him try to get in," gravel-voiced Margaret reassures her.

I put my arms around Charlotte, alarmed by her fragility. Her heart beats like a caged parakeet. "You're safe. No one can hurt you."

"You don't know him," she whispers.

"I am at the gate," Margaret crosses sinewy arms.

"He's very determined."

The buzzer jolts us. It's the doorman. Fred has pushed past him and is on his way up. Should he call the police?

"Not yet," responds Margaret.

"I'll stand by," replies the doorman.

Seconds later, there is a knock. "It's me," Fred addresses the bolted door.

My mother emits a cry, little more than a whimper.

"Go away," orders Margaret.

"I want to see my wife."

"She doesn't want to see you."

"Just two minutes. Please, Charlotte. Give me two minutes and then I'll go away. A minute. That's not too much, is it?"

I hear him draw a breath, cough, clear his throat. Charlotte shakes her head, trembling in her housecoat.

"She doesn't want to talk to you so you might as well go away and leave us alone. If you try to come in, the doorman will call 911."

His hands slide down the door, scratch at it with his nails. He rattles the knob as he pleads to speak to his wife. Margaret's gaze can freeze grease in a broiler.

"You've got to give me a chance, darling," begs Fred. "Just a glimpse of your face." He speaks as through a mouth full of pebbles. His words fall on the threshold outside.

I recall his red wigs, the way he served hors-d'oeuvres in his rubber foam multi-breasted apron; his uncanny skill with the whoopee cushion delighted Claude and me, not to mention his expert placement of fake turds. Fred had shared Charlotte's journeys through Christian Science, Yoga, Gurdjieff, Ouspensky, and the teachings of Manly Palmer Hall. For his wife's sake, he had mastered the pasadoble, mambo, and Argentine tango, tried his hand at oil painting, served canapés at soirees in which divorcees and theosophists mixed with Republican politicians from Queens. He had taken her sons on vacations, and cared for their teeth. He set off cherry bombs in garbage cans for Claude. He was always kind to me.

"Charlotte, I love you."

His words hang in silence for a minute before his palm falls away from the door. I can't help but identify with him, standing in the hall, locked out and abandoned by my mother. Through the peephole, I watch Derfydiddle shuffle toward the elevator, recalling one of the nonsense lyrics he used to sing to us:

We were strolling through the park,
Goosing shadows in the dark,
If Sherman's horse can take it,
Why can't you?

***

Two weeks later, Claude writes:

> Mom offered to let me stay with her if I come home this summer, but I've been down that road before. Besides, I'd rather travel in Europe with David before we dig in for the second year, which they say is the hardest. She called last week. Sounded tearful. What happened?

I answer him:

> She left Fred. He moved out. More, I can't say. He may have been a "latent." Speaking of which, I've started psychoanalysis at the Karen Horney Clinic. They prorate the fee. I go four times a week and pay only a few dollars a session. My analyst, José, is from Spain and has read Juan Ramón Jiménez. I'm determined to track my suffering to its lair. I'm also concerned about my suspicion that the life I'm living isn't mine. I am imprisoned in the center of a jelly doughnut.

Our next letters cross. My brother doesn't say much about the news of Fred's departure beyond the fact he liked the man. But Claude is far too busy meeting the demands of medical school to think much about it:

> We bang the books all night, go to class, and then quiz each other some more. Thank God for Uncle Irving. I'd never get through without uppers! I'm fluent enough in French to take the exams, written and oral, and make diagnoses that surprise even me. I seem to have Dad's gift of being able to point out the etiology of symptoms that elude my professors. It's exhausting, but I've passed the first year with *Grande Distinction*, which is the same as our *Summa cum Laude*.

Over the summer of '67, I receive cards from Malta, London, Paris, and Bruges. A few months into his second year, Claude encloses a snapshot of himself dancing in front of his apartment holding a box over his head. His letter explains that the box contains his new cockatiel. Before the following spring he writes:

> I've traded the bird in for a cat the size of a raccoon and a girlfriend. Le Chat is a Belgian breed. He licks my ears in the morning. My girl, Marianne, grew up in the Congo until it became independent. She licks other parts of me. Marianne is a physical therapist. You might say that I'm taking a real licking in Brussels.

Snapshots confirm that Le Chat may in fact be the size of a raccoon. To say that Marianne is a buxom girl doesn't do her justice. I'm not sure that she has the range of motion necessary for a physical therapist, though my brother finds no fault with her technique. My only concern is raised by what Claude calls *her free-spirited philosophy*, which includes visits to a former boyfriend with whom Claude

suspects she is still sleeping. In January, as the snow falls, I
write to him:

> You may want to find a good analyst to figure out why
> you tolerate Marianne's visits to a former lover with
> whom she's still having sex. This can't be good, even in
> the name of "freedom." For me it would be
> excruciating. But then so many things are. I rattle
> around United Artists unable to understand why
> watching John Schlesinger direct *Midnight Cowboy* or
> hanging out with Arthur Penn and Arlo Guthrie on the
> set of *Alice's Restaurant* should generate suicidal
> fantasies. The Director of Publicity asked me to
> publicize *The Bride Wore Black*, Francois Truffaut's
> homage to Hitchcock, then told me that UA views
> foreign films as penance and budgets nothing for
> promotion. Still, I arranged to fly Truffaut from Paris
> for an in-house screening. No attention from the press.
> We filled the room with staffers. The screening ended
> to polite applause. I asked Truffaut to say a few words.
> He told us, "The creative act is a match struck in a dark
> room; a second of light, then it goes out." Then we
> whisked him to the airport.

I hang on to the letter. Something tells me that I am not ready
to send it. There is more news to come.

> Yesterday I read the City Lights edition of *Paroles*, by
> Jacques Prévert. Afterward, everything was clear; I
> would leave UA to be a poet. This afternoon, at the
> urinal next to one of the VP's, I gave my notice.
>   "Murray," I said. "I quit."
>   "You can't do that."
>   I told him that I'd be gone in two weeks. I made
> him so nervous he sprinkled his shoes. This is no place
> for artists, united or otherwise.

Claude's answer, a week later, brings tears to my eyes. The message is even briefer than Truffaut's:

> Dear Saigon Rose, *C'est bon*. It's not right to suffer for being who you are. Do what you must.

***

Charlotte invites me to meet her for lunch at the Rainbow Room. Her makeup can't cover the shadows around her eyes. Her hand shakes when she raises her martini. She has just broken up with the Judge after a six-month affair she may have begun during the final days of Fred. She does little more than poke at her *salade nicoise* and stare at the basket of popovers in front of us. I urge her to get help, but I know that she won't.

I met the Judge at Charlotte's one evening as Andy Williams sang "Tenderly." An intense little man graying at the temples, he drank Dewar's on the rocks and gazed longingly at his inamorata through black-rimmed glasses. Only later did I learn that he also had a wife and children. But his adoration for *"Carlotta"* seemed boundless. He moved into the Pierpont Hotel with the intention of filing for divorce to marry his beloved. The Judge's wife and her *famiglia* let the errant jurist know that if he continued to humiliate his wife and blight the sacrament of marriage, there'd be consequences. Fearing danger to himself—and to his Carlotta—the Judge returned home.

I scribble my analyst's name and number on a piece of paper, then watch it disappear into her purse.

A week before Christmas, I receive a letter from Claude which reads like an SOS:

> She wants to come over during intersession. What can I do? After two years in Europe, with my command of French, she expects me to make her stay memorable...

I respond: *Wear your trench coat.*

On the eve of Charlotte's departure, Claude sends up another
flare. His anxiety is evident in his writing which wiggles on
the page.

> She wants to meet at the Hotel Geneva, in Switzerland,
> two days after my orals. I'll be a fucking wreck. I'm
> already a F.W. I've spent the last month on bennies and
> four hours' sleep a night. But it's not her fault, I keep
> telling myself. Why shouldn't she have a break from
> her problems? Wish me luck.

His next communication arrives in January:

> Oy veh, Paulie! I can't tell you how I felt at the sight of
> Mom wearing a blond wig and leopard-skin coat in a
> hotel lobby full of bourgeois Europeans. Everyone
> gawked. When she threw her arms around me, my legs
> turned to jelly. I stayed up all night staring at the patio
> outside my window. In the morning I took her to a
> farmers' market with vegetables, fruits, and cheeses on
> display. She admired some cherries and because I
> speak French, thought I'd know what to do and asked
> me to buy some. I bought a kilo. She paid for it, and
> then complained a kilo was too much. Hadn't I learned
> the European system of weights and measures? How
> could we possibly eat all these cherries!
> I apologized. Maybe things would get better. I took
> a long nap in the afternoon. When we met for dinner,
> she was wearing a fox stole over a gold lamé dress. All
> eyes in the dining room were on us. As we were eating,
> a man approached the table and started a conversation.
> He was European, Swiss, possibly German. Harmless
> enough. I assumed that she would handle it. She's no
> stranger to male attention. And you can't expect not to

have some when sheathed in gold. He asked how long she'd be in Geneva, then invited her to join him later for a drink or a walk in the garden. Mom told him that she was here with her son who is studying medicine in Brussels. He bowed graciously and said adieu. No sooner was he gone, than she asked why I wasn't more protective. She actually scolded me. Why hadn't I intervened? As her escort, it was up to me to handle strangers trying to pick her up.

I was speechless. I never thought of myself as *her man*. I'm her son. It's up to her to accept or reject a suitor. The man had been perfectly civil—frankly, innocuous. And here she was...

I went up to my room, locked the door, and braced myself for a confrontation in the morning. I couldn't find her at breakfast. No one answered when I rang her room. Then the desk clerk told me that she'd checked out and flown back to New York. Paulie, I still can't bring myself to call her. Every time I touch the phone I start shaking.

Claude's letter reminds me of a dinner I had with Charlotte at the Copley Plaza during my freshman year at Boston University. It was the only time she visited me there and it came at a point when I felt miserable in my situation. I spoke openly about my impatience with the academic drudgery and social isolation, and my plans to move to San Francisco to live among the Beats. When I finished, she gazed across the linen tablecloth and told me that she loved me. At first I thought this a touching affirmation. She went on from there to confess that it had taken every ounce of her will power not to actually seduce me.

My heart stuck in my throat. Confused by my own responses to my early images of her posing like Venus fresh from the bath, I felt a wave of guilt and desire. We finished the meal in silence. In front of the elevator, she held the back of my head tenderly. I kissed her cheek and left.

Claude's letter brings the evening back. I replay the conversation at the Copley, then decide against writing Claude about it. It will only muddy the water. But as I consider Charlotte's revelation, her words that evening are more redolent of the confessional than seduction; I hear in them the unaddressed longing I had glimpsed as a child under the piano when she played her violin. What could I say to make it clear to my brother what he has never seen for himself? The woman he had encountered at the hotel in Geneva and I at the Copley in Boston had surfaced briefly from a hidden depth. It had been Thaïs speaking.

Glens Falls/Rye NY
June 3rd, 1987

"I thought you should know," Michaela tells me over the phone later that afternoon. "Claude has asked me to sell his Australian mining stock. Something about raising cash to get away after pushing an old lady at the bank."

I phone Highcliff. Someone picks up the receiver. I assume its Claude, but recognize Wallace speaking so quickly that it takes me a minute to understand what he's saying. "You have to do something. Everyday he gets more aggressive. Now he's barricaded himself in his room with that smelly cat. I called him for dinner and he walked past me without a word. Yesterday, we were watching, A Night at the Opera. *Everyone was laughing, except Claude."*

At my request, Wallace knocks on my brother's door upstairs to tell him that I'm on the phone. I hear them in the distance.

"Claude, are you in there?"

"No, I'm not in."

"Paul, you've got to do something." Wallace is back.

I remind him of our talk when he and June first invited Claude to move in, how he'd dismissed my concerns. Wallace brushes this aside. Claude is deteriorating and he is my responsibility.

"What do you intend to do?"

"Let me speak to him."

This time Wallace sends his teenage son upstairs. When told that I am on the line, my brother screams, "I don't give a shit!"

My brother avoids my calls for a week. Finally, I reach him on the upstairs phone. "Hello. Claude? It's me. Are you there?"

"Paulie?" He speaks my name softly, then yells, "Hang up the phone downstairs. Dammit! Hang up the phone!"

"What's going on?"

"Okay. I don't give a shit. Goddammit, hang up the phone!"

I hear a click.

He quickly tells me of his plans to cash in stock and get out of Rye.

"Maybe you should find a motel room. Claude? Are you all right? I hate to hang up and leave you in this condition."

"Everybody hates to hang up and leave me in this condition, but everybody does. Fuck it! I'm gonna take off. If they follow me, that's it."

IX

Claude has been accepted at Albert Einstein College of Medicine for his last year. He writes that he'll finish his third year in Brussels, then one more at Einstein. The Bronx calls out to him. This summer he and Marianne will travel in Europe. He will come home in June with Le Chat. His girlfriend will join him later, when he is settled. Claude has informed Charlotte on the phone. There was no mention of Geneva. They are both ready to put it behind them.

My brother's decision to move back to New York takes me by surprise. My thought is, if something works, don't mess with it. But he might as easily point out that I've given up a fast-track career as a movie mogul to teach at Metropolitan Academy, a private school for dead-ended rich kids on 28th Street, one flight above The World Wide Detective Agency. Every Thursday I read Baudelaire with a munchkin who smokes hashish with his uncle and travels in Morocco at Christmas. Another student has produced a cookbook for anarchists and is certain he will make millions on it.

I can't argue with Claude's decision. I let him know as much, then inform him that I am trading in Baudelaire for *Old Mr. Boston*. I am learning to tend bar at a bohemian oasis in the lobby of the Broadway Central Hotel. As weekend setup man at St. Adrian's, named after a painting by John Clark that spans the thirty-foot bar, an air-brush imitation of Franz Hals's "The St. Adrian Company," I draw beers for painter Larry Rivers, whose work hangs in the Museum of Modern Art, and poets like Paul Blackburn and Jack Michelin. Charles Mingus drops by for clams on the half-shell. My buddy is a rock-guy, Alan Vega, aka Suicide, a soul on ice.

I don't tell Claude about the cocaine folded into dollar bills that end up in my cup. My buddy Suicide has given me the largest rock I've ever seen. He is like a shaman who inhales the pain of others, then exhales compassion. For most at St. A's, he's our resident saint.

I tell Suicide I'm working with dreams, describe one in which I am pursued by the same ghostly ectoplasm that rose from the darkness of the linen closet at Lincoln Road. In the dream I walk through a desolate alley full of garbage cans. Suddenly, a trench-coated figure wearing a fedora, gloves, and a gas-mask steps out of a doorway. I stand paralyzed by the sum of my fears finally taking on human form. The figure faces me for a moment before uttering words that echo in its gas mask: *Get out of here, fast!*

"Those were my father's words of warning to me as a child when his anger was about to explode. Now I know who I've been running from in my dreams."

"Yeah." Suicide nods. A tear visible behind his dark glasses, wordlessly, his gloved hand folds a solid object wrapped in foil into my fist.

I pick up Claude at LaGuardia on a warm June afternoon in 1969. He stops by the gate to stare at a beefy cop carrying a sidearm. My brother has forgotten the explosive culture we live in. One doesn't see guns in Belgium, or most of Europe. The customs officer removes his baggage from the conveyor belt and tosses the crate containing Le Chat at his feet.

"That's all right," jokes the customs officer. "He's dead."

We are faced with the riddle of Schrödinger's cat—it could as easily be alive as dead and there is no predicting which; Chat, fortunately is only semicomatose.

On our way to Forest Hills my brother informs me that our mother has invited him to stay with her until he can find a place of his own. But it's clear when she opens her door that Claude's arrival is a surprise. We're interrupting a client conference. Charlotte introduces her sons to a young divorcee, then reschedules her appointment.

"How sweet." Our mother peeks into the crate.

Under the Moorish lamp, martini in hand, Claude discusses his plan to send for Marianne after he finds an apartment in the Bronx, close to Einstein. Suddenly there is rumbling from the crate. First one huge paw, then another appears, followed by a huge body of hair that just keeps coming. I see Charlotte's jaw drop, her eyes glance from side to side.

My brother calls three days later.

"Things aren't working out here."

Apparently, our mother found the raccoon-sized Chat snoozing on an evening gown she'd laid out on the bed, too full of cat hair to wear to a political function that night. The prospect of a life full of cat hair was more than she could take. Once again Claude is asked to leave by a lady who he is shocked to see looks old without her makeup. My brother and Chat move in with me.

In July, 1969, Second Avenue below 4th Street is rife with derelicts, hustlers, and junkies. My brother sleeps long hours on the living-room couch. He ventures out only when necessary, mostly during the late afternoon to buy cigarettes. Inside, Chat growls like a dog walking protective circles around his sleeping Lord.

I am the weekend bartender at Phebe's, on Cooper Square, a cafe haunted mostly by gay actors from La Mama and the Truck and Warehouse Theater on 4th Street. The money is good, and I have never been hit on by the clientele. Strapping men from the Ballet de Monte Carlo, who perform *Swan Lake* in tutus, strut around the juke box to Bette Midler singing "Bugle Boy of Company B." Tennessee Williams cruises with his eyes from a nearby table. Straight from Warhol's factory, Rollerina, in drag, arm-wrestles me for Golden Dreams.

As I return to my penthouse this morning, my feet hurt. My arm, too. Rollerina may wear a flared skirt and blonde wig, but he usually beats me for the Golden Dream. The elevator is out, and I must walk up ten flights. I expect to find Claude asleep or with Chat in front of the tube. I reach the door breathing heavily, pause for a moment, reluctant to wake him. The place is small. There's not much I can do with him around that requires privacy, like have a sex life.

I tiptoe to my bedroom in the dark, wanting nothing more than to throw my body down on my bed, which I see in the light of the rising sun, is ALREADY OCCUPIED!

Michaela stirs, sees me through half-closed eyes, smiles, waves.

Claude raises his head, asks what time it is.

"Ssssssix thirty," I hiss. "In the AM."

"I should be going." Michaela slips out skillfully, careful not to reveal too much.

More out of pique than politeness, I retreat to the living room. Michaela, dressed, waves again, then slips out the door. Claude, in his underwear, stands rubbing his eyes.

"Just getting back in touch," my brother explains.

"Like saying Hello?"

"Exactly."

"In my bed..." I tell him it would be best if he left, then fall on my bed, redolent of my brother and his lover. By the time I wake, Claude is carrying his bags into the hall, where Le Chat waits in his crate.

"Wallace and June are on their way to Haiti to oversee their factory in Port St. Jacques. They're glad to have me house sit. So, you know where I'll be."

Our parting is freighted with accusations and recriminations, but I suspect that my brother is as glad to leave as I am to see him go. I know that there will be little to no communication between us unless there is a crisis or breakthrough event. He will knock around the empty mansion in Rye with Chat, swim in the pool, walk the sea wall, and fish for blues from the dock.

I don't feel sorry for him. In fact, I've almost forgotten about Claude entirely by the end of the month when two guys from the neighborhood approach me to ask if I'll help them set up and run the burnt-out wino bar they've just leased on Bowery and 2nd.

They have stars in their eyes, see themselves as principals in their own version of saloon society, but neither has any idea of what it takes to run a bar and restaurant.

"You'll have my answer in a week."

The following week they agree to remain silent partners and to let me bring my Cherry Lawn friend, Michael, on board. Mike has years of business experience working with his father in the Garment District.

Claude's call in the middle of July is more of an interruption than a relief. He's rented a one-bedroom apartment on Gun Hill Road, five minutes from Einstein. Marianne is here. She arrived yesterday and wants to meet me. Is it all right if they stop by in the morning?

I am hardly ready for the bosomy young woman who enters two steps in front of Claude, buries me in an embrace before kissing me on both cheeks. "So good to know you, Paul."

X

Thc Tin Palace is my match struck in the Bowery night. In November, 1971, it burns bright. The bar had been a blue-collar shot-and-beer joint in the '40s; before that, a speakeasy run by Meyer Lansky and Bugsy Siegel. We worked through a hot summer tarring the walk-in, breathing plaster dust and polyurethane, painting the pressed tin ceiling chocolate brown—the same pattern I used to cover a fissure in the outside wall that would have caused any building inspector to close us down. My struggle from the start has been to keep the environment inside safe from the no-man's-land on the street. Michael's idea to "wash the street with light," large spots on both corners, helps to keep the forces of destruction at bay.

Michael sets up the books. I hire the help, stock the booze, book the music, and work the room on busy nights. My staff has been drawn from the hip bars in lower Manhattan, every one with a following. And the buzz among the artists in Soho and lofts along the Bowery grew during the period we worked on the place. But the real magic is the room itself. From my perch at the service end of the art-deco bar I watch rock legend Doc Pomus descend from his van in a wheel chair. The man who wrote "it's my party, you can cry if you want to..." rolls himself to the table reserved for him. Rolling Stones drummer Charlie Watts sips a beer while waiting for Eddie Jefferson, the father of vocalese, to step onto our stage with his protégé, tenor man Richie Cole. A limousine pulls up. Out walks the Countess, Charlie Parker's mistress.

During the '60s, I had watched Slugg's Saloon on 3rd near Ave. C become a junky hell that culminated in the shooting of Lee Morgan as he stood on stage playing his horn. My rule for musicians as well as customers is, NO DRUGS ON THE PREMISES. Except after hours. My coke habit expands with the business. I'm sure I can control it. Except at those moments when I spiral down from the heights to find myself overwhelmed by an inexplicable sadness.

"Yes, Dad," I whisper. "I've ended up on the Bowery."

"Phone for you, Boss." The bartender I call Diamond Jim calls out. "It's your mother."

I take it reluctantly. It is hard to make out what she's saying, only that this call is an SOS. She'd been trying to reach Claude for weeks, but he wasn't answering the phone. Just as she was about to call the police, he picked it up and told her the news.

"Your brother has dropped out of Einstein. I'm worried about him."

The room is filling with regulars: the Laughing Budweiser, a parole officer, stares at himself in the bar mirror, chuckling quietly. There is Bosomy Diane, with a jones for bass players; Buddy, a gambler from Chinatown; vocalist Joe Lee Wilson and sax man Monty Waters drift in from The Ladies Fort on Bond Street looking like Elders of Zion; Barry Altschult, a drummer from Sam Rivers's loft, comes to see Squeak, one of our waitresses; the young horn player, David Murray, and his critic/mentor, Stanley Crouch, drift down from their apartment upstairs.

"I'll talk to him."

"You can't reach him by phone. He's stopped picking up again."

"I'll go up to the Bronx."

"I quit months ago."

We sit among the ruins of his Gun Hill Road apartment. Claude is lying back on a couch so woven with cat hair that I can't discern the original fabric. Le Chat rests across him. My brother sports a week-old beard, matted hair, and clothes that look as if he's slept in them for a year, which he may very well have. Paper plates, old Chinese and Italian takeout, newspapers, cigarette butts and ashes are strewn on the floor. The air is saturated with the vapors of unchanged kitty-litter.

"So close to your degree?"

"Less than six months."

I see an emptiness in his eyes that frightens me. When the phone rings, he picks it up as if saved by the bell, only to shake his head and whisper his answers, then hangs up.

"Einstein." He is pale. "One of the physicians wants me to take a leave of absence and see a psychiatrist on staff. I won't go back."

My brother sinks deeper into the couch. This morning, when I knocked at his door, he was reluctant to answer it, even after he realized it was me. *What do you want?* He asked through the closed door.

"I'm a fucking wreck. The competitiveness, I couldn't handle it. After awhile, I could hardly get out a word on clinical rotations."

"Marianne?"

"Gone, as soon as it became clear I wouldn't become the brilliant American doctor..."

"Oh, Claude."

"Actually, she's been defecting little by little all year. She's fucked practically all my closest friends. Including Wallace."

"How do you know that?"

"She told me." My brother lets go of Chat. "You know the funny part? I picked the same kind of woman Dad did, an opportunist like Betty."

"What about going back to Brussels?"

"I'll never become a doctor."

I feel like a priest talking to a lapsed Catholic about his denial of faith. I find it too hard to accept that Claude will never become a doctor and find a cure for Saigon Rose.

"But why? Help me understand."

"I'm sorry. It's none of your business."

***

On cocaine all things seem possible. Certain moments open like miraculous improvisations that blow through me. Most of the time I'm unaware of the changes in my relationships, the cuticle developing around my heart. Today, I am the evangelist, touched by divine madness, hurtling uptown on the A Train to give my brother his first sniff of the new gospel, sure it will lift him from the depths, renew our friendship.

I haven't seen Claude for nearly three years, since he dropped out of Einstein. During that time he's moved to a basement apartment on West 75th Street, qualified for a license in bacteriology, and begun working in the lab at Montefiore Hospital. When I told him last night that I had a surprise for him, if he was game, he seemed to know exactly what I meant and invited me up. I ring the doorbell under the steps of a brownstone a block from Central Park wondering if I'll find myself surrounded by half-eaten chicken wings, old Chinese noodles, rock-hard burgers in rigor-mortis rolls, the spoilage at our last meeting.

The man who opens the wrought-iron door is razor thin. He is wearing a plaid shirt over chinos and pats me on the arm as a token greeting.

"Hi, Paulie. Come on in."

My brother slides the police bar on his apartment door so I can enter a space with room enough for Chat, a bed, desk, two large chairs, a bureau and TV. The only two windows look out at street level and let in minimal light. There are piles of books and elaborate devices everywhere; I recognize the microscope on his desk half-hidden behind machinery for repairing rods and making lures.

"There's something I want to show you."

He disappears behind a door to the left of his small kitchen, then emerges in a leather apron and head phones holding a sonar-like disc at the end of a pole that resembles an alien vacuum cleaner which he passes over my feet. My brother strikes a heroic pose.

"Sorry, we've disbanded the Ghost Riders," I tell him.

"This is a metal detector," he announces. "I find all kinds of lost or buried things with this—old coins, jewelry, historical artifacts."

I am uncomfortable with this brother who looks like a galactic refugee. Mercifully, he strips off his gear, but insists I look through several coffee-stained catalogues advertising outlandish equipment at bargain prices.

"What do you think of this?"

He takes out a blowgun and a few industrial-strength darts, then shoots them expertly at a target taped to the bathroom door.

"Handy, if you find yourself among pygmies."

He makes me try it. After five unsuccessful attempts to hit the bathroom door, I tell him I've had enough. We sit facing each other across a littered coffee table. I unfold a dollar bill, lay out lines of white powder on his coffee table, then show him how to vacuum up the coke. He bends over, sniffs up the crystal as though he's been doing it for years. The telltale smile appears, and I know he's on his way up, out of the darkness of his life, the gloom of his apartment.

"It's been a long time," I say.

"I haven't seen much of anybody. After Einstein, I spent most of the year on Gun Hill Road looking out the window at the parking tickets accumulating on my car."

I scrape off a few more lines for him to suck up.

"One day the door bursts open. Four or five big guys, a sheriff and his deputies come to evict me because I haven't paid rent for six months. *Six months?* I had no idea that much time had passed."

His gestures are suddenly alive, his eyes gleam with crystal fire. Soon we are laughing together as we did long ago. By the end of the afternoon, my brother, already in the thrall of Xanax, Dexies, and gin, acquires a new addiction, which he will maintain at a level subject to his volatile relationship with his dealer.

Glens Falls/Rye NY
July 10th, 1987

I stop by Highcliff on my way to hear poems of mine set to music by composer Daniel Asia performed at the 92nd Street YMHA. I would rather have driven straight into town, but I am haunted by Claude's words at the end of our last phone conversation: "Fuck it! I'm gonna take off. If they follow me, that's it."

June is in the kitchen wearing a housecoat. Her square jaw trembles as she describes a confrontation with Claude that morning.

"He was in bed with Chat beside him on the pillow. At first he just yelled about people eavesdropping on his phone calls. I told him his behavior was unacceptable. He quieted down and said that he was leaving soon, though he didn't have a destination."

Is he taking his medication?

"Not as far as I can determine. And he hasn't eaten for two days. I told him to go downstairs late at night and fix himself leftovers."

My brother is waiting in his room, chinos bagging beneath a blue windbreaker. He appears leaner than ever. Shadows circle his eyes. On our way to the Mamaroneck Diner, he checks the rearview mirror. We drive in silence. At this hour the tables are empty. Claude demolishes the Early Bird Special roast beef dinner, then ends with coffee and a wedge of banana cream pie. Between bites he says that he's going back to Portland. He'll get a night job and save enough money to go back into therapy. Only a brand new therapist might think he's crazy.

I drop him back at Highcliff. He lingers in the driveway, two fingers held in the shaky victory sign used by another paranoid, Richard Nixon. Only Claude's smile isn't nearly as convincing. No way around it. I can't put it off any longer. I have to hospitalize my brother.

I reach the 92nd Street Y at 9:00. Seated in the middle of the half-empty hall, vaguely aware of the ensemble, Musical Elements, warming up on stage, I recall Claude with his two fingers raised. Dan appears, followed by bass-baritone John Shirley-Quirk. The sound of my words in Dan's settings comes from a distance. Then the ensemble performs a particular poem; I am struck by a grief for which I'm totally unprepared. My defenses give way to words I wrote about Claude years earlier. John Shirley-Quirk's voice singing the poem, "Mein Bruder," comes through with the clarity of a code that's finally been broken.

> I want to write a poem
> to you, Claude, who never
> believed my words but endured me
> as a brother
> who couldn't see you
>
> in spite of which
> we managed to agree
> it is a pity anyone should suffer
> for being what
> one is...
>   then tell me
> why it's true
> that half-way through my life
> I rush around afraid
> the world will stop

if I do
        then stop
and realize
you are
among my deepest sorrows?

PART 3

MOTHER'S BLOOD

Diamond Jim summons me from the kitchen where I am working on changes in the menu. It is a slow night in early June, 1975. Claude's voice over the wires comes to me from a distant place, perhaps another galaxy.

"Can you hear me?"

"Just fine." A mental itch reminds me. "Happy birthday, two days late." I start to sing the birthday song.

"That's not why I called. Mom's just undergone an exploratory operation on her colon."

"What?"

"I thought I should tell you."

"You thought..." I slip off the bar stool. "Where are you?"

"Parkview Hospital, in Forest Hills."

He gives me directions, which I scribble on the back of a bar check. All the way out on the IND I'm angry. Why wasn't I told about Charlotte's procedure? Maybe because I've kept in touch so infrequently and then always with the message that my busy life demanded I fly off. Several years ago her doctor, an old German with an office in her building, advised her to remove an ovarian polyp. My mother had refused, taking her stand in Christian Science: *No surgery. I'll heal it metaphysically.*

Claude and Gerry, Charlotte's new boyfriend, meet me in the lobby of the private hospital overlooking the Long Island Expressway. Gerry, a young cop with the dark good looks of a lounge singer, puts an arm around my shoulder. "She's just coming out of the anesthesia."

"I want to see her."

My brother leads us through swinging doors, down a hall, and into a ward of beds along a wall. Charlotte lies in the middle of the row behind a half-drawn privacy curtain. Her eyes are open. She smiles and reaches out between the bed rails. I try to smile back, but her face and cheeks are swollen.

She's ghostly white. A white cap holds her hair in place. I'm surprised to realize I can't stand the thought of losing her. Steadying myself on the bedrails I fold one of her hands into mine and keep it there until she falls asleep like a child.

"So, the nightmare begins again," says my brother on our way out.

Claude and the ever-faithful Gerry greet me the next day in the surgeon's office, a few blocks from the hospital. After ten minutes in the waiting room, we're invited into the inner sanctum where Dr. Z., a pear-shaped man with a dark mustache and bad toupee, tells us there is nothing to be done for the patient. In an authoritative baritone, he describes how the cancer has spread invasively through her peritoneum.

"It's too intricately woven into the fabric of her stomach tissue to unravel."

The source of the cancer is uncertain. It might be the polyp that she was advised to remove. One could as easily point to her use of estrogen.

"I can't tell you how much time she has left. What I can do is keep her comfortable. Of course you can transfer her to a bigger hospital, like Sloan Kettering. But if you leave her in my care, I promise to look after her as if she were my own daughter."

Gerry's gaze darts between us. He would be cooler in the middle of a gang war on Bed-Stuy than he is here facing his own helplessness. Claude suggests that they might take a more aggressive approach to her condition at Sloan Kettering.

"Would that matter?" asks Gerry.

"Probably not," my brother concurs, his shoulders slumped.

In the end, we agree she will undergo radiation and chemotherapy in a place where she feels comfortable and will receive quality attention from Dr. Z., which I pray is better than his toupee.

Claude, Gerry, and I linger in the waiting room trying to figure out what we'll say to Charlotte.

"Let's tell her the truth," I suggest. "If you had only so much time, wouldn't you want to know?"

"I'm not sure." Claude can't hold my eyes. "The quality of her life might be better if her spirits remained hopeful. For the time being, let's not say anything."

There is an edge of anger in his voice; his mother is leaving him once again. With his medical background, he feels responsible. Finally, we agree to let her know only what she wants to know, nothing more. Gerry sighs, visibly relieved.

Charlotte insists that she'll be all right. "I'm working with this." She holds up her dog-eared copy of Mary Baker Eddy's *Science and Health*. Every afternoon two or three blue-haired ladies sit by her bedside in the private room where she's staying for a week of radiation treatments and chemotherapy. These are solid women in print dresses and serviceable shoes. They sit with her in her room reading the weekly lesson, moving from scripture to the concordance, reinforcing at every point that evil is an illusion and she is God's perfect child. How can anything they subscribe to fail?

Two months later, Charlotte is still in her room, but the Mary Baker Eddies are not. They come once in a while to let her know they're still working on her, but they seem uncertain, in need of a kind word. Sometimes they read the lesson, but mostly they just remind her of their Founder's revelation.

Claude, Gerry, and I pace the waiting room, visit her bedside; one or more of us are present at all times. We discuss her condition, the care she is getting. My mother moves around less, sleeps more. At times, she hovers all day on the threshold between sleep and wakefulness. She has asked us not to crowd the room so we take turns, one at a time, sitting by her bed. One afternoon, when I am alone with her, she pops out of a twilight sleep, stares at me, and asks the question, "Tell me, Paulie. Am I going to get better?"

I shake my head, and then manage to say, "No."

"Oh." She closes her eyes.

I want to touch her cheek, kiss her, tell her how much I love her. Before I can, she sits up, her face transformed into a Kabuki scowl. "You mean this is what it comes to? Everything, just....*this*!"

Her hands open to indicate the hospital bed, a stainless steel bedpan, and the rails that hold her on either side. Before I can respond, she falls back and folds her arms over her chest as if she were already a corpse.

At the end of September, Charlotte rallies. She insists on going back to her apartment. Pear-shaped Dr. Z. agrees to release her, but cautions us to watch her closely. We hire a private-duty nurse, then work out a schedule to make sure one of us will be with her at all times. Claude and Gerry take the longest shifts. I fill in where I can.

Our mother's elation at being home displaces her worst fears. Seated on her sofa, surrounded by her iridescent curtains, it's possible, for a moment, to be hopeful. But a bulge on one side of her stomach becomes visible the following day. At the end of the week it is so distended that she's unable to move her bowels. When I phone her physician, he tells me that a bowel obstruction like this can only be treated on the ward. I ask him to make the arrangements.

Claude refuses to stay while I break the news to her. When I let her know that we'll be returning her to Parkview in the morning, Charlotte jerks upright, her nightdress falling away from her ravaged body. "Isn't there anything they can do for me?"

"Not here." I stroke her hair. There's nothing else I can do.

We move her back into a ward reserved for terminal patients.

"Isn't there *anything* they can do?" she asks again.

"Just keep you...out of pain," I tell her.

Charlotte's condition deteriorates. When we try to address our concerns, we're told that Dr. Z. is either unavailable or on vacation. The oncologist fades in and out like a shadow. We stalk him through the corridors in vain. My mother could linger, perhaps for months, coming in and out of comas, unable to eat or eliminate waste. She's catheterized and kept on liquid supplements. Her bedsores grow angry. The nurses neglect to change, clean, and move her. Demerol no longer works.

Uncle Irving flies up from West Palm Beach, strides up to the nurses' station and introduces himself as Dr. Rachlin, the patient's brother. For a few days the nurses become attentive. But Irv soon loses his edge and joins our death watch in the waiting room until he can take it no longer, then departs for Florida. Claude, Gerry, and I continue to pursue the oncologist, as Charlotte is left to perish of pneumonia, if she doesn't first starve to death. Her one request, when she surfaces from her coma, to find us all around her bed, is that she be allowed to die with dignity.

"Nobody should have to endure this," she says.

I'm in the basement office doing inventory and snorting a few lines when Diamond Jim calls down to say there's a short blond guy at the bar who claims to be my brother. It's the day after Christmas. I'm exhausted after months of shuttling between the Parkview and the Tin Palace. Claude would normally be at the hospital maintaining a vigil with Gerry, who's taken emergency leave from his precinct. It's also the first time he has visited me here, on the Bowery.

"No. She's still with us." Claude, seated at the bar, lifts his martini.

"Out of pain?"

"For the moment. *Son of a bitch!*"

He curses the elusive oncologist, whom we finally

cornered on another ward and begged to up her dose of morphine. Speaking through a surgical mask, he'd refused. Morphine might depress the breathing of her already compromised lungs.

"I will not be party to euthanasia."

Claude called his Brussels friend, now Dr. Dave, a trauma surgeon in New Jersey. Dave has offered to have Charlotte transferred to his hospital, where he'd do what was necessary to keep her out of pain. We doubt the Parkview will let us move her in her present condition. But Charlotte has been at death's door twice before, and rallied, sitting up in bed, cursing the doctors and the hospital, demanding that we help her to die with dignity. At one point, she made us promise to do so.

Claude follows me to the rear, then slumps into the booth, facing me. His lips are pursed, resolved, but haggard.

"It's not your fault," I tell him.

"I'm the one with medical training. If I'd made the right decisions, she wouldn't be in this condition. The least I can do now is put her out of her misery." He puts an ampoule full of colorless liquid on the table.

"What's that?"

"Insulin. I'll do it myself. But you have to stand outside the room to tell me if anybody's coming."

"Will it put her out gently?"

"It can. But it's tricky. If I use too much, she might convulse. Not enough, she could linger as a vegetable."

"How can you be sure what to give her?"

"I learned something on the wards. If I don't do it, who will? We can't just let her waste away, Paulie. Not with that bedsore opening at the base of her spine."

"What if someone gets suspicious and orders an autopsy?"

An autopsy, he conceded, could find evidence of both the needle and the insulin.

"When?"

"Tomorrow."

"No," I tell him. "Shooting her full of insulin is a bad idea. How can you be sure you're not doing it out of anger? Can you swear to me that this act isn't your way of thumbing your nose at a medical establishment that ignored your pain at Einstein?"

"If you won't help me, I'll do it alone."

"What if you do throw her into convulsion or leave her a vegetable? Everyone will know what we've done."

"She asked us to put her out of her misery. I promised, Paulie. So did you."

"It's a setup," I cry. Someone else, a physician, could reasonably perform such an act of compassion. But killing Charlotte by his own hand will make Claude a matricide, food for the Furies.

My brother stands, pockets the ampoule. "I'll give it another day or two."

Glens Falls/Rye NY
July 30, 1987

On July 30th Claude leaves his attic sanctuary at Highcliff to euthanize twenty-year-old Le Chat, who's been dying of cancer. Over the phone he claims his only regret is that Chat died in pain and confusion. Someone has to be held responsible for that. Perhaps God. Maybe it's Claude's way of also grieving for our father, who chose a hospital where his colleagues made sure his death was quick and painless.

After putting down Chat, Claude spends mornings in bed listening to voices from Long Island Sound. This morning, he hears the gardeners at Highcliff yelling a name, Marty Cohen. He can't imagine who that is or why they're calling that name, until he realizes they aren't summoning Marty Cohen, but hurling an invective, "maricón." All those boaters near the dock gunning their motors and making duck noises, Claude knows what they're up to, accusing him of being un pato. A duck.

"They're calling me a faggot in Spanish."

I urge Claude to sign himself in to a hospital.

"Paulie, if I thought I was crazy, I'd commit myself. Maybe I should just get some peace."

"A good enough reason."

II

Two days after Claude's visit to the Tin Palace, Charlotte dies alone in the early morning hours of December 28th, on the cusp of the American bicentennial. Standing beside her open casket a few days later at the funeral home in Forest Hills, I hardly register the faces filing past. I'm aware of two things: how tiny Charlotte's corpse seems, and my brother's rage. It's as if all the unspoken sibling issues that festered for years have opened into a single angry wound. I ask if he plans to say anything at her eulogy. He glares like he's about to challenge me to a duel. The eulogy is delivered by George Kemp, a Presbyterian minister who speaks of hearing Charlotte play the "Meditation" from Massenet's *Thaïs* in the high-vaulted sanctuary of St. James's Church on Madison Avenue, and ends by affirming that "she will be with us as long as we too embrace truth and beauty, kindness and mercy."

On our way to the service, Claude stumbles into me, fists clenched.

"Get away." he mutters.

"I'm sorry," I say, uncertain what I am apologizing for.

At the end of January, I receive a telephone call from Lillian Jay, who had been the pianist in Charlotte's all-girl band. Lillian is calling from her home in Texas to say she's coming to New York soon and wants to see me. A week later I open a letter giving me the address and phone of the friend with whom Lillian will be staying. She goes on to write there are things that she wanted to tell me about the real love of Charlotte's life.

Who was Charlotte's real love?

It wasn't Larry (owner of the hotel on 86th Street to which we fled with our dying father), an old law-school crush who never merited more than a passing reference. The Judge was a very public love. Even now, he calls Claude and me on

Charlotte's birthday. Gerry, her last amour, was at least ten years her junior. At first she put him off, worried that he'd look at her one day and see an old lady. But his devotion overcame her resistance and he remained steadfast through a six-month death watch during which she deteriorated in front of him. Then there was a mysterious New Orleans lover, her first one, dispatched with a phone call to his wife by our grandmother, Fannie, after she found out the man was married with children. Had he been the one she thought of when she played her violin?

Weeks pass. I hear nothing. On Valentine's Day, a woman identifying herself as Lillian's New York friend phones with news that the pianist has suddenly passed away. It takes a minute for the news to register. I hadn't really thought much about our prospective meeting, but understand that I had given it more weight than I had realized. I know this by the depth of my disappointment. I will never know the secret that Lillian kept so faithfully all these years. Our meeting, the one I had hoped would hold the key to the mystery that was Charlotte, will not happen.

Glens Falls/Rye NY
August 5th, 1987

"Sounds like agitated depression, pain, fear, and anger coming down at once," our old friend Jeff tells me. "Call a cop and an ambulance and get him to a hospital. They might admit him on a temporary basis and medicate him. If he doesn't have health insurance, try a state or county hospital. Nothing can be done for him until he's properly medicated."

I mention that his shrink on West 9th Street has him on BusBar and Marplan.

"He's not properly medicated. BusBar is for anxiety. The

other is an antidepressant. Claude's delusional. He needs an antipsychotic."

Jeff, one of two Brooklyn chums with whom I have stayed in touch, once believed that the Mafia had taken out a contract on him. He knows the ropes when it comes to paranoid delusion. He had jumped out of the sixth floor window of his apartment to escape a hit man only he could see. After two years as a psychiatric inpatient, he emerged an empathic man who counsels others. I trust his judgment and listen to him closely.

Further phone calls yield different opinions from a variety of people. Dr. M., Claude's current therapist, thinks hospitalization is as likely to have a bad result as a good one unless he has coverage to pay for a top-flight facility. Dr. Robert London, my brother's mentor at the Université Libre, now Chief of Psychiatry at Bellevue, confirms Jeff's opinion: nothing can be done until Claude is medicated. He refers me to Dr. K. at Gracie Square, who informs me that for an involuntary admission to a county hospital I'll need corroborating letters from two psychiatrists that Claude is a danger to himself or others. Four Winds, in Saratoga Springs, won't discuss a patient who has no private insurance. Dr. D. states that Austin Riggs is a voluntary institution, but suggests I try New York Hospital, a private facility at the old Bloomingdale estate in White Plains. Sue H., at New York Hospital, wants to know if Claude has been violent.

"Not yet. He's shooting people with a camera instead of a gun."

She offers to dispatch a crisis team to evaluate him, but pulls back when she learns my brother has no insurance. He'll have to go to a public institution, unless we can pay for his first week or two at New York Hospital, until he qualifies for Medicaid. But that will cost a fortune.

The following day I drive to Highcliff. Claude is bunkered in his bedroom. I knock. Almost inaudibly, he invites me in. The drapes are drawn over the French doors. The place smells of stale kitty-litter. He sits up in bed, stares through pupils like pinpoints. I repeat the message that Wallace and June want him out of their house as soon as possible. His best bet is New York Hospital, on the old Bloomingdale estate, more like a college campus than an institution. The problem, I continue, is that no hospital will take him without medical coverage, but I've made arrangements for him to sign forms at the public assistance office in Mamaroneck.

"I'm not ready to go on welfare," Claude pulls the covers over himself. A muffled sob seeps through, the cry of a soul stuck in the underworld.

On August 27th, 1987, three weeks after I set the wheels of hospitalization in motion, New York Hospital calls to say a bed in long-term care has opened up. They'll admit him on a voluntary basis tomorrow at 9:00 AM. I drive to Highcliff with the news. Wallace and June are on the deck drinking coffee.

"Thank God," says June. "We've been prisoners in our own house."

"Especially at night," agrees Wallace.

"It's going to be all right now," she pats his hand

"Just in time." Now they will be able to enjoy the remainder of the summer, says the man who found decorative uses for chain-mail. There are such wonderful cultural events at SUNY. Wallace pulls out a catalogue from under the newspapers by his chair and finds the SUNY Purchase program schedule. Tonight they'll celebrate by going to see the Düsseldorf Ballet.

"What are they doing?"

"A Night in Dachau."

Claude is on his bedroom balcony wearing only jockey shorts. The Watchers are everywhere, he tells me, pointing at one of the Cigarette racing boats on the sound. "They even have a navy." Even worse, they have followed him into his dreams. He complains: "Now there's no place to go."

"No," I counter. "New York Hospital is a refuge. They're expecting you tomorrow morning."

"Maybe I'll learn the answer to the question I've been asking for almost two years. I want to know the identity of the person or persons responsible for this persecution."

Suddenly hopeful, he suggests we pick up a pizza in Rye, and then meet Michaela at Jo's apartment in the Village for his last supper. Later, seated at Jo's long cherry-wood table, Michaela assures us that she's sold fifteen thousand dollars worth of Claude's stock to cover hospital costs for a month, until his Medicaid kicks in.

"Wouldn't it be cheaper if I became Sri Claudeananda and joined an ashram?" Putting down a half-eaten wedge, my brother raises his hands like Christ charging his Apostles. "Tomorrow I will be a committed man."

"Think of it as going in for a ruptured appendix," I suggest.

He is composed throughout his last supper, almost happy. We talk so easily on the way back to Highcliff I forget the seriousness of his condition until we enter a Shopwell Supermarket to buy a toothbrush and shampoo. Then he notices two Hispanics in their late teens, one about 6'2". They're talking about someone's girlfriend and what one of them did to her.

"Those are the people I have to deal with, assholes."

I have visions of trying to explain to those guys why they shouldn't trample my brother, that he's a sick man. Fortunately, I manage to herd him into another aisle.

"I'm sick of their dirty little minds. I hear them say, 'He's angry.' So I put on another face. Then they say, 'He's laughing.' I don't know what to do with them anymore."

At 8:00 AM on August 28th, my brother is waiting in front of Highcliff armed with his Minolta. He takes a few steps toward my car, then wheels and aims his lens at a corner bush.

Click! Click!

I throw his old suitcase into the back seat as he walks around the house, his step defiant, head thrust forward. He wears paratrooper boots laced around his jeans. The collar of his blue windbreaker is turned up to hide his face. He is a crazed paparazzo. Claude snaps his shutter again in the direction of Long Island Sound, then stalks back to where I wait, ready to drive us to New York Hospital.

"Ha! That'll show 'em. I won't take this lying down. I've got them right here." He pats his Minolta. If only they would stop sending signals about him from Manursing Island. Oh, they pretend to be pruning trees. But who do they think they are kidding? He snaps a road crew fixing potholes, then anyone who looks our way in the town of Rye. "There are themes running through this experience," he offers. "Fat women. Old ladies with canes."

We stop for gas and coffee on the way. An old lady with a cane pays her bill at the cashier's. Claude snaps her picture. She regards him quizzically.

"You notice the United Parcel truck that just passed?" he asks as we mount stools at the counter.

"How did United Parcel get into this?"

"I can't tell you. Only that I kept packages for other tenants on 75th Street because I was in the basement. They're slandering me, Paulie. They say I'm cheap. They talk about my sex life, accuse me of all kinds of things. If you only knew." He talks again about the gardeners around Highcliff screaming, "Marty Cohen," those in boats gunning their motors and making duck noises, then comments: "Maybe I am a queer duck."

Claude falls silent on the highway and through the streets of White Plains. We find the entrance in the black fence surrounding the old Bloomingdale estate and start up a road through verdant lawns toward a gray stone building at the top of a hill.

"Maybe I spent too much time at Schrafft's with Mom,"

he reflects on our way to the parking lot. "The way she used the word latent, you were never sure it wasn't true of you, too—that you'd wake up with an overwhelming urge to chase little boys or hang out in the men's room at Grand Central. The message to me was: 'One day there's going to be a sea change, and WOW!'"

BOOK II: A MULTITUDE OF FISH

Most men live in the social body as unconsciously as cells live in the physical body. Or they are like the multitude of fish in the sea, which cry out the glory of God, but not in a voice which fish can understand or readily discourse in.
William Bronk, *The Brother In Elysium*

PART 1

FISH IN THE SEA

I

At 8:35 AM, on August 28, 1987, Claude and I drive through the gate of a black fence encircling New York Hospital, aka Bloomingdale's, in White Plains on what had been a grand estate in an age of Robber Barons. We continue up the tree-lined hill to a gray stone building surrounded by topiary promenades and oak allées modeled on the country homes of Victorian Europe. The main building, the original manor house, is equally impressive with its thick drapes and marble antechamber. My brother carries what he needs in an old canvas suitcase. Claude leans against me as if about to fall, before straightening at the sight of a security guard.

"Who ever thought it would come to this?" he whispers.

The guard directs us to the upholstered elegance of a room that once hosted Teddy Roosevelt, Stanford White, Diamond Jim Brady, Charles Evans Hughes, and other luminaries of New York's Gilded Age. We sit on one of several Empire couches, his eyes searching the brocaded shadows until we are summoned to the financial office by a middle-aged lady with pearl earrings who verifies my brother's name and last place of residence, and my phone number as his next of kin. She scribbles all of this on a form, and then asks, "What kind of insurance do you carry? Do you have any assets?"

"I don't know." He turns pale. "Do I?"

"He has enough cash to cover the cost of his month inside," I tell her. "By that time his Medicaid should kick in."

Claude's hand trembles as he writes out a check for fifteen thousand dollars. He is sure they'll find his secret caches. We have hidden his stocks and his remaining cash from the estate. I had sold off my stocks years ago to buy a new Ford Falcon and cover the cost of college tuition and living expenses. My brother had hoarded his cash, and under Michaela's guidance made canny investments even as his world was falling apart. I have assured him that all of his assets will be available to him in the future. But he no doubt recalls how our last joint financial arrangement ended in a hail of fries and coleslaw at Becker's Deli many years ago.

In return for the check, she hands him the item he has just paid for, a commitment form stating that he is entering the hospital on a voluntary basis. He can barely sign it. She slides the form into a folder along with Claude's check.

"Someone will come for you," she smiles. "Make yourselves comfortable in the waiting room."

"Comfortable?" Claude collapses onto the Empire couch, his old suitcase between his feet. In spite of the air-conditioning, his hair clings to his forehead and stains circle the armpits of his powder-blue shirt. "It's not like I'm on my way to summer camp."

Beyond the heavy curtains I see groundsmen tending a flower bed around the flagpole, riding motorized mowers, clipping hedges. Uniformed security guards drift in and out of the building.

"It's more like the Saturday Group." My brother's voice is as shaky as his hands. "Remember that?"

"I'd rather not."

The Saturday Group was a summer day-program to which our parents sent us when I was eight and Claude six. Instead of taking us on the trips advertised in their brochure, the people who ran the Saturday Group bused us and fifteen other kids to a yard full of dog-shit behind a candy store in Bay Ridge. There was an old swing and a slide in one corner, and a sandbox that smelled like used kitty litter.

"All those middle-class parents thought their kids were putting on puppet plays and visiting the Statue of Liberty." Claude's attention shifts, his invisible antennae check for hostile transmissions. "They know I'm here."

"Already?"

"They're all over the place spreading slander. You don't believe me?"

"I believe that you believe it."

"I should get into the car right now and drive to Tucson."

"If you went to the South Pole the penguins would be slandering you."

"All right." He wrings his hands. "I'll give this place a try."

"What have you got to lose?"

"Good question." Claude's head rests against my shoulder. "If I'm right, they'll drive me crazy. If you're right, I already am."

A man in horn rims, white shirt, and tie materializes in front of us. He introduces himself as Doctor P., then bends over to shake hands. Brushing a lock of black hair from his forehead, he invites us to follow him to the other end of the lobby. We stop in front of an elderly security guard who directs my brother to put his suitcase on the table, then rummages through it, taking care to refold the clothes.

"Will you empty your pockets, please?"

Claude follows directions, placing the contents next to his suitcase.

"Keys, wallet, credit cards, medications..." The guard notes each item before placing it in a lock box. "Standard procedure. Everything will be returned at the end of your stay. Sign here."

My brother scratches his initials on the itemized receipt.

Dr. P. leads us out of the air-conditioned lobby, through a heavy firedoor, to a stairwell. The boundary we've crossed is clearly marked by the absence of air-conditioning. Hot air sticks to us like a wet sheet. We reach the third floor dripping with sweat. Dr. P. chooses a key from a ringful to unlock another firedoor, which he locks again behind us. This space is ten degrees hotter than the stairwell.

We enter a wide corridor with rooms on either side. Standing fans posted at intervals along the carpeted floor struggle to circulate the heavy air. Scarred chairs and sagging couches, small tables illuminated by lamps that hold their light close within narrow shades line the walls. The inhabitants, like refugees from Edmund Gorey's *Curious Sofa*, sprawl on the furniture. Some smile. Others stare. A few are frozen in an internal nightmare.

I'm suddenly afraid for my brother.

A nurse in whites politely asks him to come with her so she can take his medical history. They won't be long, she promises, guiding Claude by the elbow to the station at the other end of the corridor.

Dr. P. apologizes for not being able to spend more time with me this afternoon, but will be sure to see me when I come again. Claude, he reflects, is a particularly interesting case, judging by what little information he has: "Not an acute psychosis but one resulting from prolonged morbidity, developing for a long time into a florid delusional system." He states this with the satisfaction of an angler who has just boated a prize marlin. We will discuss my brother's situation next time, after he has observed Claude more closely. Dr. P. pumps my hand, then disappears.

I pace the dilapidated corridor, stopping to copy numbers from two public pay phones in the hall. Posted between them is a "Patient's Bill of Rights," and the number of a lawyer specializing in patient advocacy. Beside it, on the wall, are names and numbers scribbled by a dozen anonymous hands like the enigmatic graffiti of a lost civilization.

Claude finds me in a chair across from what appears to be a dining room. His shirt is soaking wet. He takes mincing steps, as if walking on broken glass in bare feet. Two cans of diet Pepsi from the machine cool us down and give us more time together. But I've outstayed my usefulness. He feels this too, is anxious to get on with whatever it is that awaits him. We rise at the same time, then walk back down the hall.

"If this were summer camp, I'd make you a lanyard." At

the exit door, he turns to face me. "They're saying vile things about me, Paulie."

"Who?" I gesture at the faces pinned to the TV or staring at the walls.

He pauses, and then whispers, "The penguins."

I hug my brother, telling myself that this is the right thing; he will get the help he needs. For a moment, as I hold him, he lets his head rest on my shoulder. I feel his body relax. The very things that frighten me about this scene, the sluggish bodies, the glazed eyes, the locked doors, might be for him a relief. He'll be safe here. Attendants will watch him, doctors medicate him, and nurses tuck him into bed. Cradling his head in my hand, I consider the magnitude of the indecipherable world contained by his small cranium. The wail of grief that rises in my chest never makes it to my throat.

***

I came to the locust- and maple-lined streets of Glens Falls in 1984 as the recipient of a New York State Artist-in-Residence grant at the Crandall Library. I had discovered the area ten years earlier through my friendship with the poet William Bronk who lived in obscurity in nearby Hudson Falls. During my Tin Palace days, I took R&R in his Victorian house at the end of Pearl Street. I had arrived for my six-month residency in Bronk country intending to return to Belize where I had moved after selling the Tin Palace. I hadn't planned on falling in love in northern New York.

I met Carol at the Lake George house of a mutual friend. In the kitchen, preparing salad together for a family-style dinner, we talked about our lives, mine as a writer, hers as a middle-school music teacher and former opera singer. We began walking the wooded trails of Coles Wood behind the YMCA. She showed me where lady's slippers hid near wild wintergreen and how to distinguish the female damsel fly by the white spot on her wing tip. I was amazed by her ability to identify the robin's morning song. When Carol sang, doors that had been closed since childhood opened in my heart. I had spent years searching for "my people" among seamen, saloon society, the bohemian artists of the lower East Side, and Latin American expatriates; I might've continued to live like that for the remainder of my days without ever finding in simple domesticity what I really sought all along. With Carol, such a thing seemed possible. As if in anticipation, Saigon Rose had mysteriously kissed me goodbye.

Shortly after my official residency was over, we moved into a Cape bungalow off Aviation Road, where I asked Carol to marry me. She said, "Yes." A year later, Claude, on the verge of his psychotic break, drove up for our wedding, followed by a premonitory dread that had not yet emerged as the Watchers, who would later try to run him off the road.

After our six-month Parisian interlude, during which time Carol realized she was pregnant, I occupied a studio at the Madden, a derelict turn-of-the-century hotel with a Dutch roof, where Legs Diamond ran a card room during Prohibition. With unerring radar, I had located myself on South Street, what the local OTB players called "Dream Street," the Glens Falls version of the Bowery. Now the only thing I had to figure out was how to make a living in a place stranger to me than the Belizean jungle.

Every day at the Madden I work on my second novel, *Redemption*, set in Chiapas, where a hundred thousand Mayans in Mexican refugee camps have fled to escape the genocidal terror of a Guatemalan army trained and supported by the United States.

Driving back from Bloomingdale's, I think about the challenges in front of me. With the hope for a movie based on *The Tin Angel* stillborn, a baby on the way, and my brother's madness an inescapable reality, I shudder at the prospect of shouldering demands for which I feel unprepared. Staring at the All Points Diner across the street, I am suddenly comforted by something Claude said to me on leaving Highcliff, "I'm so tired of putting on the mask of joy, then of sadness." I wonder why I never visited him much at Cherry Lawn. At least at Bloomingdale's he has a private room with a window facing the flagpole.

"Someone outside my window yelled, *His brother told them everything.*"

"What am I supposed to have told them?" I ask over the phone.

"I don't know."

"I don't know either."

"Well, if I'm paranoid, how could you?"

Ten days after his admission to Bloomingdale's the voices are everywhere, calling him gay and demanding he confess it, which Claude tells me he is tempted to do even though, he insists, it isn't true.

"Is this what you brought me here for?" he screams.

"You have a better idea?"

"Get in my car and drive away."

"You'll get to the South Pole and..."

"Fuck the penguins!" He hangs up, only to call back a minute later and apologize. Dr. P. is a nice guy, but won't or can't give him any of the answers that he came there to find.

"Be patient," I tell him.

"If I stay here, you've got to expect more phone calls like this."

Dr. P. explains that Claude's increased agitation is due to the fact that he's been taken off all medication. The hospital does this with new patients in order to get a baseline.

Does he realize that for the first time in years my brother is going cold turkey not only from BusBar and his antidepressant, Marplan, but from uppers, cocaine, Xanax, and alcohol?

Dr. P. acknowledges my concern. If Claude continues to get worse, he'll order a Valium substitute.

"Oh, by the way, do you know if your brother has had

any adult homosexual experiences? He keeps hearing voices accusing him of being gay, and, after all, where there's a fear, there's a wish."

I suggest that a strictly Freudian approach might be misleading. Maybe I can come down next week and talk to him.

But it's early October before I get to Bloomingdale's. Red and yellow leaves litter the grounds. Recalling Holden Caulfield's haunting question in *Catcher in the Rye*, I conclude this is a perfect place for ducks in winter. Strange ducks. Daffy ducks. Unfledged ducks. And in Spanish, *pato*: Queer duck. Voices outside Claude's window call out *ducky, ducky, ducky.*

A middle-aged lady in a white staff coat unlocks the fire door, then ushers me onto the ward. Patients, mostly in their teens and early twenties, sit in the corridor facing a TV. A young man in a bathrobe raises his head. I recognize a second face. It belongs to my brother.

Claude's beard has grown. There's gray in it. I see the shape of his skull through thinning hair. He smiles but makes no attempt to rise. I pat his shoulder, tell him I'll be back after my visit with Dr. P. He nods and turns back to the TV.

I find Dr. P in the staff offices. He gestures to a chair in front of his gray desk. Immediately, he broaches the subject of Claude's sex life, asks if my brother has had any adult homosexual experiences. I tell him that Claude has always been drawn to women, describe his relationship with Michaela, and Marianne, the buxom Belgian with whom he lived for three years. I speculate that this aspect of my brother's delusion has more to do with our mother's sexual paranoia than with repressed desire.

Dr. P. writes all of this on a legal pad.

I find Claude where I left him, in front of the tube. Before I can sit down he declares that he wants out. "Ward Three is no place for me. Everything is in the open. Even now people are listening all around us."

I suggest we go to his room.

We walk in silence to the other end of the ward. Claude has been instructed not to lock his door. He can close it, but not all the way. We enter. Bare eggshell walls seem coated by the suffering of past occupants. My brother sits on his bed, curtains drawn. Our conversation, he repeats, isn't private. As if on cue, an orderly knocks, peeks in for a moment, then withdraws. Claude says they do this every fifteen minutes.

"Fuck your good intentions." He stands up suddenly. "Time for you to leave."

The day after my visit, he phones, his voice full of urgency. "They showed me a paper saying I was paranoid schizophrenic." Claude's voice races. "So I asked them why they gave me an IQ test, which really makes no sense if I am psychotic." He describes the scene; they brought him into a room full of doctors in white coats, evaluated him before the whole staff. "They say that I am a paranoid schizophrenic due to an inability to accept my latent homosexuality. It's the kind of diagnosis Mom made all the time of any man who crossed her."

Claude retaliated by flashing the cover of the book he is reading, *Bonfire of the Vanities*. The head doctor recognized his non-verbal protest.

"He told me, 'I wish I could spend my days just lying there reading.' I didn't say a word. I got up and walked out rather than give them the satisfaction of saying, 'Fuck you, you're all pompous assholes.' I wanted to tell them that the whole thing smacked of the Coliseum, feeding Christians to lions, vanity and cruelty. This white-coated little Nero wanted me to explode. I refused."

One of the psychiatrists had asked my brother if he belonged there. When Claude said no, the doctor asked my brother to explain the fact that he was currently a resident of

Ward Three. Claude offered that he had been on his way to Arizona and thought he'd stop by.

"The doctor told me, 'You are psychotic.' He said it five times. 'You're psychotic. You're psychotic. You're psychotic. You're psychotic. You're psychotic.' What does that sound like to you? Accusation and punishment: I came here to get away from that. What should I say to a little prick in Gucci loafers who shows me my IQ before calling me psychotic? Give me one good reason to stay here another minute."

"Because you're psychotic," I tell him.

Dr. P. has been trying to convince Claude to take the antipsychotic medication he and his team think appropriate. My brother is refusing. When I call to find out why, Claude tells me that they are trying to poison him. On the advice of counsel he's drafting a letter demanding his freedom. I phone Dr. P. immediately, horrified by that prospect.

"I'll have him on Haldol by dinner time. Hopefully, the medication will broaden Claude's reality base enough to make him reconsider."

"If he still wants out?"

"We can only do so much."

My brother's legal advocate, whose number is listed near the public pay phone, has advised him to put the hospital on notice with a letter requesting his release, dated and signed. Claude hasn't yet composed such a letter but expresses every intention of doing so.

"If he does, we'll keep him for seventy-two hours and then let him go. Claude is a voluntary patient. The hospital has no legal grounds to hold him without evidence that he's a danger to others or himself."

I warn Dr. P. of legal action from my side. Releasing Claude after taking him off all medication is indefensible. I take the name of the supervising physician.

"I'll be sending a registered letter of my own stating that a decision on the part of New York Hospital to turn Claude out unmedicated and in a delusional state is in itself madness of a high order."

Dr. P. calls the following day to confirm receiving my brother's letter demanding immediate release.

"But rest assured they won't release him on Saturday."

Dr. M., the therapist my brother was seeing in New York, agrees that Claude's release under these conditions would be disastrous, and will put as much in writing. Armed with her corroboration, I drive to Westchester, rehearsing what I will say to Dr. P. It's harder to figure out what I'll tell Claude. How do I let him know that if he refuses to stay in the hospital voluntarily, I'll commit him?

The corridor is crowded and smoky. Before confronting my brother, I visit Dr. P.'s office to see where things stand.

"Yesterday, your brother accused me of not being honest with him. So I did something I seldom do. I let Claude read the description of a paranoid delusional personality disorder in the DSMV-IV, and then asked him if he recognized the profile. He admitted that he needed help, but not in this place. That's how much shame Claude feels at being a mental patient."

"What will it take to commit my brother?"

"The process has been simplified." Dr. P. steeples his fingers. "I can sign a paper. It's an infringement of civil rights, no doubt about it. But in Claude's case I have no hesitation. Are you prepared to support this?"

I find Claude on his bed wrapped in an old blanket, his hair and beard matted. He plans to pick up the Brat at Highcliff and drive to Phoenix where his old medical school buddy David now runs a trauma unit. "I'm out of here tomorrow."

"What if they don't let you?"

"THEY!" His face catches fire. "What do you mean, *they*!"

I tremble at his anger.

"Ok. Me. Not *they*. I'm responsible. I want them to commit you."

"You have no right to make that decision. You're not equipped. If you keep me here it won't be as a patient. I'll be a prisoner. If I'm going to be warehoused, it will be in a place of my choosing."

"Bloomingdale's is the lap of luxury."

"You're doing this for yourself. Not for me." Claude sits up straight. "You're the most selfish person I know."

"If I were selfish, I'd have washed my hands of you long ago."

"Wash your hands of me. You and I haven't gotten along so well anyway over the last few years."

We sit in stony silence until I say that I'm leaving. When I reach the firedoor, I can't find anyone to let me out. Patients swarm around me like reef fish. For a moment I panic at the idea of being locked in with the rest of them. At last, the woman who let me in reluctantly stops stroking another woman's hair to let me out.

"You're not going to like the news." Dr. P.'s voice interrupts my dinner. "I'm not sure we can legally commit Claude."

"You gave me your word."

"It is not so clear that Claude is a danger to..."

"If my brother gets on a highway that he perceives to be full of assassins, would you care to be in the next lane?"

"Good point."

"You're about to give the inmate executive power over the asylum."

"We're meeting tomorrow. The decision will be made at that time."

I hear nothing by 3:00 PM the following day. I phone him. Dr. P. informs me that he and his supervisors are attempting to convince Claude to stay voluntarily.

"Dr. V. has personally told him that he is psychotic."

"Five times in a row, I heard."

"They interviewed a more psychotic patient in Claude's presence, then asked him if he would release a man as disturbed as that."

My brother had refused to answer.

"Dr. V. thinks that it would be a great tragedy if your brother left before he's ready."

"But you're willing to let Claude make that decision?"

"He'll make his decision, and we'll make ours."

"If he decides to leave, will you commit him?"

"We don't have a legal right."

"Even though you know he's a dead man if he leaves."

"You believe that?"

"I do. And will state as much in my letter."

Dr. P. plays his trump card. "We must have compelling evidence that Claude will be a danger to himself or others if released. Dr. V. points out that he has been driving in this condition for years. Dr. V. calls Claude "a capable psychotic."

Dr. P.
New York Hospital
Ward 3 North
21 Bloomingdale Road
White Plains, New York 10605

9/28/87
Dear Dr. P.:

Enclosed is a copy of my letter to your supervisor, Dr. S., describing the understanding you and I came to that Claude should be kept, against his will if necessary, for treatment at New York Hospital. In your office on the 22nd of this month, you indicated that, because Claude's condition was of some duration, it would take the medication longer to work but that at the end of his treatment, with continuing out-patient care, he might realize some of his potential. This is why I find your last-minute decision to release my brother surprising.

You stated in our phone conversation of 9/2, that Claude is a "capable psychotic" and as such cannot be considered a danger to himself or anybody else, and if you are asked to make an evaluation, while recognizing that Claude is paranoid delusional, the fact that he does not have a history of violence makes it impossible to say that he is legally committable. In reply I offer this: what my psychotic brother is capable of beyond all other things is of being psychotic. Since his paranoid delusions surfaced two years ago, he has been deteriorating at a steady rate. Both the complexity of the delusions and his level of expressed anger have increased exponentially. Recently, I have seen him make hostile moves toward utter strangers. The family with whom he has lived for a year and a half will tell you that his behavior now scares them. If you let Claude go, I believe he will die. He will certainly be homeless.

Mayor Koch's decision to open the doors of the mental wards in public hospitals in New York City and release an army of psychotics into the streets is relevant: should one be able to force critically impaired persons to comply with what is in their best interest? The Mayor has decided against imposing what might be life-saving interventions, a money-saving move in the guise of constitution protection. How cynical. The test-case of homeless psychotics abandoned to the street may well be the one I bring against you on behalf of my brother, and all those other "capable psychotics." I look forward to your decision, and hope it will be both sane and humane.

III

"We've decided to keep Claude." Dr. P. calls at dinner time on Friday. "When Dr. V. informed him of the decision, your brother told him to 'shove it up his ass.' At the mention of your name he said, 'Fuck him, too.' We've put him on suicide watch."

They can legally retain Claude for sixty days, he says, during which time he may consent to be medicated. Dr. P. is hopeful.

He is even more cheerful on Monday.

"Claude walked into the dining room and threw a can of soda on the floor. No one was hurt, but the can exploded. He spent the weekend in isolation. Now that we have evidence of his potential violence, we may be able to force him to take Haldol."

Closeted in the Madden, I struggle with my novel about a man honeymooning in Mexico who discovers that the father he long believed dead is actually a CIA operative living among the Guatemalan Mayans he had once helped to destroy. I'm drawn to this search for the father by my sense of fatherlessness in a culture that no longer seems to produce men capable of fathering. I am considering consequences this implies, when the phone rings.

"Hello?"

The silence at the other end seems to go on forever. Then I hear it.

"Ooohhhhhhhh."

"Who is this?"

Again, the muffled sound of an outboard engine underwater, a rake through dry grass becomes Claude saying, "Hello."

The last vowel stretches until it falls apart. A baffled sucking noise as if he is trying to piece the word together with his own saliva is followed by a whisper.

"It's me."

"You've taken the Haldol?"

"*Yes.*"

"Are you all right?"

"My body aches."

"You've jumped dimensions at warp speed."

"Where have you been?" he asks. "I've missed you."

I explain that after my last visit, I'd run out of steam.

He implores me to come down. The phone beeps. Would I call him back? He has no more quarters.

"You need money?"

"Yes," he says. "A roll of quarters...and a visit."

I arrive the following afternoon, pockets sagging with rolled quarters. An unfamiliar woman turnkcy asks if I have permission to see Claude before leading me to his new room on the other side of the hall. His door is closed. There's no response to my knock. I let myself in, the knot in my stomach heavier than the coins in my pockets.

My brother is humped under the sheets. At the sound of my voice, the hump shifts, then opens like a rumpled chrysalis from which my brother emerges, beard and hair coiled with static electricity. The eyes that meet mine are anchored to a muddy bottom. He is stoned on his antipsychotic. In slow motion, he rises to his feet, and then embraces me. I hold him, utterly unprepared for the sensation of his body rocking gently against mine.

"I can't believe it," he exclaims when we sit facing each other on the bed. "It all seemed so real."

"And now?"

"What the mind can do. It's incredible."

More incredible to me is that in the blink of an eye the medication has dissolved a delusion that's been years in the making. *The mind*, he keeps repeating, as if in shock. "Paulie, you don't understand what it's like to realize *you've been betrayed by your own mind.*"

His words are full of panic. He says as much. At times the panic feels like a band of steel tightening around his chest and he can hardly breathe. He repeats in a tiny voice: *You don't understand...*

No, I don't know what it's like to be trashed by ten million neurons. At Cherry Lawn, I had a glimpse of transcendent mind that shaped my conviction in the ultimate purpose and benevolence of human experience. I further believed that the impulse toward wholeness, in both healing and development, is inherent in the psyche, but can hardly say as much to my brother, whose ten million traitorous neurons have made him distrust the logic of any construction. I am grateful that with the help of the antipsychotic he can now distinguish his delusion from reality, but have no idea of what this experience has cost, or where it will leave him.

He can't sit in one place for long. We walk the hall. A young man in a bathrobe and a teen-age girl with long hair and circles under her eyes turn from the TV set when we pass. Two men in white coats follow us with their eyes. Everyone seems to know the earth has shifted. He settles on an empty couch.

"I feel like I'm slipping off. Am I?"

"No."

We walk back to the dining room. Claude adjusts his posture in his chair until he is ramrod straight, then starts to shake. "I have a meeting with my lawyer in two days to prepare for the hearing on my release. How can I make it in this condition? I can't even talk on the phone."

"You should stay here."

"Will you call the lawyer, and talk to Dr. P.?"

"We did the right thing," says Dr. P. when I enter his office. He drops the report he's reading and leans back in his chair. I express concern for my brother's panic attacks. Dr. P. isn't sure if the attacks are the result of the antipsychotic. Panic is a natural response for a man breaking out of a two-year nightmare.

As he speaks, I realize that the brother I lost, the infant in front of whose crib I danced at the dawn of memory, has come back to me—desperately wounded, but alive.

"I'd given up hope we'd ever talk this way again," I tell Claude when we are seated once more in the Edwardian corridor.

"It's good to be back," he says trembling. What if the panic attacks don't go away? Was the delusion worse than this terror? He fidgets with his hands, complains that he doesn't know what to do with them, asks what I do with mine.

I lace my fingers on my lap.

He tries to do the same, but his hands shake too much. I turn away, unable to watch. How unprepared I am to receive the brother I lost, the part of myself that haunts me like a phantom limb. My own body starts to tremble. Spasms rise from my stomach, tears fill my eyes. I hear stifled sounds from Claude. He is crying, too. But his sobs are feeble, pumped full of Haldol.

A week later, Claude is still tremulous.

"The situation with Betty was real, wasn't it? I didn't imagine it?" He slumps over on the couch, elbows on his knees, head in his hands. "I was so loyal to him."

"Yes," I touch his shoulder. "That was real, too."

"Betty, at Bellevue?"

"Real."

A year after the estate was settled, Betty had been found unconscious in her living room from a nearly fatal blow to her head which rendered her permanently catatonic. We'd learned from a detective Charlotte hired that she had been bringing men back to Sutton Place from the Tattler bar on 57th Street. At thirty-five, Betty was a vegetable. In the summer of 1969, before Claude started at Einstein, Irving phoned to tell us that Betty was in Bellevue awaiting transfer to a long-term state facility, and he agreed to meet us there. At the sound of Irving's name and title, the guard on duty opened the heavy door. A nurse directed us to the middle of a long corridor where a woman in a wheelchair sat framed in the doorway facing the hall. She stared straight ahead, unblinking, an Inca mummy freeze-dried in her prime. Her baggy green hospital gown gaped at the knees revealing calves not much thicker than her ankles. Hair sprouted from her head like shredded fiber-glass.

"She knows we're here," Claude muttered, then approached the wheelchair. He bent over to place his mouth on her ear. Betty stared blankly past my brother's head, which appeared to be resting on her shoulder as if this were an occasion of intimate sorrow.

"Do you know what I said to her?"

I shake my head. Claude's hands rest on his knees. They start to tremble as he speaks. "I remember it word for word. 'You poisoned Barney, turned my father against me, and stole our inheritance. Now I'm going to walk out of here, but you'll never leave this chair.'"

"So, that was real."

"Now I'm the one in the hospital." He smiles.

I ask him about the little old ladies in his delusion, their fish-mouthed pocketbooks open as if tempting him to criminal activity. "Betty had accused you of taking money from her purse."

"They were also Mom. I remember going to see her one morning when she answered the bell in her housecoat, without makeup. I wondered what this little old lady was doing in our mother's apartment."

"The high-testosterone women at salad bars?"

Claude shrugs; the legacy of our afternoons at Schrafft's? Who thought that those pinafore-and-doily ceremonies would leave my brother huddled in a corner taunted by cries of *Marty Cohen*?

He reminds me of a time when Charlotte, gazing at him from her hospital bed through a Demerol haze, recited "Little

Jack Horner," before telling him to go home, shower, and brush the cat hair off his clothes.

"The implication was that I smelled. Another time she said, 'Claude, you don't seem to be the marrying type.'"

"How did you respond?"

"I couldn't. She was dying. But inside I felt, *Oh God, Mom, are we through now?*"

PART 2

TROLLING THE WOUND

I

In his third month at Bloomingdale's, Claude's paranoid delusional system is replaced by depression. Dr. P. informs me that it would be helpful for me to meet his therapist, and whenever possible participate in family sessions. Judith, the social worker assigned to us, has long brown hair she wears loose and the nose of an Akkadian warrior. In her early thirties, there is also a hint of wildness in the way she swings her mane. I trust her immediately and agree to drive down once a week. Family therapy is considered an integral part of Claude's treatment. My brother, on the other hand, is agitated in her presence.

"When can I get out of here?" he crosses his arms at the beginning of our first session. She compares his question to that of a child on a road trip. We sit in Judith's office watching the afternoon light trapped in the dormers. Afterward, Claude and I retreat to the pool table in the recreation room on Ward Three. A thin man on a nearby Exercycle introduces himself as Keith. He lets us know that he'll soon be released. I ask if he's excited. Keith shakes his head. "My presence in Bloomingdale's is just a temporary battle in a great war."

"I don't have any friends on the ward," says Claude when we're alone. "Most people here are younger and have been in and out of these places. They develop a way of handling things."

"Like cons."

"They talk about beating the system, but not what they're feeling. It's bad form to ask someone's diagnosis. Patients speak about issues with their therapists, but not each other."

I give him a roll of quarters, some books-on-tape from the Rye Library, and a new radio-cassette player. He turns the radio on. The Four Freshmen are singing, *There is someone walking behind you...*

"The Paranoid National Anthem," says Claude.

My brother's chief complaint in the following weeks involves the side effects of Haldol. The antipsychotic eliminates his delusions but leaves him with a dry mouth, shaky hands, and generalized weakness. Claude claims never to have been more miserable, that neither Judith nor I can imagine the weight of his sadness—an actual, physical weight in his belly. He is pregnant with it. If words are tools, why is no one on the ward willing to talk?

"Sometimes there's the feeling that if you can find the right listener, you can get it all outside of yourself, but it doesn't work that way," replies Judith. "The weight, that false pregnancy, will diminish slowly on its own."

Dr. P. suspects that Claude's stiffness and dry mouth may be signs of *tardive diskenesia*, sometimes irreversible Parkinsonian movements that develop in a small percentage of those on Haldol. He's already dropped Claude's dosage from 20 to 15 mgs.

"Claude is like a creature that has shed his protective exoskeleton, which is what his delusions were. Of course he's in great misery. Hospitals are places for people in great misery."

By early November, Claude is allowed to walk the grounds in the company of family or staff. Following our grueling standoffs in family sessions, I become his co-conspirator as soon as we're outside. Strolling past topiary hedgerows, he confesses to plotting a Thanksgiving escape. Instead of going to Jo's for dinner, he plans to drive west in the Brat.

"I'll be in Ohio before anyone misses me." He pauses. "So, why am I suddenly having second thoughts?"

"Maybe you're getting better, as Dr. P. himself observed."

"He's a little young and a little slick," Claude smiles. "Did he tell you about my *exoskeleton*?"

Carol, baby Charlotte, and I take Claude out for Thanksgiving dinner at Cousin Jo's. My brother says nothing about escaping to Ohio, just stares with eyes like headlights at our one-year-old making faces at him from her car seat. No sooner do we arrive at Jo's than he checks the liquor cabinet. She's hidden the hard stuff, but left a six-pack cooling in the fridge. Before we know it, Claude is in front of the TV with a beer. After emptying the can, he returns to the kitchen, where I wrestle with him for another Budweiser in his hand. He won't let go. I give up. He finishes the six-pack and passes out in the bedroom before we carve the turkey. Jo is serving coffee when he staggers in to let us know the mix of booze and medication had made him sick. We rush him back to Bloomingdale's.

At our next session, Judith asks about our holiday.

"A disaster." I tell her.

"Seems like you took your problems with you," she comments. "Up until now you've blamed them on the hospital."

Claude insists that he's ready to cope with the outside world. All he needs is an apartment and a TV.

"What about booze and drugs?" I challenge.

"As far as I'm concerned, you two can get together alone. It will be easier on all of us. You speak the same psychiatric language and agree on everything."

Judith asks how I feel about what my brother has said. Before I can respond, Claude's anger boils over. He wants to know why she is addressing me; I always get the attention.

"I remember when you were grounded; you'd gotten drunk or refused to cut your hair. Dad took me to Coney Island as a reward for being a good boy. At last I had him to myself. We walked the boardwalk, went to the fun house, drove bumper cars, and ate hot dogs at Nathan's. *But all he could talk about was you.* What would become of you if you didn't straighten out?"

"Hold on a minute." I lean forward in my chair. "Who

put himself between you and Dad when things got rough, arranged for you to go to Cherry Lawn, put you up when you had no place else? I pushed our father's wheelchair when he couldn't walk, told our mother she was dying, spoke to you through your delusions, fought to get you into this hospital, then to keep you here to get the care you need...and no one, ever, ever, told *me* I was a good boy!"

Claude stares dumbfounded, then scratches his head and sighs. "So I guess you turn out to be the hero after all."

A week after Thanksgiving, I sit in the Hotel Madden reviewing employment options. I'm a writer with no market, with a psychotic brother in a locked ward and a year-old baby. I had resigned myself to tending bar again, but discover that I've aged out of the competition. Those I know in Manhattan still walking the duck-boards, like Ken Brown and Big Charlie, complain about back pains and burnout. Best to press forward with article proposals. I've done pieces for *Adirondack Life* and *Motor Boating & Sailing*. The idea is to sell to a venue where moguls troll for books and movies.

I prepare proposals for my upcoming lunch date with Bruce Weber, features editor at the *NY Times Sunday Magazine*, arranged by a mutual friend. I have high hopes for a piece on aging New York bartenders. But Weber might prefer my proposal on Clint Eastwood's new movie purported to be the life of Charlie Parker, *Bird*. I had an inside track on this through horn-man Red Rodney, who played with Parker and was Eastwood's musical advisor on the film. Red had told me: "They had Bird cursing like a rapper. I told Clint to take all that out. Charlie didn't have to say *mothafucker*." Or *The Real Mambo Kings*, Machito and Chano Pozo and their impact on Dizzy and Bird, who regularly crossed from 52nd Street to the Palladium.

Proposals are tricky. Even if one manages to get a contract, there's no guarantee a magazine will use the article. The enterprise can go wrong a hundred ways. I pump out proposals, and feel my life as a writer drying up. In a recurring dream I uncover a lost novel sealed in an envelope. I wake in a panic actually ready to search for it until I realize that the book has yet to be written.

Only the prospect of the publication of my *Hotel Madden Poems*, a collection few will read, keeps me going spiritually, if not financially. Between its covers I have stamped the image of my daughter "in the tub/ conducting her first/ nine months/ as if her life were/ a symphony," and of my brother who "assures me he's not crazy/ anymore, just pregnant/ with a hidden language."

I arrive early for my lunch with Bruce Weber at the Sea Palace on Ninth Avenue. A clean-shaven man with Clark Kent glasses, the editor locates me at a table in the rear looking over my proposals, sure one of them will work in *The Sunday Times Magazine*.

When I ask how he's been, Bruce complains that he finds his job a bit stifling. "I'd love to do nothing but write a novel. You know how that is."

I say I do, but for the time being will be happy to work on a magazine article.

"All right," he adjusts his glasses. "What've you got?"

I pitch the Clint Eastwood piece.

"Good for eight hundred words in *Arts and Leisure*," pronounces Bruce.

"How about aging bohemian bartenders in Greenwich Village and the lower East Side? There's playwright Ken Brown at The Corner Bistro, pulp novelist Shayne Stevens at Chumley's..."

"Try *New York* magazine," he shrugs. "Too regional for a national publication."

"'The Real Mambo Kings: An Untold Story,' especially now that the movie has made..."

No, he shakes his head.

I am about to suggest a profile of Wynton Marsalis when Bruce inquires, "Who's the *new* Wynton Marsalis?"

The question stops me. It didn't occur to me that Wynton might be old news. What about the *new* avant-garde? These young Turks display a pointed arrogance, a talent for self-promotion, and an exhaustive theoretical knowledge which included European classical tradition.

"Possible," Bruce nods. "Why don't you write me at the *NY Times* proposing a first-person piece on the changing styles and attitudes in jazz that draws on your own experience. Of course," he adds, "the article will have to be written on spec."

I sit stunned. He wants me to work without a contract. How can I? Not with a baby and a household to support.

Bruce says I know where to reach him if I change my mind, then nixes coffee and dessert. It suddenly dawns on me that I might propose an article on my brother's struggle to find his way back from paranoid schizophrenia. But I am too late. He has already picked up the check and is on his way out the door to his next meeting with a doctor who's just finished an article based on his experience in a Louisiana leper colony.

II

When I am about to despair of ever making a living in the land of wrap-around porches, novelist Jean Rikhoff, whom I met through William Bronk, hires me for the spring semester to teach creative writing at Adirondack Community College, where she chairs the English Division. I am grateful, but two classes as an adjunct are hardly enough to pay our phone bill. I stumble into another offer while visiting the new halfway house on Maple Street, in Hudson Falls, as a possible place for Claude upon his release.

It is a two-story glass-and-concrete building among mill-town Victorians. A smiling man with a fifties pompadour introduces himself as Mark, and then shows me the "cooperative apartments," emphasizing that the residence is staffed by mental-health professionals. Clients pay for the service by signing over their monthly disability checks to the Mental Health Association, from which they draw a small allowance after costs are deducted. The beds are currently full, but Mark puts my brother's name on a list and promises to let me know when one opens up.

"By the way," he lingers at the door. "Our group home on Pearl Street is looking for a relief counselor, if you know anyone interested."

The group home is a white Victorian, two blocks from Bronk's. I enter from the mud-room off a gravel driveway. A twentyish man with wire-frame glasses and a frayed maroon sweater greets me in the kitchen like an old friend. He's moving to San Francisco next week. They need a replacement for him right away. Would I like a tour?

He leads me into a living room furnished with Empire sofas and chairs, which I have come to think of as the décor-of-choice for the mentally ill. In the library, purple drapes and electrified sconces highlight half-empty bookshelves.

Residents stare from the shadows, pop out of bedrooms upstairs. I smile, trying to hide my growing alarm.

All those I see are either overweight or skeletal. A few have distended bellies on otherwise normal frames, a condition I've come to recognize as the "false pregnancy" of ongoing psychosis. Women in faded housecoats shuffle worn slippers over hardwood floors, smoking and coughing. This is a space turned inside out by sorrow, a liminal zone where things usually hidden are visible. I trail my burned-out Virgil to the dining room, residents in our wake. They sit at the long wooden table. My host and I disappear into the administrative office.

"This is where you'll spend the night. It's the graveyard shift. Day staff relieves you at eight."

There's a large desk, with a couch in front. He points out the first-aid cabinet, small refrigerator, Rolodex on the desk. When extended, the pull-out couch fills the space between the desk and the door. The bed frame is bent, but I can always fold up the springs and put the mattress on the floor. Can I handle two nights a week?

The hours won't interfere with my teaching or writing time. Between the two jobs, even at slightly above minimum wage, I'll make enough to carry a small part of our expenses.

"Can you start tomorrow?"

My job is to be on the scene in case someone sets fire to the curtains or falls down the stairs. If a resident becomes violent or suicidal, I can intervene myself, or use the Rolodex. Senior staffers are on call. In a pinch, there's Glens Falls Hospital or 911.

The shift begins at 8:00 PM. I arrive as residents are clearing the table and washing dishes. Everyone is responsible for their own dinner setup. After chores, they regroup in the dining room, a designated smoking area, or disappear into their bedrooms. A few introduce themselves. Larry, a razor wire with straw hair and glasses, speaks brilliant

Whitmanic phrases at burp-gun speed. His buddy, Clem looks out through the cow-eyes of moderate retardation. Lucy carries herself like the winsome teenager she may have been ten years ago, before her hair turned brittle and her belly grew as a side effect of meds she takes to quell auditory hallucinations: the false-pregnancy of psychosis. The most daunting residents of all are the bulky white women in housecoats, high-testosterone ladies who regard me with suspicion as they puff and cough until the dining room ashtrays overflow.

This Greek chorus of smoking women in housecoats keeps an insomniac vigil, wheezing through the night. I hear them as I read Nietzsche's *My Sister and I*, written during his last days in the madhouse: *"I once thought that a bird which passed this same window might be God on an inspection tour."* Heavy slippers shuffle as I unfold the bed and stretch out on the mattress praying I'll be spared a crisis. The fact is that I have been less frightened in the free-fire zones of Vietnam or working the door of my Bowery jazz club than I am here among the population of Pearl Street.

At a little after 1:00 AM, I wake to shrieks, like the blaring of an air-raid siren. I race upstairs, follow the sound to Larry, seated on the edge of his bed, mouth agape. He stops when I burst in and accuses Clem of flashing his penis and trying to get him to touch it. Clem denies the allegation, then stares at the floor. Larry wants to change his room. I assure him that we can discuss it in the morning. For now, he can sleep on the library couch. Larry decides to stay where he is.

I manage to sleep and dream that the Hudson Falls Fire Department is heading for Pearl Street. The siren this time turns out to be Lucy who has forgotten to take her meds. She is screaming back at voices accusing her of things she dares not repeat. Her face is a replica of Edvard Munch's *The Scream*. By the time I quiet her, morning light creases the sky. I sit with her until the day counselor appears and transports her to the unit at Glens Falls Hospital.

My second night finds me on the phone at 2:00 A.M. with a Maple Street resident who calls to say she's been drinking earlier with friends, only to waken with suicidal thoughts. I talk her through the crisis over the phone, aware of the women in housecoats gathered outside my door.

By Christmas, I can distinguish their coughs. Most heave their chests quietly. Some pace to the muffled growling of their lungs. Others are cataclysmic, tectonic plates shifting with every puff. A few sound as though they are literally coughing up their lungs. One of these, a woman in her sixties, recently returned from the hospital less half a lung, has resumed smoking. I think of them as the chorus of Medea trying to tell me something I only vaguely understand.

Claude loves to tell about the time he went into the common room and sat down between a patient talking to himself, a catatonic woman, and a young man nodding out in front of the TV. One of his doctors peeked in, then told him, "Very good, Claude. I'm glad to see you're socializing."

In spite of my brother's vaunted isolation, Claude has gotten to know several inmates on Ward Three. Closest to his age is a shy woman he met in the lounge when protesting to anyone who would listen that he didn't belong in the hospital. So, what was he doing here, she asked. Getting away from the accusations and humiliation he suffered outside. Gently, she had assured him that he was where he belonged, and so was she. She might otherwise have died of anorexia.

Claude has also made friends with two other patients: Keith, the lanky man on the Exercycle; and Jason, a college drop-out who draws M.C. Escher-like constructions of impossible realities. Jason majored in art at SUNY Purchase as a cover for his true identity—that of a CIA agent collecting evidence on former Nazis. He came to the attention of college security when several professors complained of being followed by one of their students. His cover was blown once and for all when campus police found him at 1:00 A.M. tearing apart a brick wall with a spade. Jason claimed he'd found the entrance to Hitler's bunker and intended to seize the files.

"When they collared him," says Claude, "he told them, 'I'm a top agent for the CIA. Make some calls.' They replied, 'All right, come on, buddy.' He still isn't sure why the CIA hasn't come to his rescue."

Walking in the garden, my brother compares his delusion to Keith's and Jason's. Keith, who believes himself a rock star, goes out on his veranda and sees thousands of adoring fans. Jason's delusion glorifies him as the CIA's top man.

"They're paranoid, but not like me. I was despised by everyone. Why is my psychosis so cruel?"

He leaves the question hanging to invite me, Carol, and the Poose to the ward party on Christmas day. I tell him we'll make it if we can. There is light in his smile.

When we arrive for Christmas day at Bloomingdale's with our one-year-old daughter, the ward is done up with crepe paper and balloons. My wife presents Claude with a Grand Union fruitcake.

"There are some who might question the idea of bringing a fruitcake to a nut house," observes Claude. "But not me."

Carol points out her cake is hardly noticeable on a buffet that includes a mocha cake, cherry cobbler, pumpkin pie, banana cream pie, and a tray of cheese and cold cuts.

Claude serves us red Kool-Ade from a crystal tureen. We sit at a table with the actress-sister of an unidentified patient and the mother of a tall, cranelike man in his early twenties. The cranelike man excuses himself to join the crowd on the floor.

"He's saying goodbye," his mother explains. "He's coming home in the morning."

The cranelike man works the room like a politician. I congratulate her on getting her son back. She gulps a breath of air, then confides she has taken her son home from six hospitals only to have to recommit him after he's medicated himself with free-base cocaine and grass.

"He still doesn't accept that he's schizophrenic. It's everybody else's fault—my fault, the world's fault. The old schizzes burn out after forty. But he's not only crazy," she gazes at her boy. "He's young."

Before the evening ends, Dr. P. volunteers that Claude may be ready to leave by February. My brother's face lights up like a Christmas ornament. It's all he can talk about at our next session. Walking away from Bloomingdale's is one thing, Judith advises, finding a destination another.

He can't go back to Eastcliff, but wants to remain in the area. Maybe stay at the YMCA, until he finds something else. But what can he tell the Y when asked where he's spent the last year?

Claude's anxiety over logistics builds. At the end of March, he announces that he's found a basement room in Eastchester and put down the first month's rent.

"Will you look for a lab job?" asks Judith.

"No. I'm forty-three years old. I should be doing something meaningful, like horticulture."

At our last therapy session, I expect to find a scrubbed and hopeful Claude. Instead, he appears dazed, his beard a bird's nest, his back hunched. He's anxious to confess that he's terrified by the prospect of leaving. Judith sidesteps his declaration by summing up what she sees as our accomplishments over the last six months, the foremost being our re-established brotherly communication. I add that I've come to appreciate Claude's courage.

"*Courage*?" He tilts his head, and then asks how I can apply that word to one who feels so impotent.

Before I can explain myself, Judith wishes Claude the best of luck, hugs him, and declares with misty eyes that she will miss us.

My brother's Brat, packed with most of his worldly goods, waits in the parking lot. (I drove it from Highcliff earlier this morning while Carol followed in our Toyota.) Claude steers it down the oak-flanked allée, haloed in budding April green, and out of Bloomingdale's, without a backward glance. We tail him out to the Flagship Diner, where he tells us that his new place is dark, reminds him of his old basement apartment on West 75th Street. Poosie eats Cheerios while calling out his name.

"Caw, caw," she sings like a little bird.

"Paulie, the place is a hell. There are two guys next door. I hear every move they make. I'm calling from a pay phone down the street."

I share my fears with Carol. Should I drive down and get him?

"He has to do this on his own," she replies.

Claude calls at noon on Monday from a phone booth. He's having a panic attack. "I got out of bed and there was a parking ticket on my car. The second one. I thought I understood the streets, but I don't."

"Drive back to the hospital."

"I can't go back there."

"What do you want to do?"

"Get drunk."

I plead with him not to, then call Bloomingdale's. Judith isn't in on Monday. Dr. P. is out to lunch. Claude phones with his new number. I leave it for Dr. P., who returns my call and suggests my brother try 911.

Claude's new phone rings but no one answers. I imagine him passed out on a curb and dial the hospital. Dr. P. replies that his supervisor has determined Claude doesn't need a crisis team. He can wait until tomorrow.

At 2:30 AM, barricaded behind the office door of the group home on Maple Street, I listen to the insomniac smokers, aware Claude and I are trying to make it through the night in a world whose boundaries can dissolve in the blink of an eye. We're subatomic particles of energy disappearing before our existence can even be measured. He, a *gluon*, sucking on his vodka. I am a *muon*, wondering if I should go back to school for an MSW rather than continue knocking at the door of an inhospitable literary world. What makes more sense than to function as a therapist in a universe of unstable vectors?

One can think of time as a river or a wheel, the one moving inexorably toward the sea, the other around a silent center, and write convincingly about either of these as the fundamental shape of human experience. What does this mean to the women smoking outside my door, my brother free-falling through psychological space in Eastchester, myself at the center of a failed vision? I tune my ears for signs of trouble.

On Tuesday morning Claude phones from the hospital waiting room. Dr. P. has arranged to readmit him to a short-term unit. The following day he tells me, "I hate this hospital. I hate being a patient."

A week later, we face each other in Judith's office. His gray sweater has a moth hole in the shoulder.

"I can't help you, Claude." Words rush from my mouth. "Nobody can, until you've decided to help yourself."

"Now you're abandoning me, too."

"He's not abandoning you. He said that he's impotent to help you. What else is Paul telling you?" asks Judith.

"That I couldn't hack it out there."

When I inform him that he's on a waiting list for a cooperative apartment in Hudson Falls, Claude is visibly relieved. There'll be no problem transferring his Social Security payments if he wants to live upstate. Judith would like him to attend A.A. meetings and become active in the vocational program here before he goes. It takes another three months, but on a clear August afternoon in 1988, almost a year to the day from his admission, Claude again walks out of Bloomingdale's, slides behind the wheel of his Brat, and then follows me north to the Adirondacks and Maple Street.

BOOK 3: HOMETOWN, USA

How does one become a hero from a position in which
he has hardly any resources at all?
Ernest Becker, *The Denial of Death*

PART 1

BECOMING A HERO

I

Staff at Maple Street, in Hudson Falls, is curious about the new resident who has worked on the psychiatric wards in Brussels and at Einstein. Mark, the counselor on duty, a moon-faced man peeking out of glasses in tortoise-shell frames, expresses his hope that my brother will like it here.

By the end of the week, Claude complains he's surrounded by rednecks with whom he has nothing in common. His roommate, a lanky man in his twenties, lies around listening to country music and talking about cars and comic books. After two months of modulated unhappiness at Maple Street, my brother moves to a satellite apartment in Glens Falls.

Elm Street is not the Norman Rockwell part of town with lawns fronting gingerbread Victorians, but a series of two-story row houses on a strip of concrete a block from the Hotel Madden. His apartment on the first floor is at the end of a hallway smelling of damp plaster. We enter through a kitchen/dining room, which opens into the living room flanked by a bedroom on either side. The wallpaper is peeling, the carpet filthy, and the chairs and couches smell of old hair oil. My brother's roommate, Mark Koen, a rangy young man with an unhealthy pallor, sits at the kitchen table in a white T-shirt pouring over girlie magazines. He barely raises his head to nod at us, then continue his exploration of beaver shots as Claude unpacks in the far bedroom.

On Saturday morning, November 5, 1988, I discover Claude on the living room couch of our Shippee Street home reading *The Glens Falls Post-Star*. He had gone to the computer lab at Adirondack Community College, discovered it didn't open until two, and decided to kill time here. Carol and Poose are at my in-laws' a few blocks away. I'm still tired after a night at Pearl Street and go back to bed. When I rise at 1:00 PM, Claude is on his way out. I invite him back for dinner. We leave together, he for ACC and I for the Madden.

At a few minutes after 4:00 PM, Carol calls me at the hotel to report a message on our machine from an Officer Conine at the Glens Falls Police Station trying to reach Claude. I return the call immediately. Conine asks to speak to my brother. Do I know where he can be reached? Or account for Claude's whereabouts between 12:00 noon and 2:00 PM?

"What is this about?"

After a brief hesitation, Conine informs me that around noon a woman has been raped, stabbed, and bludgeoned in my brother's Elm Street apartment. The victim is a girl in her twenties.

"Evidence of a break-in?"

"Are you a lawyer, Mr. Pines? You sound like a lawyer."

I tell him I'm a writer who teaches at the college. My brother was with me on Shippee Street until 1:30 PM, after which he drove directly to the computer lab at ACC. "Claude isn't capable of such a crime. What about the roommate?"

"We're questioning him now."

"How's the girl?"

"Not good." His voice becomes cool, professional again. "We have to talk to your brother. He might have information, even if he had no direct involvement."

Even if. I start to speak, but hold the words back. It will do no good to protest his innocence over the phone. Claude would be coming back to our house for dinner, I tell the policeman. I'll let him know what happened.

"Can I bring him down in the morning?"

My sister-in-law, an intensive-care nurse at Glens Falls Hospital, confirms that a young woman was admitted with multiple contusions to the face, neck, and abdomen that afternoon. But the most damaging blow is one to her head with a pipe. She had also sustained stab wounds in the mouth, cheek, neck, and abdomen. Her condition is listed as "critical."

Carol and I wait in shock for Claude to return. I worry about the destabilizing impact of such news, not to mention any criminal involvement. Can they really regard Claude as a suspect? *Even if*, Conine said. I hear the ring of suspicion and wonder *what if?* Claude's last encounter with the law involved a false accusation of rape and sodomy. This is a link in a chain of experiences that includes Charlotte's sexual paranoia, Betty's lies, his debacle at Einstein, and a delusion in which strangers allege he's committed heinous crimes that can neither be addressed nor substantiated.

Claude returns for dinner high on his success with the computer class. Not only has he mastered Word Perfect, but he's written a probing essay on the potentials of cyber technology.

"What's wrong?" He has read the expressions on our faces.

Seated in the living room, I tell him that a woman has been raped and assaulted in his apartment that afternoon. My brother shakes his head in disbelief.

"Who is she?" he asks.

"We think it's your counselor."

"No. Kim is off on weekends. It must be the relief counselor. My roommate was scheduled to see her." He pauses. "On my way out this morning, he asked where I was going. I told him I'd be at the ACC library all day. I remember he repeated, '*So you won't be back all day?*'"

"Could he be the perpetrator?"

"No. No." Claude shakes his head. "Koen is a withdrawn guy. Hardly speaks. Though I've heard rumors about petty stuff, like shoplifting. Someone mentioned three suicide attempts. But the man is invisible."

"There has to be more," I insist.

"He complains that his girlfriend won't sleep with him."

Koen's bedroom walls were papered with nudie fold-outs

and beaver-shots when Claude moved in. A few days later, Kim, their counselor, made Koen take them down. This he had done, without protest. "But they must've been concerned to send a relief counselor to check up on him." Claude's brow furrows. "They don't think I had anything to do with it?"

"They just want to talk to you. Tell the officer what you've just told us."

Claude is pale through dinner. We put him to bed on the couch. His hands shake the next morning, spooning up Cheerios. The *Post-Star*, which carries the story, states that the victim is still in critical condition and the police are actively questioning suspects.

"Does that include me?" he repeats. "I was here yesterday and at school."

At 9:00 A.M. on Sunday Officer Conine ushers us into the Glens Falls Police Station, in the basement of City Hall. A thirtyish man with a brush-cut and trim mustache, his tone is polite, even diffident. He takes Claude's testimony on an IBM Selectric. After confirming my brother's whereabouts during the crime, he tells us that Koen has confessed to bludgeoning twenty-three-year-old Amy Carpenter, but not to stabbing her. "We now have to determine if he acted alone."

Conine studies my brother for a long moment before asking if he thinks Koen might have had an accomplice. Claude's eyes dart between me and the policeman.

"How would I know? I just moved in last week."

Conine resumes the interrogation. Did Claude notice a knife? What was Koen wearing? Were there pictures of naked women on the walls that morning? He thanks my brother for his cooperation, and then signals for me to follow him outside. In the hall he explains that Koen raised the question of an accomplice without identifying anyone. They had to follow up on it. Koen's attempt to shift the blame, muddy the water to create reasonable doubt, probably. This has become more important since this morning when Amy Carpenter has died as a result of her wounds.

After brutalizing Amy, Koen went to Genesis, a group home in Glens Falls, where he told a counselor about finding a woman's body in his apartment.

"We arrived at Elm Street to discover the body on the floor, the walls covered with pornography. If he was wearing clothes, he'd disposed of them." Conine sighs. "He probably lay in wait naked and attacked her when she stepped inside. As careful as he'd been, he missed the blood evidence on his shoes."

The policeman gives us permission to remove Claude's clothes and TV from the crime scene. He also returns to my brother an envelope containing seventeen hundred dollars after Claude identifies the amount and the pillow where he squirreled the cash. When we get to Elm Street, the apartment is still posted, but there's nobody at the location. We walk past peeling paint, over blankets and sheets; pooled blood stains the carpet and has splattered the walls. Koen must have dragged the girl all over the place. The centerfolds and beaver shots have been taken down, but we find cheesecake photos on Claude's dresser. My brother stares at them.

Back at Shippee Street we play *what if*.

What if Claude had returned to Elm Street when he found the computer lab closed? *What if* he had walked into the Elm Street apartments at the height of the carnage? *What if* they'd assigned a male relief counselor, like me?

Claude takes out a tackle box that once held fishing lures and sinkers, forages through medications until he finds his tranquilizers. After popping several, he goes upstairs and falls asleep. He's still sleeping when Officer Conine stops by after dinner with a typed statement to be signed. He agrees to wait until tomorrow. My brother, he tells us, may be called upon to testify at the trial. They've made a solid case, have a witness who saw the perpetrator leave the apartment at the time of the murder, and enough blood on Koen's shoes to make a match.

"But I don't think it will go to trial. He's already attempted suicide three times. If he wants to take his life badly enough, he'll do it."

The prospect of testifying in court terrifies Claude. He believes the police suspect he might have been an accomplice. Koen confessed to beating his victim, but not to stabbing her. My brother is frightened that they suspect him of wielding the knife. At a pretrial interview, the DA shows him snapshots of the crime scene. Buried in the pile is one of Amy Carpenter's body in a fetal position on the floor. Claude turns pale, drops the photos. On our way home he insists, "It was a setup. To see if I was involved." I want to deny this and ascribe it to his paranoia, except that it's clear he might be right.

My brother will be permanently haunted by these events and in his more paranoid moments tremble whenever he passes a police car, terrified that they have built a case against him; surely the record of his arrest long ago for rape and sodomy would indicate a possible pattern, raise suspicions. No matter that these charges were dismissed when his accuser recanted, or that he had been in the computer lab at ACC working on a paper when Koen murdered Amy. His accusers could wage a campaign of rumor and innuendo to raise doubts, perhaps even stick him with a label like Claude the Ripper.

II

First week in April 1989, five months after Koen was remanded to a psychiatric facility for observation pending trial, I drop three-year-old Charlotte off at the Center for Early Learning in the Baptist Church, and then turn onto Elm Street. Marty, a round man with black hair, is coming out of his apartment in Claude's building. He is the witness who saw Keon leave at the time of the murder. Motionless in the hall, he'd felt the small animal's instinct in the presence of a larger one. Koen hadn't noticed him. Today Marty whistles to himself. Like most other residents of the North Country, he is glad to have made it through another winter, but especially this one. Later, he will walk three miles to pick up his homely girlfriend, Clara, who works at Grand Union on the other side of town. Both moderately retarded, they are devoted to each other.

Spring light washes the gazebo that serves as a bandstand in City Park. I skirt the Civil War monument to see my brother on the porch of Freedom House, a program that tries to find employment for higher functioning *consumers*. ("I hate that term," Claude protests. "As if we did nothing but consume what everyone else has made!") I have hardly seen him since he moved into a new apartment last December. He calls now and then to say he is depressed, but forces himself to trudge between Freedom House and Cherry Street at least three times a week, certain the cops are watching him.

North on Bay, two miles past the intersection at Quaker Road, the red brick buildings of Adirondack Community College perch on a ridge between a golf course and a cornfield. Turning onto the campus, I imagine Dan Garcia pedaling his bike to Dearlove Hall, battling clinical depression. As his satellite counselor, I encouraged him to take my World Literature course. He committed suicide mid-semester. I am having better luck with Laura, who struggles with auditory hallucinations but regularly attends my Contemporary Novel course to discuss James Baldwin.

On my way back to pick up Poosie, the shadow world of Home Town USA rises to greet me like a message written in invisible ink held up to a flame; but it is spring, and buds about to break into blossom deliver a message of their own. I park in front of the Methodist Church, then cross the lawn to Freedom House. Faces stare at me from the porch. One among them lifts his head. After a second's delay, I recognize my brother.

"I could sit here the rest of my life and nobody would care." Claude observes this like a biologist examining a flatworm.

Since I last saw him, Claude is thirty pounds heavier, pale as a cod, and determined to find a job. He answers an ad at the Village Booksmith: *Three floors of used books off the main square in Hudson Falls*. They quickly hire him to replace a young woman.

Claude shows up for work in his new "dickeys," a striped blue shirt, with his hair combed and beard neatly trimmed. But his hands shake as he squints through horn-rimmed glasses. He breaks out in cold sweats and gets confused at the register. The owner fires him at the end of his first day. Claude assures me that although the owner assumed he had been either drunk or stoned, he was neither; my brother had simply buckled under the stress of a situation that proved too much for him.

Freedom House refers him to an employment counselor at VESID, an agency that specializes in placing people with disabilities.

"The first thing she did was test my aptitude for spatial relations," Claude informs me. "I have many problems. None of them have to do with spatial relations."

His employment counselor warns him off a job at Dunkin' Donuts because the owner doesn't speak much English. Claude turns down a job as a night clerk in Lake

George. The veterinarian who advertises for an assistant is inundated with applications. A real estate agency wonders why someone with advanced degrees in science and microbiology wants a job in the mail room.

"Oy!" He puts his head in his hands. "And they once called me *Doctor. Doctor Pines!"*

A possibility at Mallinckrodt Catheters lifts his spirits. "Very low key, not much pressure," he tells me. "I stand on line and put a pin through a hole." I suggest he look for lab work. No, he'll never wear a lab coat again.

"What about a hit man?" I ask.

"Paranoids have trouble focusing on a target. I've taken aptitude tests, preference tests, and spatial relations tests. According to the results I'd be an outstanding forest ranger or rabbi."

"You could be the first forest ranger/rabbi in the Adirondacks." I notice an ad for a herdsman in *The Post-Star* and urge him to apply.

"They probably want experience. Of course I can say, '*I herd you wanted someone.*'"

At the end of April, Claude breaks his vow never again to plate another slide and circles an ad in the *Post-Star* for someone to launch the bacteriology wing of a laboratory in Saratoga. After a brief examination of his résumé, they hire him. He is responsible for setting up the physical plant, ordering and installing the equipment, in addition to qualifying the lab for state certification by identifying blind slides in a four-hour exam. He works furiously, setting up the plant by day, then hitting the books at night. He qualifies the lab in four months with a flawless series of blind identifications. At the celebration party the following day, Claude is nowhere to be found, though his colleagues remember him at work that morning. They discover him in a nearby cornfield, assisted by vodka and Xanax, attempting to crawl away from stress.

His recovery is delayed by two other blows. The first one, which he might have anticipated, comes when a member of his therapy group with a criminal record breaks into his apartment to steal the coins Claude has unearthed with his metal detector. My brother is forced to leave Cherry Street and move to what had been a church rectory in the residential section of South Street. More unexpected is the news of his psychiatrist's sudden defection. Dr. U.'s flight surprises everyone. Eventually, we learn that Dr. U. has set himself up as a specialist in addiction and co-dependency in Sacramento. The timing couldn't be worse for Claude, who is scheduled to appear as a witness at the Koen murder trial just as he is running out of Xanax.

At the trial, on July 12th, 1990, Claude is asked if there were images of naked women on the walls of the Elm Street apartment when he left it on the day of the murder. The D.A. produces a knife my brother can't identify. He is dismissed and walks out of the courtroom feeling that the legal procedure has somehow trivialized the crime. But Claude can't forget the way Koen looked the morning of the murder when he asked if my brother was sure he'd be away all day. As if some part of him had known Koen's intention and cleared the way for the act. We are shocked two weeks later when the jury rejects a verdict of first-degree manslaughter to find Koen guilty in the 2nd degree, which will allow him to walk in four years. My brother will continue to look over his shoulder at patrol cars for much longer that that.

"The jury let him off easy because of his mental health problems."

"Probably," Claude agrees. "He's the type that gives all psychotics a bad name."

I meet Claude at the Candy Kitchen at the end of August, a few days before Carol, Charlotte, and I move to Philadelphia. My wife, on sabbatical from her teaching job, has received a fellowship to study Music Learning Theory at Temple

University. The move is facilitated by the sale of film rights for my unpublished novel *Redemption* to an independent producer who hires me to write the screenplay. Wearing a blue oxford shirt and a tweed jacket, my brother informs me that he will be interviewing for another lab job at Irongate Center, a private medical complex, after lunch. His face is tanned from hours in the sun. Only his eyes give him away.

I think about his eyes as we drive past Newark Airport and over the Delaware Bridge in a car packed with pieces of our lives. It is one of those things I hadn't intended to take with us.

At the end of March 1991, he calls me in Philly. His boss has asked him to stop performing tests. He hasn't gotten a wrong result, just forgotten to fax the right ones to doctors waiting for the information. I tell him I'll be coming to Albany to interview Chief Judge Sol Wachtler at the Court of Appeals for my monthly profile in *The Upstate Legal Record*. I can meet him for dinner on Thursday. We choose Mahov's, a surreal pizza joint owned by former Detroit Red Wings goalie Pete Mahavlovitch. It features a dining-room mural of a locker room complete with sweaty socks and athletic supporters. Claude enters breathless, blown up like an over-inflated football. His speech is slurred, his eyes red. If he continues self-medicating, I warn him, he's headed for a fall. Two days later he calls to say he's been fired.

III

Sol Wachtler, Chief Judge of the NY State Court of Appeals, greets me like an old friend in the marble lobby on Eagle Street. We cross the rotunda to the elevators. Over the past two years I have profiled all nine of the State's top justices for *The Upstate Legal Record*. My interviews have become noteworthy in the local legal community. Judges, who spend most of their time listening, are eager to take off their robes and talk to me.

This is my second interview with Justice Wachtler, a handsome man in a charcoal-gray suit, dark hair salted at the temples. He has already told me about his father, a Jewish merchant who moved south to set up a store in North Carolina. The future jurist grew up fascinated by the dramas in the local courthouse. Sol, the son of a Jewish immigrant father, reveals that he has decided not to run for governor. The common opinion is that he will do so when Mario Cuomo retires. It is the natural steppingstone for Wachtler, a political lion whose future seems unlimited. Instead of the lion's roar, he gives me a sad smile when confessing that he will not run for governor or any other political office.

"I no longer have the fire in the belly."

The fire, as I later learn, is buried elsewhere, in the secret chamber of personal obsession that will explode into public humiliation: the revelation of Justice Wachtler as a socialite stalker and would-be kidnapper.

At our second interview, Wachtler's conversation remains seamless.

Eight months later, he will be apprehended by the FBI in the disguise he used to spy on his former mistress outside her Park Avenue pad. The doorman will identify the cowboy hat and false mustache as items worn by the man who leaves notes threatening to abduct the woman's daughter. Everyone will wonder how the man who wrote brilliant legal opinions and had been seriously considered as a gubernatorial candidate could embody such madness.

Willie Bosket is another story.

Penthouse magazine gave me a contract for an article on Willie, known as the most dangerous prisoner in the New York State penal system, held under conditions worse than those imposed on Hannibal Lector in *The Silence of the Lambs*. Willie is being held in a sub-dungeon below the SHU (Special Housing Unit) under constant surveillance by video cameras. Before he can receive food, protocol requires that he be chained to the door. Willie's lawyer doesn't deny that he is dangerous. He's killed inside and outside of prison. He is also highly intelligent and has recently converted to Islam. Most interesting to me is the fact that his voluminous files contain no more than a page of psychiatric evaluation or intervention. I exchange letters with Willie.

Shortly after our move to Philly, I learn that he's to appear in the Monticello Town Court representing himself on his own appeal. I reach Monticello the night before. The next morning, I catch my first sight of Willie, a black man in a green prison jump suit. Chains around his ankles jangle with each step. His mother abandoned him to the penal system at the age of ten after she was abandoned by her husband, Willie's father. He thinks of the penal system as a parent. At the first recess, I try to meet him in the holding room, but the correction officers refuse to let me in. On his way back to court Willie says he'll put my name on his visitors' list tomorrow at the prison. But they do the same thing at Warwick. I talk to William Kunstler of the ACLU and state Democratic representative Maurice Hinchey. Both try to help me. *NY Times* reporter Fox Butterfield is also waging a campaign to see Willie. So far, not even The Gray Lady can force open the gate. As Hinchey puts it, "When the Department of Corrections closes ranks, nothing can open them."

They are keeping Willie on ice because of a hearing scheduled in the Brooklyn Supreme Court to determine if the conditions under which he is being kept constitute cruel and unusual punishment. There will be no reporters at the proceedings.

I try to reach Claude on the phone, but he is either not in or not answering. I know he has taken a blow with the loss of his job, but I am struggling with issues that seem more immediate. The prospects for my screenplay are dim. The producer has replaced my storyline about a man discovering his CIA father still alive among the Mayans he had once persecuted, with his own plot about a road-builder who falls in love with the daughter of a Guatemalan general. By the summer, it becomes clear that the project is doomed. My childhood asthma grows worse by the day.

During the week I pick up four-year-old Charlotte at Penn Wynne Children's House, a Montessori school in a church beside a park in Bala Cynwd. The park is bisected by a brook running past a playground bordered by a verdant hill and an arboretum of indigenous trees. We play there. She is *Lady Lovely Locks.* As the arch-villain *Hairball,* I chase her over wooded banks, my lungs rattling, fingernail beds turning blue. Theophyllin keeps me awake, prednizone and Ventolin open my airways. But the asthma grows worse until my lungs feel like fists closing in my chest. One night in bed my lungs close until there's no room to draw the next breath. I shift to my left, the heart side, then let go of everything: my brother, daughter, wife, the novels, poems, articles, and screenplays I will never write. No sooner do I prepare myself for death than the clenched fists open.

In August 1991 we return to our old jobs in Glens Falls. A few days later, I join Claude at Freedom House for a meeting with his counselors. He is waiting on the porch, a balding man with a belly hanging over his pants. He loses no time in telling me how much he dislikes the program. Upstairs I meet the director, a middle-aged woman with warm eyes and a speech impediment, who thinks the world of Claude but expresses frustration. The system doesn't provide for consumers with his background and intelligence. While this is true, she cautions him not to become self-indulgent.

"Everyone at Freedom House has a story," she reminds us. "And intelligence doesn't determine the degree of personal suffering."

If Claude will take a job of any kind for a few months, long enough to convince the Office of Vocational Rehabilitation (OVR) that he is dependable; she may be able to help him get a better one or even financial support for graduate school. Before we finish, Claude agrees to bag groceries at Price Chopper.

I don't hear much from him over the next two months. Then, one evening on the supermarket checkout line, I find myself staring at a man beyond the register wearing a white shirt gaping under the pressure of a gut that swells over tan chinos. Sweat glistens on his forehead as he struggles to keep up with the flow of groceries on the conveyer belt. I've failed to recognize my brother. I want to change lines, but he catches my eye. A smile replaces his worried grimace. I feel ashamed.

After bagging my groceries, Claude takes a break. Some of the full-timers, he tells me, treat him as subhuman. He's trying not to personalize their remarks. And there is this one special cashier.

"I bag my heart out for her, but she's married."

When I meet him again at the register a week before Thanksgiving, his back aches from carting frozen turkeys from the stock room. A few days before Christmas, he informs me that customers occasionally ask him when the new semester begins at ACC.

"They think I'm you. I don't bother to correct them."

It tickles my brother that people assume the novelist,

poet, teacher, and father of the Poose spends his intersession at Price Chopper bagging groceries.

***

"I hate the job," Claude tells me. "Forty-seven years old and bagging fucking groceries! The cashiers at the register just shove the stuff at me. There are one or two very nice cashiers, but to most of them I'm dirt. I'm 47, not 18. And they're shoving stuff, won't even talk to me. There's a supervisor, an obnoxious self-important little shit. I go over to get the orange vest with reflector strips you're supposed to put on and she's talking to somebody else. I stand there and say, 'I don't want to interrupt but...' She just keeps on talking as though I don't exist and then after about ten minutes, still talking, without even looking at me, gives me a vest. I swear to you I'm not a violent guy, but I want to grab her by the throat and tell her, 'Who are you? You don't treat people this way.'

"When I was working the line she'd come by but she wouldn't look at me. She'd say, 'Take a break.' But I didn't hear it, didn't know it was directed at me. Then she'd come back later and say, 'I told you two hours ago to take your break.' I had no memory of it at all. I told Janet, I really have no memory of being told that. I began to have paranoid bleed-throughs. I asked Janet, 'Do you remember Dale telling me to take a break?'

"Janet said she did.

"Dale would laugh. 'Claude, you're losing it.'

"It happens this way all the time. For a while I was going to my car during breaks, just for a change of scene. I was trying to quit smoking. And I don't smoke pot. That's like smoking a cigarette. So, she writes me up for that. She said, 'You know when you're on your break, you're supposed to be around in case of an emergency. And you've been seen'— I had been seen—sitting in my car, smoking. Judy tells me— like I've committed a major crime—'You know you have been seen going out to your car for a smoke.'

"I can't really defend myself. 'Yeah! I do go to my car on my break and quiet down, smoke a cigarette if I have to. And I'm being written up for that!'

"I asked older full-timers, 'Are you not allowed to go outside and smoke?' Everyone said, 'No, I go outside and smoke.'

"The whole job is humiliating. It's a minimum-wage, no-benefit job set up for six months by Freedom House so you can't claim unemployment. You're cannon fodder. If you prove yourself, you go to VESID, the agency that's supposed to help the handicapped find decent jobs. That's the ultimate object. But they're very tricky, too. You really have to prove yourself and be very specific about your job goal—which is a problem I ran into with them. They ask, 'What do you want to do?'

"I feel like a medieval philosopher defining God in the negative. I say, 'I don't know. I don't want to bag groceries, mop floors, or be a janitor.' I don't know what I want to do. I don't know what I can do."

PART 2

POSTER BOYS

I

From where Claude stands, I have everything: a wife, a child, meaningful work, a white ranch-style house with a fenced-in yard on a street shaded by ancient maples. Every Sunday he comes for dinner, cuts enormous wedges of cheddar from the appetizer cheese, demolishes huge portions of pasta followed by mountainous bowls of ice cream, and then leaves without a "Thank you" or "Goodbye." As far as we can tell, he seldom arrives sober.

Tonight, with several ACC colleagues in the living room, Claude shows up wearing his leather apron and head phones. Spade and metal detector in hand, he is a hesitant superhero somewhat diminished by the instruments of his power. He says he would like to scour the backyard of our new home on Garfield Street.

"It's not a good time."

"Why is that?"

"I don't want spade holes in our lawn."

I wonder if Claude is aware of my discomfort at the spectacle he presents. The sight of him grazing with his inverted satellite dish outside our living room window as we entertain friends would embarrass me. He isn't happy with my response. I read anger in his stare. Not the explosive outrage of our youth when he would cut me off without a word because I'd stolen his allowance or made his private life public. Nor is it the simmering bile that spilled from his lips at our mother's grave. What Claude conveys to me now is a calculated hatred, so certain of itself that it takes the moral high ground. *I played by the rules. You didn't. And look what's happened!*

His anger spills onto Carol. She clears his empty plate, dishes up his ice cream, and brews his coffee. He treats her as he has been treated bagging groceries at Price Chopper, as if she doesn't exist.

Only the Poose is proof against his anger. At ten, her delicate face beams when Claude appears in the living room. She is affectionate with most people, but throws her arms around her uncle with a lavishness she shows few others. Sensing his fragility, she snuggles beside him on the couch or curls up on his lap. In those moments I can see the pain of his existence fall away. He holds her carefully, like an exquisite piece of porcelain. Their attachment has evolved into weekly "dates." Instead of eating with us on Sundays, he has begun taking Charlotte and a friend of her choice to their favorite pizza places. She becomes known to him as "Pizza Girl," and they have developed their own code for conversations over the phone.

When she answers the ring with "Pollywanacracker?" I know its Claude. He arranges to pick her up with unreal precision at six-twenty-three-and-thirty-two seconds.

Now, he stands in the hallway in earphones and leather apron. I say, "Leave your gear in Charlotte's bedroom. We'll be serving dinner in a few minutes."

Reluctantly, he trudges down the hall, untying his leather apron. When guests are seated and he still hasn't returned, I go in search of him. He's sitting in Poose's room staring at the Wicca shrine next to her bed. Beside her offerings to the elements, power crystals, and incense, lies a book. Claude picks it up and examines the cover, *Astral Travel For Beginners*.

"Does it come with training wheels?" he asks.

"Dinner's ready," I announce.

"You know, at least once a month I dream about leaving my body. I shed all this physical weight, become light, luminous, more whole than at any other time or place, and remember what it felt like to be free. I hope it never stops. I never look down, never look back."

***

In the spring of 1995, a feature writer for The *Glens Falls Post-Star* asks to interview Claude for a feature on the local mental-health community. He makes a date to meet the journalist, Hope Ferguson, at my home where (Claude tells her) he is most comfortable. I am a fly on the wall as they face each other on the couch. An attractive black woman in a business suit, she opens by asking Claude what life is like for those in his community.

"Not as bad as it was in 1797," he replies, "when Philippe Pinel went into the *Asylum de Bicetre* to unshackle the mentally ill from the walls. But the invisible chains are there: poverty and stigma. Remember Thomas Eagleton, the Democratic vice-presidential candidate in '68 who had to withdraw when it came out he'd been treated for depression? Instead, we elected an untreated paranoid named Richard Nixon."

"What about the system itself?"

"More shackles. Medicaid doesn't allow for periodontal work. If my tooth is abscessed, they pull it out. Most mentally ill people eventually get false teeth. Medication dries out their mouths and they develop dental conditions. From the outside they appear to be people with no idea of how to care for themselves. Low-lifes with bad teeth. The fact is that their condition produces this result and poor medical coverage makes it a given."

The article appears on the front page of the *Features Section* a week after his 52nd birthday, with photos and generous quotes. Shortly thereafter, the Mental Health Association hires Claude as a "counselor" at South Street. It's a part-time, minimum-wage job, but they assure him there are bigger things ahead.

Bigger things turn out to be organizing a consumer self-help group for which there are federal funds. The funding requires a majority of the board to be consumers. As one of a handful of high-functioning consumers in the area, Claude has become an important player.

At an early meeting, my brother and four other high-functioners agree on the mission: *to reclaim dignity and self-determination.* The suggestion is made to model the program after one in Albany, *Consumer Voices.* Claude objects to the name. People unfamiliar with mental health issues might mistake them for an offshoot of *Consumer Reports.* Besides, the label of "consumer" is anything but dignified.

"It describes this population as a parasitical form of life that eats up resources and contributes nothing," Claude tells them. "Let's call it *Voices of the Heart?*"

As a new star in the mental-health firmament, the pain of Claude's past humiliations is replaced by anxiety. The idea of becoming a mental-health advocate leaves him breathless. My brother sighs, "I don't know if I'm up to this."

At times he feels people are eavesdropping on his phone calls, watching him on the street. He monitors himself for delusional "bleed-throughs," checks with Dr. L., a highly regarded Park Avenue psychopharmacologist, about balancing his medications.

"It's the hard-wiring," Claude says. "Dance of the neuro-transmitters. Only some of mine aren't dancing."

Dr. Roger Longo, professor of psychology at ACC, is a small man with a kind smile and eyes that peer out of Coke-bottle lenses. He and his wife often dine at our house. From the time of their first meeting Roger and Claude began a conversation few of us could follow that has since moved beyond the dinner table.

Both are convinced that reality is chemistry. Roger holds that the internal environment of the nervous system is constantly being altered by external delivery systems. Food alters brain chemistry. So does music. Or bungee jumping. Some people get hooked on their own brain chemistry (*the basis for all addictions*), or become cross-addicted by using others as delivery systems. Dysfunctional families, couples in abusive relationships trigger emotional swings that produce cycles of engagement and withdrawal around the rush of adrenaline. Roger and my brother discuss such things late into the night. It forms the basis of their friendship.

In November 1996, Roger invites Claude to participate in a conference on psychopharmacology at the Queensbury Hotel. My brother demurs. But Roger persists. Claude's medical background and first-hand experience give him a unique perspective on psychotropic drugs. My brother will be one of four panelists. There's no reason to be frightened. As moderator, Roger can run interference if necessary. Claude gives in.

I arrive at the Queensbury Hotel on the appointed day to find the banquet hall filled with doctors, nurses, and mental health professionals. Claude sits at a table in front flanked on one side by a psychiatrist, and two pharmaceutical representatives, and Roger on the other.

Each makes an opening statement about the use of psychotropic drugs in the treatment of psychosis and depression. Claude speaks last. When his turn comes, he gazes at the audience for what seems a long time. The silence becomes almost unbearable. Finally, he begins to speak slowly, as if feeling the words take shape in his throat. Strides have been made targeting the limbic system, he declares. Schizophrenia is now understood as an excess of dopamine. "But I don't believe for a second it's that simple. It's the interplay between neurotransmitters that determines any state of mind. Like physicists trying to figure out photons, we're shooting in the dark."

Most of the questions are directed to him. While the others address the action of specific drugs, Claude alludes to the broader implications of neurobiology. In his closing statement he points out what no one else has mentioned: the chameleon ability of mental illnesses to shift symptoms from one diagnostic category to another. He ends by recalling a David Frost interview with futurist Isaac Asimov.

"Frost asked what he thought would be the greatest breakthrough of the coming century. Asimov answered: understanding of the human brain. Strides over the next fifty years will make the answers of today seem primitive."

I am blown away by the intensity and duration of the applause.

Claude and Roger, the Mr. Bones and Mr. Interlocutor of mental health, are in demand. They appear two months later at Glens Falls Hospital for the local NAMI (National Association for the Mentally Ill) meeting, their topic: "Survival in the Street."

My brother, in pressed chinos, a white shirt and a tie that ends half-way down his belly, trembles slightly when he stands to face the audience. His puffy face, red-rimmed eyes, and distended belly mark him as one of those about whom he speaks. It also gives his voice a unique authority.

"Where does one start talking about the system? With the infantilizing day programs, forty-minute therapy sessions twice a month, the absence of vocational training or economic initiatives? 'Survivors,' in the Mental Health Community is a code word for people trapped in a system that dehumanizes and holds them economic hostage."

Claude recalls that Philippe Pinel, the chief physician at Salpetrière Hospital, observed that the asylum wards emptied at the time of the French Revolution when patients left of their own volition to join the battle for *liberté, égalité,* and *fraternité.* They had been drawn out of the lair of their self-loathing by a heroic ideal.

Those in this audience, either directly or through a loved one, have shared Claude's experience. It isn't what he says, but the way he says it that moves them.

"Might not the best medicine of all be the possibility of some meaning...a way to let those who have struggled with the pain of mental illness see themselves as, dare I say it, heroic?"

He stands before them like the one-eyed man in the kingdom of the blind, an embodied voice-of-the-heart. In Roger's terms, Claude has become a delivery system that changes the internal environment of everyone in this room.

II

A change of the division chair at ACC places my job in jeopardy. My choice not to try for a tenure-track position is based on the idea that I still want to write, but my literary career has ground to a halt. I apply to Rockefeller College, at SUNY, Albany, as a candidate for a master's in social work with the idea of becoming a psychotherapist. To complete the degree in three years I must take two graduate courses over successive summers in addition to the standard course-work and two years of internships while I am still teaching full-time at ACC. Better, I reason, to embrace a new life as a psychotherapist than sink into the quicksand of the old one. With the encouragement of Bernie, my Buddhist shrink, I do my best as the oldest student in the program to assume the attitude of "beginner's mind."

The first of my two required practicums is with Washington County Hospice at Mary McLellan Hospital. Nursing my father and mother through terminal illnesses did not prepare me for my first assignment: to attend to a seventy-year-old woman dying alone with her senile husband on a rural road. As soon as I enter their home, I want to run away.

Amy, my mentor, is young enough to be my daughter. She combines the serenity of a Mahatma with the openness of a sunflower. I marvel at her courage and console myself with the observation that when Amy sits by a deathbed she sees someone else; when I look at a dying client, I see myself. I am even more at sea when my own daughter, perhaps eerily sensing my preoccupation, but also keenly aware of mortality, asks me not to die when I tuck her in at night. I recall my own attempt to grapple with this issue at her age by holding the pull-cord of the Venetian blinds beside my bed and repeating to myself that I would one day be unable to feel the knotted rope. Fifty years later, I am still scared that I will someday *have* to let go of the pull-cord.

I watch Amy prompt loved ones to give the dying person permission to die: "You can go now. We will miss you, but we'll be all right."

It will help if my Poose can say as much to me.

In the last month of my internship I sit with Mary, an elegant woman of seventy, as her husband in the last stages of dying moves in and out of consciousness. A retired engineer, he designed boats and houses, including the one in which he now lies. On my second visit, she tells me about recurring dreams he's had over the past week. In the first, he walks up a dock toward a boat with teak decks tied fore and aft by green ropes. In the second dream he is on the boat. The bow line has turned white, but the stern line remains green. In the last dream he stands in the housing, uncertain that the waters will be calm or the boat seaworthy.

I ask Mary if they have discussed the dreams.

She says, no. They've become increasingly estranged over the past few years. Alone together, they share less and less of their inner lives. Now, she is waiting for him to die, unsure if he even knows that he's dying.

That morning, as he comes out of a deep sleep, I let him know that Mary has talked to me about his dreams, then ask if he understands them. He replies that he doesn't but wants to. I suggest the images reflect his inner situation. Green lines are vegetal, his organic tie to life. Beyond, the sea, that which waits. The bow line has turned white, waiting to be cast off. The stern line, still green, holds on because he's afraid. In his third dream he's uncertain the seas will be calm or his craft seaworthy. I recall my own grip on the pull-cord by my bed. The cord that holds him is about to dissolve. His craft, I assure him, will be up to the journey. I leave Mary holding her husband's hand as he slips the line and sets out to sea.

"I've given it a lot of thought, and I'm not prepared to assume that kind of responsibility." Claude declines the invitation from the director of the Mental Health Association to serve as president of *Voices of the Heart*. He agrees to train as a respite counselor in a program that offers the consumer in crisis an alternative to hospitalization. The association sends him to a conference on peer advocacy at the Nevele Hotel, in the Catskills, and asks him to attend the national NAMI convention at the Crowne Plaza, in White Plains. Claude's presence in a mental health fund-raising film gives the documentary a haunting depth. My brother is suddenly very visible.

"I recently heard the Human Services Director discuss a plan to introduce sex-offenders into the mental health population. *Can you imagine that?* I told him, 'You're about to give predators grazing rights; put wolves in a pen with ducks, don't be surprised if they end up with a mouthful of feathers.'"

At Roger's invitation, Claude addresses the Washington County Rotary in West Fort Ann where he puts his hand on his heart and sings the Star-Spangled Banner. "After dinner, I told them what it's like to be a recovering psychotic in the mental-health system. The good-old-boys loved me."

Other invitations follow. My brother accepts them without hesitation as long as they include Roger, whom he refers to as "my safety net." Claude appears to have retrieved a piece of the destiny that had seemed to be lost to him forever.

Following my second internship as a psychotherapist at a local out-patient clinic, the director invites me to stay on staff. Ironically, my position at the college has become more secure, so I'm able to do both. But there is something profoundly compelling about my new career. As a psycho-therapist, I see myself in boys labeled with Attention Deficit-Hyper-Activity, all of whom are responding to family dysfunction. The child I was at the same age would today be on Ritalin. I see Dad in every depressive and Mom in every narcissistic personality disorder. In all of them, I find fragments of my brother.

III

On Friday, October 30, 1998, I pick up Claude at his apartment on Sherman Avenue. This afternoon we are driving my van to NAMI's Sixteenth Educational Conference in White Plains. I find him upstairs at the computer. His new couch smells of cigarette smoke. Everywhere ashtrays overflow. Newspapers and empty Coke bottles litter the floor. A TV faces the couch, a chart with chemical symbols on the wall above it. Similar symbols are scribbled on a chalkboard beside it.

"The Krebs Cycle," he stretches. "The way glucose breaks down."

"Why are you studying glucose?"

"Glucose produces lactate, and there's an action in lactate that triggers anxiety." He sees a direct connection. Injections of lactate can make a calm person anxious. Lactate production is a side effect of his antipsychotic, Malarial. "I'm now a B cup."

On the floor are *Receptors*, his favorite book on neurohormonal transmission, and *The Dancing Wu Li Masters*, which discusses the universe as a dance of energy, Claude's vision of brain chemistry. Our father's intuitive sense of the body and the dynamic interaction of its systems remains alive in him. More remarkable, *it exists in the same person who can no longer work a cash register or remember where to find the soy sauce in aisle four.* I step over paperback thrillers by Ross Thomas, James Lee Burke, and Lawrence Block. He likes the last two because their heroes have drinking problems and attend AA. Mysteries solved are a comfort in the face of impenetrable ones like that of glucose.

"I'm ready." My brother puts on his coat.

We are off on an adventure together. I feel like Dr. Watson when Holmes declares "the game's afoot." We exit the Cross Westchester at Bloomingdale Road. The Crowne Plaza Hotel, with its Miami-style porte-cochère, rests on the slope of a hill blocks from where Claude was hospitalized more than ten years ago. The activity in the lobby reminds me of an ant farm. We wade through "The World Cruise Association" conference in search of our own in the lower lobby without live music, bar, and canapés. A young woman at the registration table hands us packets and name-tags, then points to a room where people are "caring and sharing." Claude flattens his hair with his palm, then poses the question: "Do I look sane enough?"

We enter the room in which a dark-suited man with a gray goatee nods as we take our place in a row of folding chairs. He introduces himself and his wife as parents of a schizophrenic son, then asks, "How many people in the room are on some kind of medication?" Ninety-five percent of the audience, including my brother, raise their hands.

Early the next morning, people fill the Crowne Plaza's banquet hall. Identifiable among them are the parents of consumers who have forged this coalition of health-providers and politicians to advocate for their sick babies. The first speaker points out that the mental health system refuses to recognize meaningful work as a step toward recovery. "As a counselor, I took over a bakery, and employed twenty-two consumers at The Pie in the Sky Bakery. We ran a movie theater in Malta and a bagel company in Otsego County." Claude's fist is clenched in solidarity. He knows what it's like to have no other option but bagging groceries.

After lunch, I attend a seminar on "Borderline Personality Disorder." The speaker describes the condition as *being born without an emotional skin.* "They don't let you help them. If you get close, they push you away."

Like a client I'm treating who is engaged in self-mutilation and high-risk sexual behavior, *and my mother, who so altered her appearance at one point that I didn't recognize her.* I imagine Charlotte at the head of a conga-line of would-be messiahs that includes Gurdjieff, Mary Baker Eddy, and Manly Palmer Hall, or herself as Thaïs on the violin playing to fill a bottomless borderline emptiness.

At night we crowd into the banquet hall for the "Celebration and Awards Ceremony." Guest of honor, Fox Butterfield, of the *NY Times,* who also tried to write a piece on Willie Bosket, can't be here. His stand-in happens to be working on a book about former Chief Judge Sol Wachtler.

My missed opportunities ganging up on me!

The speaker declares the world's largest mental institution to be the Los Angeles County jail, holding fifteen to seventeen hundred mentally ill inmates, one in ten of whom suffers from schizophrenia, bipolar disorder, or major depression. I drift off into personal regret: Chief Judge Wachtler's story had been mine to tell. Like Butterfield, I could have stepped around the Department of Corrections to locate Bosket's father on death row in Texas to explore the roots of homicidal behavior. That I did not, I tell myself, marks a failure of nerve and imagination.

Keynote speaker Lynn Redfield Jamison, Professor of clinical psychiatry at Johns Hopkins, glides to the podium in a long gown, bare white shoulders and arms. Her book, *An Unquiet Mind: A Personal Account of Manic Depressive Illness*, in which she admits publicly to being bipolar, spent five months on the *NY Times* best-seller list. Her desire to disclose her illness emerged while directing a mood-disorder clinic at UCLA where she realized that most clinicians had no idea what the illnesses they were treating actually felt like. As a doctor with state licenses and hospital privileges at Johns Hopkins, she had risked malpractice claims and the loss of professional credibility, but decided it was more damaging to remain silent. The result of her action surprised her. "The sheer numbers who call to request consultations...if anyone has a clinical practice that's not currently peppy I recommend you say that you're psychotic as hell." The applause is deafening. For Claude, she is Joan of Arc after Orléans.

On Sunday morning Claude's other hero, Dr. Lewis Oppler, stands in front of a projector screen looking out through horn rims at the banquet hall, and declares, "I'm a great warrior. But I have yet to know one person who has won a war without a great army. So—*hello, army.*"

"Hello," Claude's voice rings out among the rest.

His troops are those who fight to balance their medication, struggle with side effects. Also in the ranks are soldiers who refuse meds or take them and become zombies. The Director of the Office of Mental Health for New York City briefs his army.

"There's no such thing as a bad patient, only those who haven't yet found the right treatment."

"Amen," says Claude.

"Armies can do wonderful things." The audience claps long and hard. When they are through, their general invokes his weapon system of choice in his great war: Clozapine. He describes his twenty-year battle for FDA approval of the drug used with such success in Europe. "Sandoz and Lilly say that their drugs with similar structures are just like Clozapine. Wrong! It's a waste of money and lives to be dragged through long trials with drugs that aren't effective. The drug of choice in patients with refractory schizophrenia is..."

"*Clozapine!*" my brother rises to his feet, foremost among the troops ready to do battle.

"Together, we can work magic. Remember when Mary Martin was playing Peter Pan on TV with Tinkerbell dying and we all had to do was clap as hard as we could to make her well."

On the drive back I observe that Oppler was okay, but Jamison pretentious and histrionic. Claude insists that I am wrong. She has done what every high-functioning consumer wants to do, step out of the closet and flourish.

What does this gorgeous, accomplished woman have in

common with the ladies in housecoats at Pearl Street, or any other so-called "consumer" he knows?

"She's so bright," Claude says. "That woman risked her career. Can you imagine what kind of courage it requires to put everything on the line like that?"

We fall silent. There is something unbridgeable and perhaps even dangerous between us. It is a shadow cast by a darkness that holds us both.

"Tell me she doesn't remind you of Mom."

He dismisses me. "How can I expect you to understand?"

"Ahab in a ball-gown."

"Now I get it. You think it should have been you up there."

BOOK 4: VOICES OF THE HEART

"Brother," whispered Feirfiz, "is the Grail
not very like the human heart?"
Parzival, Lindsay Clarke

PART 1

LEAKY VALVES

I

Things have been tense between Claude and me since we returned from NAMI a week ago. His invitation to have coffee takes me by surprise. Nor can I read his mood when he gets into the van, except that he won't meet my eye. Driving down Glen Street, he informs me that he has seen a cardiologist who confirms that his childhood mitral prolapse, the barely audible whisper our father heard long ago and dismissed, has gotten worse. It's clear to me that the stress of his condition and the effects of alcohol, drugs, and his clinical medications have played a significant role. At this point, the valve is so stretched out of shape that a large portion of his blood is regurgitating back into the artery with every heartbeat.

"The condition is common among schizophrenics."

I tell him that I know as much. It is cited in the *Diagnostic and Statistical Manual of Mental Disorders, Fourth Edition.*

"Surgery is inevitable."

"Don't be melodramatic," I reply, unsettled by the news. "You're not going to die of this."

"Do you ever think about death?" he asks.

"Not a day passes that I don't."

My brother is surprised. As he sees it, I have so much to live for. Why should I be haunted by death? He has forgotten who saw both of our parents into their final days, and spent time working with Hospice.

"Everyday I rehearse letting go."

"Really?" Claude regards the golden maples along the main drag of Hometown, U.S.A. against a turquoise Indian-summer sky. "I would leave the world with one less consumer," he smiles.

"One less advocate," I counter.

"Being an advocate was never my choice."

"A part of you always looked at those people and felt repulsed."

"They are me. And they aren't."

"But you've made their cause yours."

"Not all consumers walk around feeling about their lives the way I feel about mine. Most don't even walk around. When they do, they're usually alone."

"Why is that?"

"Mentally ill people don't like each other. They see in the other what they despise in themselves. Those who have mental breakdowns spend the rest of their lives trying to figure out what became of them, and how to live with this creature everyone treats with contempt."

"I see Marty and his girlfriend walking together all the time."

"There are touching stories. This guy Ken is really retarded. His wife, Sue, is dual diagnosis. They met at Freedom House. She cares for him like a baby. When they're out walking she's got her arm around him. Is it a normal relationship?"

"Don't give up on them," I blurt out. "On yourself."

"I love the idea of Philippe Pinel going into the pits of those French institutions to free the mentally ill chained to the walls. But I don't have the ego for it."

"You stir people. I've seen it."

"In therapy Elizabeth says, 'You're an advocate.' But I'm full of self-hate. A shriveled ego...with heart problems."

"A great heart, one that people recognize."

"The rational part of me thanks you. The other one isn't even listening."

***

By Thanksgiving, cracks in Claude's new life look like fissures in the walls of Highcliff. His mood is unpredictable. Over brunch at the Silo, he gripes that the Association director drives a Mercedes but nickel-and-dimes the consumers. My brother is also angry at what he calls the *social hypocrisy*. "When I make public appearances or discuss brain chemistry with professionals, they sing my praises. Have any of them invited me to their home for dinner or out to a movie? They expect me to perform at a high level, then communicate my inferior status at every turn. They touch me with rubber gloves. I find the situation tiring."

A week later, at Ashleigh's Cafe, in Saratoga Springs, Claude tells us that he stormed out of a VOH board meeting when they refused to pony up money for pizza at a party to promote their respite program in spite of an eleven-thousand-dollar surplus. "They held the line at cookies. I went home with a six-pack." My brother orders a sausage omelet, then notices my Sunday *NY Times* with the post-impeachment photo of President Clinton in the Rose Garden surrounded by party faithful. "Now there's a guy with a personality disorder. Instead of getting clinical help, he surrounds himself with clergy."

"That's what I want for breakfast." Carol puts down the menu. "Scrambled eggs *surrounded* by ham, mushrooms, and onions."

On our drive back to Glens Falls, my brother announces that he intends to open his own cafe: The Personality Disorder Bistro. "Featuring a brunch special of *two eggs stalked by a rasher of Canadian bacon, o*r, if you prefer, *borderline bacon*, it's half-cooked. For lunch I suggest our 'Paranoid's Delight,' *half a chicken pursued by Brussels sprouts;* for dieters a 'Dysfunctional Marriage Medley'..."

Claude's misery increases. He complains about the lack of leadership in the Association, a borderline consumer volunteer spreading vicious rumors about him. It's clear that he is drinking again. He snaps at me when I ask him what's wrong.

"If I wanted to talk about it, you wouldn't have to ask."

I hear warmth in his voice only when he talks to Poose, who invites him for Sunday breakfast at The Peppermill. In a booth bordered by calico wallpaper, Claude tells us that he's going to spend Christmas with Jo at their friend Susan's cottage in High Falls. As a devout member of AA, she allows no booze in her home. It's a way for him to get back on the wagon. Turning back to the menu, Claude is inspired to add a dish to his own at the Personality Disorder Bistro. "How about a 'Schizo-Affective Special,' *French toast adrift in tomatoes?*"

Claude's hope to regain sobriety at Susan's the following week is a failure. He claims to have been distracted by Susan's new boyfriend, and Jo's endless talk about her computer courses. He should have stayed home and gotten drunk. "But drinking makes me angry. And Mellaril makes me impotent, gives me breasts and escalating cogwheel movements of my arms, dry mouth, and shakiness." He's lowered the dosage, but is hearing bleed-through voices on the street and in messages over TV. "Think my menu is a joke? Not to me. *Je suis Eggs Florentine penetrated by pork patties.*"

"Claude wants to celebrate New Year 2000 at the Rainbow Room," Jo giggles through static on the phone line.

"He met our mother there for martini lunches," I tell her.

"He likes to relive his outings with Charlotte," notes Jo. "At Christmas he drank martinis and talked obsessively about what a charismatic woman she was, then described how cruel she could be."

"How did he manage to drink three martinis at Susan's house?"

"Dinner was at my place." Jo long ago stopped policing Claude's drinking habits. "Two Beefeaters and he talked to anyone who'd listen about the way men and women alike stared when Charlotte entered a room."

"He was in love with her." I'm surprised by my own words.

"I didn't want to say it exactly that way, but it's what I was thinking," sighs Jo. "He still is."

New Year 2000: Claude dreams that his blue Festiva has petered out in the middle of the highway and ups his prolactin-producing Mellaril. At night he says he can lie in bed and listen to his heart regurgitate. This hasn't stopped him from taking home six-packs from the corner convenience store. If only he could find a decent rehab, he tells me.

"I've tried AA but can't stand the God stuff. If you're taking any meds, they say you're not clean. Four Winds won't take Medicaid."

For relief, my brother calls Poose. She answers, *"Pollywannacracker?"* When an ice storm prevents their pizza date, he goes on a two-week bender. At the end of it, Claude tells the director he can no longer execute his duties in the Respite Program. He stops attending VOH board meetings and gives notice at South Street, where he worked as a counselor.

I phone him once a week, more out of duty than a belief that I can stop his slide downhill.

"There's nothing to say," he responds to my inquiry. I am put off by his angry tone. He hangs up without saying good-bye. My Buddhist shrink Bernie attends my lament; I can't stand being bound to the burden of my brother any longer. Claude's anger is focused on me. He is quicksand, will swallow me whole if I don't pull free.

"You have no choice but to hang in," replies Bernie. "The problem is that Claude wants more attention than you're prepared to give him."

"I need what energy I have for my wife and daughter, to say nothing of my teaching and clinical practice."

"Call him before he goes to sleep and tell him how much you love him," urges Bernie.

Every night for a week I approach the phone intending to call. The following week, Claude phones me. The shadow falls. Only it is not his anger that swallows us, but mine that explodes before I know what's happening. I tell that I can hardly stand the sound of his voice. His constant complaints, personal disregard, lack of appreciation have created such distaste in me I can't think of him without acid reflux.

"What about family therapy?" he asks.

"We tried that."

"At Bloomingdale's I choked back my feelings. I was afraid if I spoke honestly you'd stop visiting. You and Judith ganged up on me. You've never shown the same concern about me as those at NAMI do toward their mentally ill children."

"You're not my child," I remind him. "I've stuck by you, fought for you, even with you when necessary. I don't expect gratitude, only a little civility. When have you directed anything toward me but resentment?"

Claude considers my point, and then declares: "You must be aware that self-absorption is part of this pathology. But that would take the focus off of you."

He hangs up.

In the silence at the other end of the line I hear a mitral lisp followed by sloshing blood. I am immediately remorseful. He is sick. I am well. How could I have forgotten that!

My brother will not return my phone calls. Weeks pass. I leave messages and e-mails. Finally, at eleven one morning, I catch him when he's just waking up.

"I'm sorry," I blurt. "Are you all right?"

"Yes."

"Do you forgive me?"

"No."

"Why not?"

"Because you make me feel like an obligation."

"Sometimes you're more weight than I can handle."

"You've always patronized me. It's been very destructive."

"Remember how happy I was when you broke out of your delusion, how proud when you spoke publicly about it?"

"Your pride is worthless. You always tell me how busy you are."

"I have a wife, a child, and two jobs."

"There's no talking to you. You deflect everything with cleverness. People ask, *Why don't you talk to your brother.* I tell them, *There is no talking to Paulie. He doesn't hear a thing.*"

His words are poison darts. He has turned the voodoo mojo on me. I am his pin-cushion effigy. Once again, the shadow falls between us.

"Your anger is misdirected," I protest.

"Convenient for you to pass this off as my problem. You're like a vampire. Paul, you can't see your own reflection."

"At least I function in the world." My words are pressure-driven. It is too late to step back. "You, on the other hand, are locked in a dirty apartment blaming everyone else for your condition."

"Giving you a smattering of psychology is like putting a gun in the hand of a five-year-old."

"One who has pulled your fat out of the fire."

"That's what you think. You've been a relentlessly destructive force in my life. It's your fault that I am the way I am. You did this to me."

Before I can respond, he's gone.

II

Our break should be a relief, but instead of feeling free I feel like the fool who punched a tar baby. Even as I tell myself that I have been relieved of an unbearable burden, I hear his charge: *You've been a relentlessly destructive force in my life.* And again: *You did this to me.*

Neither of us can unsay what's been said. Unlike past breaks, even ones that have lasted years, I am convinced that this one is final. While he was psychotic, I remained outside the compass of his paranoia. My betrayals in the past in fact resulted in years of silence, during which I was convinced he might never speak to me again if I did not pursue him. But in this last encounter I feel so deeply and totally buried in his outrage, and he in mine, that I can't imagine a way to repair it. We have leveled our lances and wounded each other one too many times.

"He's out there telling people there's no talking to me," I tell Carol.

"He's always said that. When he was concerned about your health he'd repeat to me: *Paul doesn't listen to anyone.*"

I recall the bitterness in his words during one of our family sessions at Bloomingdale's. *So you turned out to be the hero.*

I can't let it go. At my next session with Bernie I talk about saving Claude's life when we were kids, maybe five and seven. My brother had slipped out of his tube at the deep end of a pool at the Miami Beach hotel where we were vacationing with our father. No one was looking. I swam out in my tube and pulled him back to the shallow end.

"I knew I had to be secure in my own tube or we'd both drown. Now Claude has slipped out of his tube in a larger, deeper pool, and I can barely hang on to my own."

"Maybe that's the point," observes Bernie gently, sure to

convey the absence of censure. "Claude needs to swim on his own. How else can he cast off your oppressive heroism?"

I hear this claim with alarm, but have to admit there may be something to it. From Claude's point of view, I am glib. Answers and insights roll off my tongue while he struggles to find a reason to get out of bed. Might he be the brother in my Katzenjammer Kids dream who could not speak but experienced consciousness on a far deeper level than the one for whom words came easily.

You're like a vampire, Paul. You can't see your own reflection.

I remember how he'd cursed me at Bloomingdale's for committing him. I hadn't wanted to do that.

You did it.

Is there an assassin in the caretaker?

"You've acted heroically," says Carol.

"I'm a legend in blood."

A blustery winter turns the streets of Glens Falls into a geometry of snowy barricades and slippery surfaces. By the end of February, Claude seems to have melted into the drifts on Sherman Avenue. Then, on a Wednesday night in March, after my last session, I glimpse a figure approaching the clinic through the parking lot, recognize the rounded shoulders and Black Watch cap. Peeking from behind a door, I observe him enter the lobby, announce himself to the receptionist before shuffling off to the waiting room. When the coast is clear, I slip out into the darkness, angry and ashamed of my cowardice. Two weeks later, I run into Claude talking to the receptionist. He regards me with an embarrassed smile. I say a curt hello and continue to the filing cabinets in secure territory.

As a psychotherapist I learn how the body speaks what the mind refuses to articulate. I listen to symptoms; the message sent by a six-year-old bed-wetter, a hand-wringing grandfatherly man who inappropriately touched his teenage foster girl-child.

"*I can't stomach this*," says the spastic colon.

"*I can't support this*," cries the aching back.

"*I'm holding my shit together*," barks constipation.

"*The center will not hold*," declares the panic attack.

"*Open the door or I'm going to break it down*," pounds the migraine.

"*You're eating yourself alive*," hisses the ulcer.

"*You're disappearing*," murmurs anorexia.

Homeopathy tells us the cure lies in the disease; unheard, the message turns into Blake's "invisible worm," a somaticized darkness.

During weekly staff meetings five therapists, the clinical director, and the staff psychiatrist discuss current cases. How do we deal with the abused child whose family remains untreated? Is this sex-offender too great a risk for our program? Does the client's coverage allow for further sessions? How much time can we devote to this problem when there are other, more urgent ones waiting to be treated?

Time is money.

It is no longer cost-effective to practice therapy in depth, see a client once a week, work with dreams and the slow unknotting of developmental issues. I would like to discuss Claude with the team, but he is my brother, not my client. Still, I wonder what his symptoms are saying right now; what is the statement made by the high correlation between schizophrenia and mitral prolapse?

Suddenly the light goes on.

I recall what Wynton Marsalis once observed about Bix Beiderbecke: "*He heard so deeply into the meaning of the music, it broke his heart.*"

***

News of my brother comes through others. Roger Longo tells me that he and Claude are giving a presentation in western

New York. When Carol and Poose chance on him at Price Chopper, he seems happy to see them and says that he's doing fine. Stewing in my own juices, I am disturbed by Claude's *sang froid* and resolve again to bury my brother in my heart next to my parents who, defying entombment, still surface in my dreams. Every morning on my way to ACC, I replay his invectives, shake him by the collar until he apologizes as I try to find a space in the dog-eat-dog college parking lot.

One afternoon in April, on my way to pick up Poose, I see Claude's Festiva under the giant maple across the street from his apartment. At St. Mary's, where she is a sixth grader, my daughter comes down the steps in her gray plaid skirt and white shirt, heaves a full backpack into the rear of the van, and switches my NPR program to her favorite rock station before fastening her seat belt. I pull out from a line of parent vehicles stacked like departing planes at JFK, then stop for a red light at the corner. I recognize the lyric coming through the speakers, and make a right onto Warren Street repeating, *I miss you, do you think of me...*then realize I am singing to Claude.

NYC in May, a week before my fifty-eighth birthday, I am lunching with Susan Sherman at Sidewalk on Avenue A. She laments how quickly her efforts as a political activist and poet have disappeared from cultural memory. "Speaking of which, you'll never guess who I bumped into at Alex Kates Schulman's reading. Shulamith Firestone. She asked to be remembered to you."

Shuly, the rabbi's daughter. *Shulamith*, named ironically for Solomon's concubine. Her book, *Sexual Dialectics*, set the standard for the feminist discourse. I haven't heard her name for decades. Susan confides that Shuly suffered a breakdown and was hospitalized.

We pay our bill and walk to Tompkins Square. The park is crowded with people out for an airing after a long tenement winter. We head toward the band shell. I am about to

comment on the splendor of the trees when Susan points to
the benches facing the stage. I follow her finger to a smiling
woman with gray streaks in her dark hair. She wears baggy
green pants and a plaid jacket. As we approach, she stands
and gives us a little wave. Her chocolate eyes peer through
thick lenses. When she smiles, I see teeth missing at the rear
of her mouth. I hug her for a long time. It's Shuly.

I tell her that I'm living upstate, have a wife and twelve-
year-old daughter. She relates that she had a nervous
breakdown, is living on 11th Street, and doesn't see many
people. Hospitalization was difficult, being confined to a
ward where people just lie around, nobody really speaking to
anyone else. When she talks about it, I hear Claude.

I tell her that I've become a psychotherapist. Shuly
laughs. So many of the people she has known have become
psychotherapists, or mental patients.

"That's the way they see me now: Shulamith, the mental
patient."

I let her know that my brother has been through a similar
experience and describes it in the same terms.

"What was his diagnosis?"

"Paranoid schizophrenic, but that's a moving target."

"Same as mine," she answers. "Did you commit him?"

The question takes me by surprise. Yes, I nod. I did in
fact commit him. If I hadn't, Claude would probably be dead
by now. But still he's angry at me for doing it. Angry at me,
period.

"I'm still angry at my sister, who probably says the same
thing you do."

"He recently told me to fuck off and get out of his life."

Shuly claps her hands. "Good for him. I don't have the
courage to do that to my sister. I would if I could. I'd like to
meet your brother sometime."

On June 1, 1999, a week before his birthday, Jo calls to tell
me that Claude will be entering Brigham and Women's

Hospital on July 6th for heart surgery. She and Susan are driving up to Boston, and Dave, with whom Claude studied medicine in Brussels, is flying in from O'Neill, Nebraska.

How do I feel about this? asks Carol.

Hurt and angry, like the person he accuses me of being, neglectful, uncaring, a vampire who feeds on his brother's blood. My wife advises me to send him a birthday card with a note inviting Claude to call when he wants to. "Let him know you're there for him in any way he wishes."

The day before Claude turns fifty-six I pick four cards from the rack at Hannaford. The first shows a penguin in an easy chair scratching his head with one hand, a pipe in the other: *Now, just because you're older doesn't mean your mind is going.* Inside, the same penguin comments: *Happy birthday, fruitcake!* Card number two pictures a long-necked creature floating in an inner tube. *Hey! Its another mid-life birthday and you're still afloat.* Inside, the caption reads: *Your valve may be a little leaky, but, yep, you're still afloat!* Number three has a tongue-in-cheek message: *Happy Birthday to you, and the child in you who laughs and plays and jumps on the bed when no one's around. Happy birthday to the dreamer in you who wishes on pennies and candles, and still knows the words to 'star light, star bright, first star I see tonight...'*

I had once joked with Claude that if he traveled to the South Pole he would think the penguins were conspiring against him. But maybe my peace-offering birthday card should focus on the future rather than anchor him in the past. My third choice directed to *one who makes everyone else believe in the magic of wishing and dreaming* is too flagrantly satirical. I choose a fourth card to drop in his mail box. On it, a cartoon cat in a ten-gallon hat conveys the message that the recipient has earned the item enclosed: a sheriff's badge *for one who has survived everything.* My note to him says that I understand his heart operation is imminent. "It seems you have covered your bases pretty well, but if there is anything I can do—anything at all!—before or after, please let me know. Your brother, Paul."

III

The evening of July 10th, I enter a curtained cubicle at Brigham & Women's Hospital. Propped up in bed, my brother opens his eyes at the sound of my footsteps. I stop in my tracks. Seeing him in a hospital gown, an IV in his arm and a groin tube from his femoral artery flushing out the dye from his angiogram, brings back everything I felt during Ben's and Charlotte's final days. I start to cry.

"I'm all right." He holds out his hand. "According to the test I've got the cleanest arteries in town. I am a chain-smoking, overweight, mentally-ill alcoholic with pristine arteries."

He stares out of blood-shot eyes. They've taken him off his antidepressant and all but eliminated the antipsychotic. Is he experiencing any paranoid "bleed through?"

"My surgeon's name is Cohen."

"Marty?"

"Larry." We laugh together and agree this is a good sign. The wall between us is down.

A male nurse enters. He wants to help Claude change his "johnny," which is stained with Betadine. An anesthesiologist drops by to discuss Claude's medications. He's followed by a blonde physician's assistant who hands him a release form on a clipboard. My brother will be prepped at 6:00 AM and in the operating room by 7:30, she says. It won't be necessary to crack his ribs. They'll use a "keyhole" technique developed by his surgeon.

"Dr. Cohen tries first to reconstruct the valve..."

"If I need a prosthesis, I want a pig valve."

"The pig valve is good only for ten or twelve years."

290

"I don't want to spend the rest of my life on blood thinners, which I'd have to do with a mechanical valve."

"I'll relay your request to Dr. Cohen."

Just when I think we're alone, a dark-haired woman steps in and introduces herself as the chaplain. She glances at my brother's chart, then asks if he'd like to see the rabbi.

"I'd rather talk to you. But can you ask the rabbi to bless the pig valve before they put it into my heart. Can he make a pig valve kosher?"

The chaplain looks confused: "Good question."

"It would help. Especially when I squeal at dinner."

Jo, Susan, and I enter the ICU on the fortieth floor of the circular tower known as the Heart Wing. We've been told that Claude spent five hours under the knife, but the doctor was able to reconstruct his valve. I am stunned by the sight that greets us from the doorway: my brother in a web of tubes, one down his throat, and another in his urethra, a third from his coronary artery regurgitating blood. His face is swollen, eyes puffy, as though he's been mugged. Wrapped in a cocoon of sounds, gurgling, ticking, beeping, his arms jerk like an insect pinned to a pasteboard.

Beeping from the monitor over his bed displaying pulse rate and oxygen level is suddenly replaced by a keening sound. I run to his bedside, then turn helplessly. Jo freezes. Susan's face pales. She steadies herself on the door frame. A nurse rushes in to make an adjustment. The keening stops. The nurse explains that Claude isn't fully out of the anesthesia, but can hear us if we talk to him. I bend closer.

"You won't have to find a rabbi to bless you. No pig valve."

He twitches. Blood bubbles from his chest. Out of the corner of my eye I see Susan slump to the floor.

The nurse reappears. "Claude needs sleep. He will surface slowly. By the morning he'll be wide awake."

Gently, we help Susan to her feet.

***

I drive to meet David at Logan Airport. My brother's oldest and most loyal friend has long been a successful surgeon at the head of a trauma unit in Nebraska. The bond established between them, first at Bard, then as medical students at the Université Libre, has weathered the separations in time, space, and circumstance in both their lives. When Claude became psychotic, David flew in from the mid-west to see him at Bloomingdale's. This morning, he is flying into Boston.

I have no trouble recognizing him at the terminal. Wearing a plaid shirt and jeans, he is more portly than I remember but gazes at the world through the same black-rimmed glasses. At the hospital, he introduces himself around the ICU as Dr. Young, a trauma specialist, and speaks to the nurses with a paternal concern they find engaging. But David is disturbed to see Claude on his back, asleep, blood bubbling from his chest two days after the operation. He checks Claude's vitals and the tubes in his chest and groin.

We lunch with Jo in the hospital cafeteria. Cousin Jo is a Microsoft trouble-shooter at Pfizer. She and David talk drugs and software. We return to discover that Claude has been moved to a recovery room where he wakes long enough to take a Perco-et and cough up phlegm before falling back to sleep. Nurse Jenny comments on the patient's somnolence. David jokes that his medical school buddy has always been an Olympic sleeper.

At dinner David suggests that he arrange for Claude's rehabilitation in Nebraska. David's hospital has a state-of-the-art facility, and Claude will be better off with him and his wife, Mary, an R.N., than at Susan's in High Falls. Again we return to find Claude as we left him, a heaving mound, a tomb filled with old bones. The nurse puts a cool compress on his forehead. I worry aloud that he is still asleep.

"Sleep is the best medicine," the trauma surgeon tells us.

The next morning, I learn that Claude's blood pressure has been falling. He's been put on oxygen to support what appears to be a failure to oxygenate on his own. His condition is now that of unconsciousness interrupted by brief periods of disorientation. David huddles with the resident cardiologist who orders a regimen of Lasix, a diuretic to drain the liquid from my brother's tissues and an echocardiogram to see if Claude has thrown a clot. My brother wakes long enough to tug at his mask. David puts it back over his mouth.

"I want it off!"

"You're hypoxic, Claude. If you don't stop, they'll have to intubate."

My brother's hands drop to his sides. He is once again asleep, fishing, perhaps, from the bank of Lake Ixelles.

David tries to rally us with tales from their student days. Claude made the European newspapers on two occasions, he tells us. The first, while visiting David's British relative, the Sheriff of Hull. In an interview with a local reporter, Claude revealed he was the nephew (through Irving's wife's sister) of Bob Kane, the creator of Batman. The banner headline reading *Batman's Nephew Visits Sheriff of Hull* was syndicated all over England. A year later, walking along a beach in Corsica, they heard a man in the water call for help. Claude jumped in with his clothes on and saved a middle-aged swimmer who had misjudged the distance to shore and his endurance. The next day's headline read: *Drowning Man Saved by Monsieur Penis*.

These, I realize, had been David's and Claude's golden years. It is what keeps David at his bedside, has tied them with a bond that survives even the radically different trajectories of their lives.

I wonder if my brother is reliving them as we speak.

X-rays on the following day show his lungs still wet. Claude's hands are tied to the bed-rails. His nurse explains that without the restraints he can pull off his mask and become hypoxic in minutes. I mention Claude's psychiatric history, what it might mean for him to wake and find his hands tied.

At lunch David observes that one should never enter the hospital for a serious procedure in July. "All the big guns go on vacation and patients are left with residents on rotation and no attending in sight." One resident wants to lower Claude's Mellaril. Another suggests his antidepressant, Marplan, might be working against drugs Claude is receiving to stimulate blood flow. David wonders that even with a strong cardiac function no one can explain why Claude is unable to rid himself of the water or oxygenate on his own.

Alone with my brother, I watch his hands tug against the restraints, his eyes flutter beneath his lids. Perhaps, as in dreams he once confessed to having with some regularity, Claude is a body of light, flying free, reluctant to re-enter a world in which he is damaged physically and mentally.

IV

Ten days after his operation, my brother sits up in bed, a clamp on his nose instead of the scoop mask, and reveals what he has experienced. "I thought the nurses were keeping me prisoner and couldn't understand why they wouldn't let me go." Claude angrily recalls his struggles with David whenever he tried to pull off the mask. I urge him to forgive his friend, who has flown back to Nebraska. He nods, then tells me he recalled a primal fear.

"Whenever we drove with Dad through the Holland Tunnel or over the George Washington Bridge, I'd be terrified we'd get stuck and die of thirst or starvation. I couldn't have been more than three." Deep in his post-operative tunnel, disoriented, unable to pass liquids or breathe independently, he had revisited this. Claude wants to know why they are keeping liquids from him.

His tissues are saturated, I explain. X-rays show his lungs are wet.

The nurse puts my brother in a walker. He makes it twenty feet into the hall before turning back. In bed, he winces from a pain in his side. Water trapped in his tissues rolls like a wave. I straighten the wires of the monitor blinking out his oxygen level, and BP. We try taking off the nose-clip. In thirty seconds his oxygen falls below seventy percent. I clamp it back on. After lunch his sluggish colon, which hasn't processed food in so long, swells with gas.

"Some things never change," he notes.

Before dinner, a neurology resident at a computer screen points out that Claude's CAT scan indicates a small stroke in the right parietal region of his brain. He doubts there'll be any lingering effect, but it explains the disorientation and slow recovery. The following day a pulmonologist declares Claude has pneumonia, probably not advanced. His ability to oxygenate will improve as they treat it.

I remain troubled by his slurred speech and a slight paralysis on the right side of his face. A psychiatric resident informs me he is going to reduce the antidepressant which may be retarding my brother's ability to absorb liquids. The following day his chest X-rays look better. For the first time I hear the word "rehabilitation." The resident cardiologist has mentioned a place in Boston where he would receive excellent care. He can be transferred directly from the hospital. Susan's home isn't viable. David still wants him in Nebraska.

Claude says he'll think about it.

I drive back to Glens Falls for Poose's appearance in the Lake George Youtheatre, planning to return to Boston early next week. This is the second in a three-show series of performances in what has become a major event in our daughter's budding theatrical career. I've already missed the first one, *Little Shop of Horrors*.

I make it back in time for Thursday's matinee performance of *Rags*. Sitting in the auditorium of Lake George High School, I watch blue-eyed, blonde Christian children play Jewish immigrants on the lower East Side in the opening decade of the 20th century. Except for my daughter's dark eyes and shell-like ears, there are no others equipped with the cellular memory of peddlers on Rivington Street, and Alphabet City tenements flooding when the East River rose in the only part of Manhattan not built on bedrock. Charlotte is an apple-seller in a babushka.

> *Open your eyes, Papa, let me tell you what I see*
> *Rags! Rags! this land of freedom we had to run to,*
> *where now we're free just like everyone to wear rags...*

Few in the audience have references for this drama. But when my daughter turns toward them, her radiant face resembles that of her paternal grandmother, after whom she is named. Not the blonde Charlotte who became a Republican celebrity,

but the dark-haired woman with Portia's elegiac gaze, herself
the daughter of a stunning immigrant girl who married the
local pharmacist at sixteen to get away from her Broome
Street tenement. My daughter sings with the other
shopkeepers and peddlers:

> *...it's all day seeing them, all day sewing them,*
> *all day listening to peddlers selling them, rags!*

When Poosie meets my eyes a shock goes through me. I
stare back at her from that plateau which no longer sees the
passage of time but the pattern of eons. The actors continue
to belt, now about "greenhorns," as recent Jewish arrivals to
the New World were called somewhat derisively by those who
had been here and understood what was required not only to
survive, but to get ahead:

> *...a wave of refugees to fill the mills and factories*
> *It's a bunch of greenhorns greasing the wheels...*

But neither these children nor the man who directed them
has ever heard the contempt suffusing this word, greenhorn,
in the mouths of those for whom it had meaning.

> *...a little oil for the machine. Greenhorns, let 'em come*
> *if we can get 'em while they're green...*

Poose stands close to a character named Ben, a young
man who has fled the Polish pogroms as had her grandfather
of the same name. I grieve that our Ben didn't live long
enough to hold his granddaughter as a baby, see her as she is
now, at twelve, a beauty he would have loved with every
ounce of his life and who would have loved him as he had
dreamed of being loved. But they are both present, in some
form, on this stage, in psychological space and cellular
memory, in the voice of my Charlotte that rises like a thrush
above mourning doves. She is calling out to her ancestors,

the close but unknown stirrings in her blood, and through her, for a moment, they stir in me. I see my father, Ben, and my mother, Charlotte, come together in my daughter and I think of my brother, Claude, who has fought so hard to claim whatever life might have to offer him after withholding so much, and wish he could be here, too.

ENVOI: THE HEART OF HEAVEN

And if there was a war in heaven once, then we
who are neither wholly good nor wholly bad, we
who consist both of shadow and of light, we sad
wounded creatures standing between earth and
heaven, striving to be whole—can, if we are truly
human, choose to be among the healers too.

Parzival, Lindsay Clarke

I

A month after he checked into Brigham and Women's Hospital, his Medicaid has run out and Claude has to vacate the bed. A black limo driver known as Mr. Happy transports him two hundred miles from the curb at Francis Street to Sherman Avenue in Glens Falls. There, without fanfare, Mr. Happy carries my brother in his arms up two rickety flights of stairs.

I am troubled by the possibility that he will also go back into his old routine of daily six-packs, cigarettes, and Xanax.

"Paulie, you always did like to be my jailer," he says.

David calls from Nebraska insisting that it would be best for Claude to fly to Lincoln. He promises Mary's home care, pretty nurses, and a treadmill. My brother demurs. He is glad to be back in his own apartment.

In February of 2000, five months after his return from Brigham and Women's Hospital, June calls to let Claude know that Wallace has had a major stroke. My brother, now much stronger, drives down to the hospital in Rye where Wallace lies, his left side paralyzed, slipping in and out of consciousness, uttering phrases like, "It's a mystery," and "When do we leave for Haiti?" Like our dying mother, Wallace spends time in *the tropics*.

"June keeps me at a distance," reports Claude. "She's pleasant, but makes sure I understand the boundaries. I haven't been invited to Thanksgiving dinner at Highcliff this year."

My brother continues to visit Wallace first at the hospital, then at the nursing home. Claude's experience has given him insight into what it's like to have a stroke. He speculates that his stroke in Boston was preceded by one or more during his early days at Bloomingdale's, when they pulled him off all the meds he'd been taking for fifteen years to get a baseline.

"It hurt to walk. I was lying in bed. I said to myself you've got to get up and take a shower and everything in me screamed NO. There were razors in my joints. Putting on a bathrobe, slippers, walking down the hall, turning on the tap were my way of fighting back. I remember sinking to the floor under the spray like this suffering animal."

By the time the Bloomies decided to give him something to calm down, Claude was convinced they wanted to kill him. Then, one day watching the WFT, he saw Hulk Hogan pounding this guy who kept trying to fight back. What a beating! Hulk threw him out of the ring, but this man stepped back into it. The whole place started cheering.

"Like angels singing hallelujah! I believed you had somehow presented this on TV to let me know what I had to do. That's when I agreed to be medicated and woke from my brain fever feeling like a James Bond martini, *shaken, not stirred.*"

"And now you look like a million bucks." I compliment his new haircut.

"The Adonis Barber Shop."

"They made you a god."

"I stand in front of a mirror and see Truman Capote."

His last few weeks have been dry. He still smokes one to three packs a day and eats huge servings of red meat and starchy potatoes, but he's getting better. He can tell. His breath doesn't run out before he reaches the top of the stairs. He also continues to open up to me in a way that is new, and disarming. Seated in a booth at Friendly's, Claude recounts a dream in which he dialed BO 8-0269, our mother's number in Forest Hills. Charlotte answered, and seemed pleased to hear from him, commenting only on how much time had passed since they last talked. There was no reproach in her tone. Claude invites my commentary. I tell him that in the language of the dream, they have reconnected; the woman on the other end had been neither the little old lady of his paranoid delusion, the unquenchable Thaïs of the Hotel

Geneva, or the libidinous Aphrodite of his idealized fantasy, but Charlotte *mater*, the nurturer she tried to but could not be in the flesh.

I ask him about the high-testosterone women.

"Testosterone was an issue. One day in the Union Temple steam room Dad gave me this clinical look then examined me. I was thirteen and didn't have pubic hair. He put me on testosterone, and I started to develop normally."

Claude isn't sure what it has to do with high-test women, but links the condition to *anosmia*, an absence of smell. Smell stimulates the release of testosterone in pre-adolescent boys. Anosmia, which has been with him since his childhood, may have been responsible for his delayed sexual development, a condition known as "Kallmen's Syndrome."

"Kalman is your Hebrew name."

"Exactly. What kind of a chance did I have? Put on a *yarmulke* and I turn into testosterone-deprived Kalman. Claude, my name in Latin, means *lame*. A hard-case hero, low-octane and lame; that's who emerged at Einstein."

I am amazed at what he is willing to share; especially his final year of medical school. As far as I knew, it is the first time he has talked openly about his meltdown.

"When I started there in 1969, Einstein was the Mecca of Freudian theory. The feeling was that every mental disorder, neurasthenia, depression, *dementia praecox* was caused by repressed homosexual drives. It was also like boot camp. Give me eleven signs and symptoms, dogface! I was so scared that I missed several classes in my first rotation in psychiatry. I'd stand at the rear of the group of students who followed the resident and attending physicians on rounds. I spoke seldom and, when I did, no one could hear me, though I made diagnoses that escaped everyone else. One attending physician shot off a series of symptoms to stump the group; I identified them as Wallenberg's syndrome. Another time, the orthopedic resident diagnosed hip pain as arthrosis, which is a viral infection. But I saw the man wince when his hip was rotated, which indicated a bacterial condition. He bet me lunch. When my diagnosis proved out, he just walked away. They didn't know what to make of me."

Dr. K., the physician in charge of students, accused Claude of trying to slip by with minimum effort. When my brother showed him the citation of Grande Distinction, Dr. K. asked about his sex life. Did he have girlfriends? Enjoy intercourse?

"The accusation followed me on rotation. In Pediatrics, the physician in charge veered into the subject of homosexuality while staring directly at me. I went to his office, but the minute we were alone he seemed embarrassed. I felt like someone had tattooed HOMO on my forehead."

By Christmas, Claude felt so beaten that he couldn't face patients and began hiding in the doctors' lounge, where a resident found him curled up on the couch. The resident was cordial, at first, then started quizzing him. His questions became insistent. Finally, he informed my brother of a meeting that night on cardiac problems. "'Be there, or I'm going to ride your ass.' I went back to Gun Hill Road, told Marianne that I was through with medical school, and stopped going. A man from Einstein called to suggest that I take a leave of absence, then referred me to a psychiatrist."

Before dropping out, Claude visited Dr. K., who asked how he was doing. My brother quoted Shakespeare, the scene in which Romeo asks the stabbed Mercutio, How's your wound? "Mercutio answers, Not so deep as a well or so wide as a church door but 'tis enough, 'twill serve," said Claude. "Dr. K. didn't get it. I explained that I was feeling like Mercutio after being run through with a sword. He said, 'Sword?' Stroked his chin and repeated the word, thrusting with his hand. 'Sword. Sword.' I saw him thinking: Long, hard, capable of penetration." My brother paused for a moment to relive this scene in his own drama, then shook his head. "Finally I told him, 'Doctor, sometimes a sword is just a sword.'"

I keep waiting for the reversal, what always happens between Claude and me: the shift from brotherly love to brotherly strife. No matter how close we are at certain moments, I hear the alarm clock ticking down to the inevitable wake-up call of explosive anger. But as we move into the great greening that is April in the North Country, in this year of the Millennium, my brother is still kind to me. We sit in the park and watch the ducks. They are back from their winter quarters, noisily engaged in turf disputes and mating dances. Some already guide formations of fuzzy babies in and around Crandall Pond, keep them close, always on the lookout for snapping turtles disguised as half-submerged logs or rocks. This afternoon Claude talks to me more openly than ever, describing his recurring fantasy that our father is living alone in the country, in a log cabin by a lake in New England.

"I drive up to visit him. He's glad to see me. We spend time fishing and taking long walks. And *he's happy*, the way he was when he laughed watching *I Love Lucy*. So I decide to live with him. He gets me a job in town, at a lab or was it a business office? Anyway, the people who hire me are glad to do him a favor because they respect him so much, and treat me that way, too. Every day I get up and go to work. At night I return and we sit on the porch having dinner."

I ask about his psychotic jaunts over the back roads of Maine, Massachusetts, and Connecticut in the florid years of his delusion; had he been looking for Ben, hoping, perhaps, to stumble upon him in a bungalow outside of Portland, or on Lake Winnipesaukee, or in the outskirts of Mystic?

Claude lowers his gaze. Two years short of sixty and my brother still fantasizes reuniting with his father. Not the Ben who allowed his sons to live in the shadow of a psychopathic wife who poisoned their dog, but the other Ben, one unafraid to live alone in quiet reflection, the father who emerges whole from my Claude's imagination.

The plot of my beleaguered second novel centers on a young man's discovery that his father, a former CIA operative he long thought dead, is still alive among the Mayans of Chiapas.

"I know it's infantile," Claude smiles apologetically.

"I'm not so sure," I tell him.

II

On a late summer evening in August, in what the Spanish call *media luz*, rosy tendrils of light creep up behind crab apple trees and forsythia bushes lining my backyard. My brother and I are seated at a white outdoor table on a lawn that slopes gently to a small enclosed vegetable garden ringed by marigolds at the other end of the yard. Behind us in the white ranch house, Carol and Poose prepare dinner. I tell Claude that I want to write a book about our lives and ask him how he feels about it.

"Otherwise, it's all lost," I tell him.

My brother nods, then adds, "Besides, what do I have to hide...or lose?"

The light deepens.

"It could be painful," I caution.

Not as painful as being persecuted for unnamed crimes by an unknown accuser.

"Did you ever find out who it was?"

"Sure. It was me." Claude sips from a glass of orange soda. "Now, that's a melodrama!"

I smell vegetables on the grill, seared chicken. Our German shepherd, Zoro, lies at my feet. Claude looks for Louie, our black cat, whom he loves in the way he does Poose, unconditionally.

And how does it seem to him from here, looking back on the entire spectacle?

"Van Gogh, you know, who was bipolar, saw the world the way he painted it. He was hooked on foxglove, the source of *digitalis* which makes all colors more vivid, especially yellows. That's why he saw those sunflowers and stars as he did. Now there's a spectacle. Most psychotics have some hyper acute sense. Mine was aural."

"But you never heard the equivalent of *The Starry Night*."

"No. I didn't hear *Peer Gynt,* either." After a pause, he

says, "I hope I haven't been too much of a burden."

"I might say the same."

Suddenly I feel free to share with him things I never would have before.

I confide my recurring dream in which I am in search of a book I've written long ago and misplaced in a drawer or beneath a stack of papers. I know every page, remember every paragraph and sentence without being able to repeat a single word. I go through my files and boxes, convinced it is in one of the many sealed envelopes. I usually wake up desperate to continue the search. Last night I found the envelope, felt the weight of the pages sealed inside of it, and knew it was the book about Claude and me, the one I am about to write, which has already been written in what the Mayans called *The Heart of Heaven*.

Hermes describes the soul as a sealed envelope. I like the idea that our book might be delivered in this way, as the unsealed content of our souls.

"Rather than a dead letter with no return address," Claude alludes to Melville's Bartleby, the most haunting nay-sayer in literature.

I want to include Claude in my experience of transcendence, the radiant well-being I glimpsed one afternoon by a stream at Cherry Lawn. But he won't let me. He rejects my vision of purpose and well-being, the cosmic container that the Tibetan Buddhist teacher, Chogyam Trungpa, calls "basic goodness." For my brother there are chemical and mathematical laws, neither of which gives any ultimate stability to our condition, one in which the mind is always at risk of betraying itself.

As if reading my thoughts, Claude talks about his last session in which Elizabeth raised the question of his spirituality. "She wanted to know how things stood in that area. I told her I have difficulty with what people call *spiritual*. But it occurs to me that I feel something greater than myself when I'm laughing; at moments when laughter takes over my whole body and sweeps me up, everything becomes laughter. Can a sense of humor be spiritual?"

We let the question answer itself.

The last rays send golden beams into the darkening sky. They arrange themselves to resemble the rungs of a ladder, like the one angels walk, ascending and descending to connect all three worlds.

Claude folds his hands on his lap.

"Just before I went into the hospital I loaded my thirty-eight shot-gun, turned on the TV, put the barrel in my mouth and my toe on the trigger. Martin Mull was on *Saturday Night Live*. It's not that I wanted to kill myself, but I had to stop the pain."

"What happened?"

"I started to press on the trigger. Then Mull jabbed a finger in the air and accused me of heinous crimes. It pissed me off. '*Absolutely not,*' I said. '*I refuse to let this guy make me take my own life.*'"

"Martin Mull looks like you."

"You think?"

My brother is quiet for a moment, then his eyes grow large. "Paulie, when you put on that play at Bard about our lives, you know what pissed me off? Bad enough you portrayed me as this whiny brat who passed gas at the dinner table, but you cast the wimpiest kid in the school to play the part. Couldn't you have picked someone else?"

"Do I get another chance?"

"Do I?"

Music from the house, Kiri Te Kanawa singing *Songs of the Auvergne*. Poose pokes her head out of the porch, calls us in for dinner. Yellow squash blossoms trailing over the fence around my garden are suddenly luminous.

"The music is not the notes. It is about the relationship between the notes. And that relationship is not complete until the last note is played.

Bernard Weitzman

THE LAST NOTE

On April 29, 2006, I drove Claude to the emergency room at Glens Falls Hospital with symptoms of extreme weakness, shortness of breath, and a slightly raised rash all over his body. He was given two liters of blood, then admitted after tests indicated acute anemia or leukemia. On Monday, the hematologist/oncologist, Dr. Mark Hoffman, a lean man with solemn eyes, confirmed a diagnosis of mylogenous leukemia, in which the marrow becomes clogged with embryonic white cells called *blasts* which never develop. With the standard chemotherapy, Claude stood a 50/50 chance of partial remission; without chemo his blood would deteriorate in weeks and he would be back in the hospital.

"So, Paulie, this is it." Claude looked at me with glazed eyes. "I don't want to be buried. Cremate me. Send me off in a Glad Bag."

After considering options, Claude's medical school buddy David recommended we contact Rosswell Park Hospital in Buffalo about an experimental program for which my brother might qualify. Within days, Dr. Hoffman arranged for Claude's admission.

On Monday, I picked Claude up on the wooden steps of 18 Sherman. He was so weak I had to carry his small overnight bag to the van. Poosie called as we headed west on Rt. 29 to remind us to fasten our seat belts.

"I will if you will."

"It's too late for me."

I reminded him that he was going to a good place, told him I was hopeful.

"We thought that about Mom." He recalled her death at the Parkway Hospital. "It was a nightmare. They dehydrated her. She dreamed of water. I should've insisted on her going to Staten Island where David would have given her palliative care. Instead, she died angry and alone."

"Are you mad at me because I'm going to go on living?"

"No. If you had gone first I would have been a basket case. They would have had to put me in the unit. I couldn't have helped you at all."

"Why are you angry?"

"I thought I had a few more years. I know I've abused my body with cigarettes and beer. I never wanted to give them up. If I'd had a lung out, I still would've smoked."

That night in Buffalo at the Double Tree Hotel around the corner from the hospital, Claude ordered a rack of ribs for himself, which he couldn't finish. His taste buds, he said, were a little off.

The following day he was admitted to Roswell Park. I stayed with him while they performed a bone-marrow biopsy. They promised there would be no pain; he was given enough Dilaudid to smile as a doe-eyed Indian physician with a thin mustache screwed what looked like a metal auger into the base of his spine. Two days later, before the start of his chemotherapy, I relayed a conversation with my friend Fred, who asked me to tell Claude that when this was over he would take us all out on his boat to fish for yellowtail off Bimini. I described *The Ebb Tide*, outfitted with a fighting chair and outriggers, urged him to think about yellowtail, picture us on the bridge under a Bahamian sunset eating fresh-grilled tuna and drinking Bud Lite.

"You know, they're going to take me close to death, within a hair of it, then bring me back to life. It'll be a rollercoaster ride."

"And then we'll go fishing."

Over the next week he moved in and out of sleep. When he woke, he spoke almost inaudibly except when talking about yellowtail. He wanted to know what kind of bait we used, did they swim deep or on the surface. I detailed the way Fred rigged baits. We agreed not to keep dolphin. The way they lost their color when beaten had such a human quality. He preferred night fishing for snapper under a spotlight from the bridge that drew the fish.

When he nodded off, I wondered if he was fishing. I would stroke his head and tell him to let out more line. His balding head with its soft tufts of hair was so like a baby's. I held him and thought, *He is my baby. I can't bear to have my baby suffer so.*

Driving back to Glens Falls that Sunday, I received a call from my other baby. Poosie announced that she and Mommy were in Cole's Woods walking Harry. "Daddy, we found lady's slippers and Dutchman's breeches and lily of the valley and a Yeagermeister bottle on a stump."

Claude returned home in the middle of June. His color was back and his strength returned slowly. He had lost thirty pounds. The space between his front teeth and the pointed tips of his ears clearly visible framing his now hairless head made him appear elfin. By the time he left for the second round of chemo on July 8th, he was weak again, dogged by fainting spells and tremors.

"Keep your eye on the goal," I told him.

"The yellowtail."

"Yes, the yellowtail."

Later I received a call from Roswell Park. "Paulie, I wanted to tell you what an ace and a brick you've been for me. I was too weak and disoriented to do anything for myself. This is the third time you've saved my life. I don't know how I can ever repay you." I told him that in the great hereafter he would save my life and I would thank him for it. He laughed, then said goodbye. I reflected that his voice had a certain gravity, came from a different place, one that saw the beginning and the end of days.

He returned to Glens Falls at the end of August. Three weeks later a bone-marrow biopsy revealed anomalous cells. By mid-October he required a weekly transfusion of two or more units of blood and platelets. Still, he insisted on driving with us to New Paltz to see Poosie play the female lead in the college production of *Urinetown: The Musical.* "You're wonderful," he told her before shuffling off to the van.

By early November he required two transfusions a week. "I'm a vampire," he said.

Toward the end of the month he called to say that he had passed out on his way to bed. He didn't recall passing out, but remembered coming to on the floor. He had made it into bed and felt better today. I found him seated on the couch in his overheated apartment wearing a down jacket and blue baseball cap, a little boy suddenly grown old. Claude explained that he'd been having unpredictable bouts of chills and fever, almost embarrassed. For the first time we both felt the palpable presence of death in the room.

On November 17th, I sat in the upper West Side living room of my Buddhist shrink, Bernie, surrounded by photos of Tibetan teachers in saffron robes, decrying the nightmare of my brother's death. His dark eyes deepened as I described a dream in which I walked along a country road between cultivated plots of land laid out in perfect squares. Smoke rose in a vertical plume from some and moved horizontally over others. I tried to explain the reason for the different smoke-trails to my father and my brother who walked on either side of me, but couldn't find the words to do so.

"There you have it. You're attempting to explain it all."

Bernie suggested that I tried to control life with knowledge, information, and the narratives I forged. At no time did those narratives actually capture the reality of my experience, only my attempt to order it according to the needs of my ego. He urged me not to impose my narrative on Claude's dying.

"You have a chance to experience your brother separately from your narrative. I'm sorry to be a hard ass about this, Paul. I really am trying to help."

"I know you are," I told him.

"Your narrative is the nightmare. His experience may be totally different. Do you know what happens when we die?" And there was the reality of Claude's opportunity to evolve in the face of the ultimate mystery. Why should I deprive him of that?

In spite of Claude's fear that his hands might shake too severely to pass the plates at table, he made it to my mother-in-law's house for a Thanksgiving dinner where he basked in the attention of a room full of nieces and nephews, the children of Carol's two brothers. He had fasted for two days so he could enjoy the meal. He was closest to Ken, who had been attentive to him throughout his battle with cancer. Brother David, an evangelical pastor, asked about his condition. Between mouthfuls of pecan pie my brother replied that he was no longer taking chemotherapy. David asked what his next move might be. Claude told him that we'd be meeting with Dr. Hoffman next week to figure that out.

"I guess I have been in a bit of denial."

On the first day of December, we huddled in Dr. Hoffman's clinic on Glen Street where he told us that Claude's marrow had turned fibrous and was no longer capable of producing healthy cells. The cancer had returned. There was a course of chemo that worked 20% of the time to produce a temporary remission.

"Without it, how long have I got?"

Dr. Hoffman was reluctant to be pinned down, but finally offered that it could be six days or six weeks. "Six months," Claude considered over breakfast at Steve's Place. "Weeks," I corrected him. "Yes," he sighed. "Weeks."

I asked him once again if he was scared. He shook his head.

"You know, Paulie, I have never had a romance with life."

Later that night, in his apartment, Claude handed me a photo-copy of Dylan Thomas's *Do Not Go Gentle into That*

Good Night which urges the reader to *rage against the dying of the light*. "I'm afraid there's not much rage left in me."

Did he still want to be sent off in a Glad Bag?

"It's the cheapest way."

"Where shall I scatter the ashes?"

The pond at Cherry Lawn. He was happy there.

I asked about other happy moments in his life. Camp Kemah, where he won the *All-Around Camper* award when he was twelve. He had enjoyed Bard. Even Belgium, traveling with Dave. If he had stayed there he would have finished medical school.

"Tell Fred the yellowtail will have to wait," he smiled.

That night Claude called at three in the morning, wanted to know the time. He had hallucinated that the clocks were moving backwards, the only safe direction left to him.

At the end of the first week in December, too weak to walk to his car, plagued by intermittent chills and fever, my brother could no longer remain at home. Dr. Hoffman found Claude a bed in Glens Falls Hospital.

"What can they do for me?"

I told him that they'd keep him comfortable.

In a soft voice he replied, "Not much to look forward to."

Dr. Hoffman appeared, palpated him, then announced that he would start an antibiotic to knock out the infection. He speculated that the infection was linked to the disease. Claude suspected pneumonia, what doctors refer to as "the old man's friend." He asked when our cousin Jo was coming.

"She'll be here on the 22nd."

"No. In the next two days."

Jo arrived two days later, her blue eyes so like my brother's. Claude seemed to rally, though he was still feverish and there were traces of blood from his gums. He pointed out the small photo of our mother, Charlotte, on the windowsill posed in a black scoop-neck dress with multiple strands of pearls above her cleavage. "Everyone asks me if she's a movie star," he smiled. "Maybe you should take it back with you. I'm getting tired of explaining it." In the end he decided to keep it.

The following day I left Jo in charge so I could see Poosie perform in a dance concert. On the way down to New Paltz I put on a tape called *The Terror of History* in which Professor Teofilo Ruiz asserted that history was a narrative written by the elite to fend off the terror of death and the meaninglessness of existence. As I pulled into the campus, Jo called to say that Claude was anxious and had the urge to pee every five minutes. I said the nurse would find Xanax prescribed "as needed" in his chart. They could catheterize him to relieve the pressure on his bladder.

I made it through Poosie's number based on *Cabaret!* before my vibrating cell phone sent me racing out of the theater. Jo informed me that Claude had been medicated and was resting easier, though she had heard a nurse say earlier that he might be "crashing." I raced back up the New York State Thruway to find my brother awake, attached to machines measuring his BP and breathing. The nurse let me know they had put him on a catheter and changed the antibiotic.

"They play you like a violin in here," Claude was sitting up in bed. His fever had broken. His teeth were no longer outlined in red.

Carol entered with a box of Godiva chocolates. Claude had mentioned Belgian chocolates when my wife asked him two days earlier what he would most like to have, if he had a wish. Carol opened the box. Claude chose a dark chocolate with the Belgian lion stamped on it, and then selected a praline. "One more," he said, picking the white chocolate, savoring it. "I can taste Brussels." He had a dreamy look on his face. We closed the box with three more pieces left and put it on his bedside table. I told him that he would sleep well tonight now that his fever had broken.

"You sleep well, too," he replied.

The phone rang at 2:15. Carol answered, then handed it to me. A male voice on the other end said, "I have unfortunate news." Claude had passed away. I rang Dave's cell. He and Mary had arrived after midnight from Nebraska hoping to visit Claude. Mary picked up. I gave her the news, then let her know that I was going to the hospital.

Dave greeted me in front of the building. We hugged each other, then went up to the second floor. The nurse, Barb, a middle-aged woman with salt-and-pepper hair stacked elegantly on her head, told us that she had bathed Claude, after which he had said goodnight, then drifted off. When she returned a half hour later he was gone. We found him in bed, the sheet turned down, his mouth slightly open but his face otherwise at ease. Everything around was clean, his clothes packed. Barb said we could sit with him as long as we liked. I bent to kiss my brother on the forehead. His skin was still warm. Suddenly I realized that there was no evidence of the Belgian chocolates in Claude's room. The box was gone. It was the last note, one he had played quietly, but which I now heard as clearly as the sound of a choir of trumpets. My brother had finished the remaining chocolates before he died. Then I heard his voice in my head as I would never hear it again: *It's all right, Paulie. You can go home now.*

PAUL PINES grew up in Brooklyn around the corner from Ebbets Field and passed the early 60s on the Lower East Side of New York. He shipped out as a merchant seaman, spending 1965-1966 in Vietnam, after which he supported himself driving a taxi and tending bar until he opened his own jazz club, The Tin Palace, in 1970 on the corner of 2nd Street and Bowery. A cultural watering hole for the better part of the 70s, it provided the setting for his first novel, *The Tin Angel* (William Morrow, 1983). Pines lived and traveled in Central America during the 80s. The genocidal policy targeting Guatemalan Mayans became the basis for his second novel, *Redemption* (Editions Rocher, 1997). Pines has published six books of poetry: *Onion, Hotel Madden Poems, Pines Songs, Breath, Adrift On Blinding Light*, and *Taxidancing*. Selections set to music by composer Daniel Asia appear on *Songs from the Page of Swords* and *Breath in a Ram's Horn* from Summit Records. His poems have appeared in *New Directions, First Intensity, Café Review, Pequod, Ironwood, IKON, Prairie Schooner, Mulch*, and *Contact II*. Pines was a featured poet at the Tucson Poetry Festival in 2004, and at the 4th Annual Latin American Poetry Festival in El Salvador in October 2005. He presently lives in Glens Falls, NY, with his wife, Carol, and daughter, Charlotte, where he practices as a psychotherapist at Glens Falls Hospital, and hosts the annual Lake George Jazz Weekend.

Curbstone Press, Inc.
is a non-profit publishing house dedicated to multicultural literature
that reflects a commitment to social awareness and change, with an
emphasis on contemporary writing from Latino, Latin American,
and Vietnamese cultures.

Curbstone's mission focuses on publishing creative writers whose work
promotes human rights and intercultural understanding, and on
bringing these writers and the issues they illuminate into the
community. Curbstone builds bridges between its writers and the
public—from inner-city to rural areas, colleges to cultural centers,
children to adults, with a particular interest in underfunded public
schools. This involves enriching school curricula, reaching out to
underserved audiences by donating books and conducting readings
and educational programs, and promoting discussion in the media.
It is only through these combined efforts that literature can truly
make a difference.

Curbstone Press, like all non-profit presses, relies heavily on the
support of individuals, foundations, and government agencies to bring
you, the reader, works of literary merit and social significance that
would likely not find a place in profit-driven publishing channels, and
to bring these authors and their books into communities across
the country.

If you wish to become a supporter of a specific book—one that is
already published or one that is about to be published—your
contribution will support not only the book's publication but also its
continuation through reprints.

We invite you to support Curbstone's efforts to present the diverse
voices and views that make our culture richer. Tax-deductible
donations can be made to:
Curbstone Press, 321 Jackson Street, Willimantic, CT 06226
phone: (860) 423-5110   fax: (860) 423-9242
www.curbstone.org